Esther Jacobs

# What is your excuse?
## No money, no time, no experience; no problem!

**NO!**
**EXCUSES!**

# Reader's comments

'Esther has shown me that problems don't exist; only challenges do.'

**– reader Danielle**

'Reads like an adventure story. Inspires readers not to walk the beaten path.'

**– Santé Magazine**

'I have quit my job and I am going to start my own business.'

**– reader Bert**

'I now realize that things won't happen just like that and that I will have to persevere,'

**– reader Iris**

'I don't like books. Got this one for Christmas. Read it in one go. Thanks for the wise lessons.'

**– reader Ruud**

'The book moved me to tears.'

**– reader Angelique**

'I have taken unpaid leave to travel around the world – ready for adventure!'

**– reader Saskia**

'The book is inspiring, which you should expect from a "make your dreams come true" book, but it has also been written compellingly.'

**– Susan Smit, Happinez Magazine**

© 2017 Esther Jacobs

This book was previously published in The Netherlands as 'Wat is jouw excuus?' in 2009. Reprinted in 2013.

Translated to English by Nienke Visser- Goodenough
Edited by Judith van Beers - www.judithvanbeers.nl

**Cover design**
Plan B Grafimediabureau, NL

**Formatting and design of the book interior**
Marieke Rinzema, Fuig tekst en ontwerpburo, NL

**Adaptation of layout for English version**
Velin@Perseus-Design.com

**Cover picture**
Dick Duyves, NL

**Photo of the author on back cover**
www.eefphotography.com

**Print book** ISBN 978-90-6523-321-9
**PDF** ISBN 978-90-6523-641-8

**The last day**
© Universal – MCA Music Holland B.V./Music Corp. of America Inc.

www.estherjacobs.info

For my niece Zarah.

I wish for you to grow
up confident that
anything is possible.

your auntie 🙂

Esther

# Other titles by Esther Jacobs

*What is your dream?*

*Have you found your Mr. Wrong yet?*

*Digital Nomads: how to live, work and play around the world*

*How to write a book in one week*

Visit www.estherjacobs.info
for more information on her books,
workshops and keynotes.

# Contents

*If today were the last of all days*
*Would it change how you feel, who you are?*
*Would you rise for a moment*
*Above all your fears*
*Become one with the moon and the stars?*

*Would you like what you see looking down*
*Did you give everything that you could*
*Have you done everything that you wanted to do*
*Is there still so much more that you hold*

*Follow your dream to the end of the rainbow*
*Way beyond one pot of gold*
*Open your eyes to the colors around you*
*And !nd the true beauty life holds*

*Would you live for the moment*
*Like when you were young*
*If time didn't travel so fast*
*Be free in the present enjoying the now*
*Not tied to a future or past*

*Follow your dream to the end of the rainbow*
*Way beyond one pot of gold*
*Open your eyes to the colors around you*
*And !nd the true beauty life holds*

*You probably said all you wanted to say*
*But doesn't that strike you as strange*
*That we only begin to start living our lives*

*If today were the last of all days*
*If today were the last of all days*

*Of all days.....*

**Marilyn Scott,**
*The last day*

# What's your excuse?

I had been away for weeks, surviving on a deserted Malaysian island for the European version of the popular reality TV Show Survivor. Suddenly I was back home, three weeks earlier than expected.

Before anyone was aware of my return, I decided to fly straight on to the US where my younger brother lives. He had been out there for a few years, living in an artists commune in North Carolina. I had never seen where he lived, and this seemed to be a perfect opportunity for an unexpected visit. I had taken care of my little brother, who is twelve years my junior, for a few years when he was a teenager. We still remained very close.

I listened to the song playing on my I pod: 'The last day' by Marilyn Scott. I did like this song, but I had never really listened to the lyrics properly. Until now: *'What would you do if today were the last of all days?'* Staring out of the plane window, I thought about it. What if this were indeed my last day, how would I want to spend it? I concluded I would be doing exactly the same as I was doing right now: visiting my brother. This moved me deeply, while the thought of spending my day as if it were my last filled me with energy. Never before had I felt so alive!

When I was sixteen, my clairvoyant neighbor told me that within a few years, our world would come to an end. *'I don't know exactly how or when it will happen. It could happen within a year, but it also might not happen for another ten.'* She said, *'Don't let it affect you too much. Just do the things you really like doing, but make sure you don't postpone for too long what's really important to you.'* For the first time I realized we are only here for a limited period of time. Until then, my whole life had been out there, ahead of me. But what if something would really happen to our earth or, for that matter, to me?

How would you live your life if you knew you were living on borrowed time?

I did not really believe this doomsday scenario would become true, but it did affect my future decisions. I opted for a business study that only took a few years, and, when finished, I did not take up a nine-to-five job, but worked as a freelancer on projects which only lasted a few weeks at the most. I never planned for my long term future. This outlook on life allowed me to be open to anything crossing my path, to do things which were out of the ordinary. I never

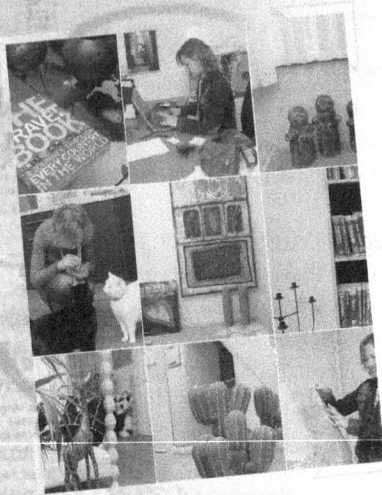

worried about having a career, and I lived for the day as much as I could.

When I was in my twenties I made a wish list of all countries I would want to visit, and decided I would tick off my top ten within a few years. I walked the famous Inca Trail in Peru, visiting the beautiful ruins of the holy city of Machu Picchu. I travelled around Brazil, lived on a tropical island for a while, and had the wonderful experience of swimming with wild dolphins. I once had the adventure of flying a plane and a helicopter myself, and I parachuted down to earth after a skydive which seemed to last an eternity. It felt absolutely great to make my dreams come true!

There were times, of course, when I wondered where I was going, especially when most of my friends were in very good jobs, and were starting their own families.
As for me, I was still putting all my energy into new projects, some not all that feasible. More than once I had to pick up the pieces and start all over again. I learnt a lot during this time though, and somehow I always managed to bounce back.

While traveling, I became convinced I wanted to do something charitable at least once in my life. It was the end of the nineties and the Euro was about to be introduced. This new currency would replace the local currencies of 12 member states of the European Union. I thought it might be an idea to collect

obsolete coins. Many people liked my plan, but told me it would never work.

To tell you the truth, as a 28-year-old marketing consultant who did not have any experience what-soever with large projects, I did not know what I was getting into. I did not have any knowledge about charitable organizations or money-processing; I was not a celebrity nor did I have a large network, and, above all, I did not have any starting budget. However, I could see this project becoming very successful and even securing my personal financial future. Let's be honest about it, I did start Coins for Care to make some profit as well.

Turning Coins for Care into a big success was easier said than done, as lack of funds forced me to take an unconventional approach. This was not always appreciated by the established charities. Fearful of being asked to work within much smaller budgets, they were opposed to my ideas and methods. I found them very difficult to work with and, having collected millions of Euros myself, I started questioning what actually happened to the money they were receiving, which wors-ened our relationship even further.

I was shocked to discover that Dutch charities have no obligation to register and are not monitored. There was, for example, no regulating body representing donors in case of complaints against the charities. Involuntarily, I became a point of contact for thousands of donors. People wrote to me from all over the country: *'We have a right to know how our donations are spent!'* and: *'How do I know what a 'good' charity is?'*

At the end of 2003, together with a few other like-minded people, I founded the first Dutch Donor Organization (Donateursvereniging). We would try to get an under-standing of how the charity industry works, and make it more transparent. This would turn out to be a very slow-moving process.

I feel I have learnt so much in those seven years working for Coins for Care and the Donor Organization. Although it never was a paid job, it has been such a valuable expe-

*On the cover of Communi-cation magazine, April 2004*

rience to have worked with people and organizations whose aim it is to make a real difference.

In 2005 I applied for the European reality TV-show Survivor. I felt I needed to get out of the fundraising limelight for a while. *During the selection procedure, I remember saying 'Two whole months.....! Great!' Not realizing that this reality TV show would put me in a completely different spotlight.*

Illustration: Ecocomics/LexDirkse

It has been more than a quarter century since my neighbour's doomsday prediction. The world is still going round, and I have been very lucky, having settled in the Caribbean after visiting over a hundred countries. I was knighted by the Dutch Queen for Coins for Care, but was taken to court by a few donors when, after seven years, I decided to stop volunteering for the Donor Organization. I was able to gain a lot of experience in dealing with the media and creating free publicity, but it still came as a surprise just how much attention was generated by a reality TV-show. I found out the hard way how the corporate world works, and now I help professional individuals and organizations to realize their dreams: by encouraging them to change their perspective on how goals can be achieved.

This book is about my experiences. Even though you can learn from your own mistakes, sometimes it's easier to learn from someone else's…

I got to know myself under extreme circumstances. This book tells my story of what it feels like to follow ones heart and chase dreams. To actually do what other people deem as impossible. And if my story supports some other people along their path of life, it has been absolutely worth it.

*'Winners make goals, losers make excuses.'* is a famous motivational saying. Starting every chapter with one of the most commonly used excuses for NOT doing something, I will tell my tale.

This book should by no means be seen as a guide-book or a to-do list. I would rather compare it to a buffet with lots of different

Photo: Dirk de Jong

12

dishes: there will be things you won't like, and some of the flavors will be completely new to you. Ultimately, you can pick and choose what you're going to eat. My wish is for everybody to find something to their taste so you go home contented. Or maybe even, off on a new adventure, realizing your long cherished dream.

Who knows? What's your excuse NOT to follow your dream?

Esther Jacobs

Illustration: Ecocomics / Lex Dirkse

# Excuse 1:
## 'I don't dare...'

'There are people who prefer to say 'Yes',
and people who prefer to say 'No'.
Those who say Yes are rewarded
by the adventures they have,
and those who say No are rewarded
by the safety they attain.'

– Keith Johnstone –

Photo: hraudiovisuals.com

# Robinson Crusoë

'This is not quite what I had in mind.' I said to myself, 'Where are the white beaches, where are the palm trees with the coconuts and the exotic fruits?' I stared at the bare walls of a dark, empty cave. We were on a deserted island, somewhere off the Malaysian coast, and this gloomy tomb was a far cry from the beautiful tropical surroundings I had been expecting. Not having anticipated this I felt a little bewildered, but I could also feel growing excitement for the unexpected challenges that lay ahead of me.

'Let's get organized and decide what to do first...' I thought. In previous years, the European Survivor show had started with eighteen candidates divided over two islands, this time they had dropped me at the cave with only one other candidate. His name was Marnix, he was a detective and house dad, and he came from Belgium. We had not received any further instructions but we did find a big wooden trunk. 'That's not a lot' said Marnix, staring at its meager contents: three pots filled with a little rice, flower and oil, a wok, fishing thread, a few fishing hooks, a magnesium stick for starting a fire, a machete-knife, and an axe. We also found an oil lamp, which shed a little light on the dark rocky walls, but by the time it had taken us to realize we could use the oil to light a fire, it had been blown out. We looked at each other, smiling sheepishly: 'What a start!'

The trunk also contained a number of framed pictures, sixteen of them to be precise. 'These must be the other candidates!' Enthusiastically, I started to line the frames up against the wall of the cave and we took a good look at our fellow survivors. They were a mixed group, young and old, male and female, a few interesting faces jumped out at us. We asked the camera crew if they knew whether the group were on the island as well but, of course, they said nothing. I examined the pictures, trying to get an idea of what these people were like, when suddenly I heard Marnix call: he had found a letter. 'Listen to this,' he said, *'Esther and Marnix, welcome to Harimau, one of the most inhospitable islands in the South China Sea. You will have to survive here in deepest secrecy, the other candidates are unaware of your existence...'*

'THIS is where we have to live?' I yelled out in disbelief. 'For how long?' Anxiously, I looked at the film crew who

© *Photo Jeroen van Amelsvoort*

were aiming their cameras and microphones at us, waiting for our reaction, but they did not say a word as they were obviously instructed not to .communicate.

Marnix and I looked around the small cave again. It was completely enclosed by the sea. Bamboo sticks, pieces of moist driftwood, and little bits of string were scattered about. It was such a cold, dark, unfriendly place, and I could not imagine the two of us living here, not knowing what was in store for us. 'How long do you think they will keep us here?' I asked, opening the little pots of food. We had about a pound of rice, and a pound of flour. Marnix and I looked at each other, both aware of what neither of us dared to say out loud: this amount of food would not keep us going for very long.

'What do we do now?' asked Marnix. The adrenaline rush made us behave like chickens without a head: we kept walking up and down the cave, not knowing what to do or where to start. I decided to make a fire, but then realized the oil lamp had already gone off. Marnix suggested going for a swim as it was very hot and we could do with a bit of a cool down, but in the end we opted for exploring the island.

When we arrived by boat we had gone past a small beach with palm trees. 'If we could walk to that beach we might find some coconuts and maybe even have a little party!' I joked. Marnix thought it was a good idea, so we set off for the beach.

Our island consisted mainly of bare, slippery rocks, which were almost impossible to walk on. It was tough finding our way, and we moved very slowly, having to wade through water and climb onto rocks again. We spotted a few bushes on a narrow ridge, with delicious looking red berries and we tried to reach them, but they were impossible to get to. The camera crew had difficulties keeping up with us, trying to protect their heavy and expensive cameras, while we clambered on. It was hot and we could feel the sun burning our heads. After a while a small boat appeared from round the corner which had Jarno on board, one of the members of the production team. Jarno started shouting at us: 'You cannot walk any further!' Marnix and I looked up, annoyed, because we did not want to stop as we had been going

ESTHER & MARNIX

WELCOME TO HARIMAU. THIS IS ONE OF THE MOST INHOSPITABLE PLACES IN THE SOUTH-CHINESE SEA. YOU WILL HAVE TO SURVIVE HERE, IN SECRET. THE OTHER PARTICIPANTS DON'T KNOW OF YOUR EXISTENCE. MORE INFO WILL FOLLOW LATER.

for a few hours already. If it had not been for the camera crew slowing us down, we would have made much faster progress. We looked ahead at the beach with its palm trees which we could see clearly now... We were so close...

'You are NOT allowed to go ANY further!' Jarno yelled again. 'That beach is forbidden territory, understood?' I suddenly felt very irritated, here I was having wasted my energy at getting nowhere, and now we had these restrictions being put upon us. 'It just isn't fair! If we are not allowed to look for food, how are we going to survive?'

Photo: hraudiovisuals.com

Jarno warned us a third time. Annoyed I shouted back: 'Sorry, can't hear you!' and I took another step forward. Jarno got really mad, his face coloring red: 'You DID hear me, and I am telling you NOT to go ANY further!'
'At least it's clear who's in charge.' Marnix tried to be lighthearted about it, but he turned around, dejected.

While we walked back to the cave I said to Marnix: 'What do we do now? There is no food in the cave, and we are not free to leave, how on earth are we going to get something to eat?'
'Do you know how to fish?' Marnix asked.
Although I had been a vegetarian for years, I reluctantly accepted that our only hope of getting anything to eat was to use the fishing hooks we had been given.
'No, you?' I replied, looking hopefully at Marnix. 'I have never, ever done any fishing in my life.' he admitted, and smiled: 'but, never too old to learn!' And together we started to assemble a makeshift fishing rod. 'I think we need some kind of bait,' I said. Looking around we came across a few snails. Marnix crushed a snail shell with a big stone, and tried to pin the slimy creature that had come out of it on the fishing hook. We were both horrified and tried not to think about the barbarity of what we were doing; we just needed to survive.

Just outside the cave was a rocky beach, the water was of a beautiful turquoise color. We were lucky immediately: no sooner had we put our home-made fishing rod in the water than we caught something. 'A fish!' we yelled, not believing our luck, and we pulled the line out of the water as quickly as we could. Glistening at the end was a little blue-greenish colored fish of about eight centimeters long. 'I've only seen fish like that while out snorkeling' I said, feeling very sad. 'And now we have to kill and eat it.' Neither of us knew what to do. Should we remove the hook? We decided to put the fish into a net we had found earlier, and, while shivering and trembling with horror, Marnix tried to kill it as gently as he could. Unfortunately, it kept wiggling and squirming and, in a last desperate attempt, Marnix just cut its head off. We stared at the little beheaded fish. Marnix was the first to pull himself together, and started to clean off the scales, his knife slipping off the skin. 'You should scale from tail to head.' I said, remembering from my survival book.

© Photo: Jeroen van Amelsvoort

While Marnix was cleaning our little fish, I went to light a fire, which is not so easy when you are constantly being followed by a camera. I kept striking the knife along the magnesium stick, over and over again. It sparkled furiously, but failed to set fire to my pile of moist driftwood. After a while, the camera crew got bored of waiting for a flame and turned their camera towards Marnix. I immediately took my chance and stealthily dripped some lamp oil on the wood. A little spark off the magnesium stick set off a big beautiful flame with a loud WOOSHHH!

'How on earth did that happen?' I heard the film crew exclaim, while I put the wok on the fire and added a little cooking oil. Our freshly caught fish was ready to go in the pan, and Marnix was impressed by my fire making skills. 'I cheated a bit, using the lamp oil' I whispered. A little while later the fish was ready to eat, nicely cooked on both sides, and laid on a tray made out of coconut shell. Not sure how to eat the fish, Marnix scraped some meat off the bone with a bamboo stick he used as a fork. 'Sometimes you just need to take that extra step' I told myself, and quietly said goodbye to my vegetarian ideals, while I took a careful bite. The fish did not really smell like fish, which I thought was

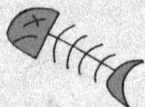

a benefit, and to be honest, the taste did not completely put me off. However, we only took a few tiny bites and threw away the rest of it. We were still not that hungry, but that small meal had, of course, by no means provided us with enough nutrients.

## A proper preparation prevents poor performance

I joined the Survivor show on the spur of the moment. I felt I needed to get away from my work in the charity industry, no more e-mails and phone calls, and away from the opposition I encountered while trying to make this industry more transparent. My friends joked the show had been invented for me personally, as they thought my style of traveling was, to say the least, truly adventurous. I admitted I really liked the idea of having to survive in the wild, but I did not think I would enjoy a reality TV-show. 'First of all, I am a food addict,' I said. 'I would not like to starve myself for a program like that, and secondly, I am far too comfortable being on my own and doing things my way. This whole group mentality thing does not appeal to me at all'. I thought I had been quite sure. However, in an apparent flash of insanity I sent an email, applying for a place on the show.

A few days after sending my email I got invited to the first audition, along with another eight thousand hopeful candidates who had signed up just like me.
We were asked to undergo a psychological test, which consisted of answering twenty five pages of questions like: 'What kind of driver are you?' (my answer: 'speedy but safe.') and 'What would you take with you to a desert island?'
The other candidates seemed to be very well prepared and very keen to win a place on the show, and I realized I had

© Eefphotography.com

© Photo: Jeroen van Amelsvoort

not thought this through properly: I had to distinguish myself somehow. Instantly this became much more of a challenge than whether or not I was going to be selected. I looked at the next question which said: 'Why do you want to join the program?' and I answered truthfully: 'Actually, I don't, because I normally eat every two hours, and I am not a group person at all.' Hopefully, this would draw some attention.

Well, it worked, because I got through to the second round in which we were interviewed by the show's production team, lead by presenter Ernst Paul Hasselbach. He tried to find out how persistent I am: 'We cannot have candidates who want to give up after a few days,' he explained.

I thought I would just go along if I would get selected, but I also knew that I would leave straight away if hunger would get the better of me. I did not think it was wise to share this with the production team, so instead I promised them: 'I am someone who does not give up easily! Have you heard of Coins for Care?' I asked. The next five minutes I spent telling them how I had collected millions of dollars for charity. 'It was a struggle at times, and my work was not always appreciated, but I never gave up!' I ended my pitch.

Next, I saw a psychologist who tried to judge my behavior in a group of people. I told him I am a bit of an outsider, and that food is one of the most important things to me. 'When I am hungry, all boundaries go.' I tried to think of an example: 'Say, I find a mango on the beach, and I have to divide it evenly among all the other people, well, by the time I've figured that one out I'm sure I will have eaten the mango myself, sorry.' I sounded a bit embarrassed, and the psychologist looked up to check if I had been serious. Then he jotted down something and said: 'Thank you for your honesty, I think we will leave it at this.' Had I told him too much?

The show was looking for people with strong characters, especially personalities which were likely to clash, and I think I fitted this profile perfectly, as I made it to the last round: the medical test. I had lots of wires attached to my upper body, and under the scrutinizing eye of a doctor I had to work out on an exercise bike. Having a bit of a cold and worried they would not think

me fit enough, I had eaten a lot of vitamin pills, and when we handed in a sample of our urine, my tube stood out fluorescently yellow between the bottles of my fellow candidates, how embarrassing! Fortunately, I did pass the test.

Finally, our swimming skills were tested. The production team told us that a lot of the activities during the show would take place in the water, so it was very important we could swim reasonably well. The test took place in a tiny swimming pool which was about three by five meters. Just as I started to wonder how they were going to assess us in such a tiny pool, it became clear this was not about swimming. Every candidate was asked to swim up and down a couple of times and then climb out of the pool. 'Can you climb in and out of the water one more time?' the camera assistant asked while the camera kept running; it was nothing more than a bikini contest!

© Photo: Jeroen van Amelsvoort

'Being part of a group is not your strong point, you can be such a loner sometimes. I think you will need to find another way to stand out.' One of my best friends was giving me advice: 'What are you going to do? You need to think of something that makes you invaluable to the rest of the group.' I knew she was right. 'Well, fishing is not my thing,' I said bluntly, 'I'm not very strong physically, and my social skills are not up to scratch either.

But...' I jumped up, '...once, when I was visiting the native Maya people of Guatemala and Belize, they taught me a lot about their plants, some of which have healing abilities. What if I try to find out everything I can about the plants of Malaysia? That knowledge would surely be of some value wouldn't it?'. My friend agreed this was a very good idea, and I immediately set out to work. I made a phone call to the Royal Botanical Gardens and was given the name and number of a tropical plants expert. He agreed to meet me, and kindly showed me around the gardens himself. 'I know very little about edible plants,' he said, 'but I will tell you everything I know.' Desperately, I tried to keep up with him, memorizing what he told me, but all the plants seemed to look the same. I tried to focus on the basics like the shape of the leaves of an edible turnip.

After a few hours I realized it was simply impossible to gain all knowledge necessary in such a short space of time, for surviving on a deserted island (and among a group of people).

I also searched the Internet for someone with an extensive knowledge of how to survive in the wild, and posted the following message: 'I'm going to spend some time on a desert island, does anyone have any useful tips?' A Belgian survival expert wrote back to me saying:' Are you, by any chance, a candidate on the Survivor TV-show? I was on the show a few years ago, and I think I can teach you a thing or two.' He was willing to help under the condition not to publish his name, as he was officially not allowed to talk with new Survivor candidates.

A few days later we met up in the Belgian Ardennes, a beautiful mountainous region, covered in dense forests and steep valleys, the perfect place for a survival trip. The survival expert was going to be my guide for the day, and the first thing he showed me were different ways of making a campfire without any matches. Sadly, I was hopeless at remembering the various techniques. 'Why is it so hard.' I shouted, frustrated by the complexity of it all, but he patiently continued to show me how to tie some branches together with a few easy knots, which would be useful for building a hut or a tripod above the fire. 'You will definitely be able to do this.' he said confidently.

What I enjoyed the most was making dough by mixing water and flour. 'When you mould this to a stick, and hold it above the fire, you will have a lovely piece of bread in no time!' my survival expert said, his eyes sparkling with excitement.' You will be given flour and rice, but this is by no means enough to survive on, so you must get your hands on anything edible in order to feed yourselves. This will include bugs and stuff…!' He smiled, and then, to my astonishment,

© Photo: Jeroen van Amelsvoort

got a bag out which contained a variety of frozen grasshoppers and beetles, and once they had been defrosted he started roasting them above the fire. 'You can eat the beetles whole, but you will need to remove the grasshoppers' legs and wings,' he explained while putting a beetle in his mouth, chewing enthusiastically.

I nearly felt sick. 'Come on!' I said to myself, 'This is part of surviving!' and bravely I picked up a beetle and a big grasshopper. According to some people they have a nutty flavor, but I would not know, I just tried to get them down as quickly as I could, never really tasting them and shivering as I attempted to swallow this unusual snack. 'I don't think it's too bad,' I said with a quivering voice. The guide looked at me expectantly, 'Do you want another one? There's plenty…!' but I thought I had learnt enough for now, and politely declined his offer. 'These do taste a bit spongy, I suppose it's because they've only just been defrosted,' he apologized, 'but I assure you, when you roast them fresh they really are delicious.'

'Wow, I have learnt so much already!' I said to my guide when we were preparing to leave. I was trying to take in what he had told me, but I still could not visualize those damned knots! 'Can you tell me your three most important tips for being on the Survivor show?' I asked him instead. He thought for a moment and then said: 'If you are ever offered a proper bed, don't take it, you HAVE to refuse it, no matter what! Secondly, take some vitamin pills with you: you won't get a lot of nutrients in, and every single pill will help you to stay strong physically. And finally, just let it happen, go with the flow and enjoy the experience!' Back in the car, driving home, I got really excited at the thought of joining the expedition. I thought about everything I had been taught that day, about the edible plants in the botanical gardens, and the advice my friends had given me. But then it dawned on me: I would have to cross my own borders, I would have to push myself further than I had ever done before, I could feel my confidence seeping away, no longer feeling so sure anymore. It felt as if the grasshopper and the beetle were still crawling around in my insides. I struggled to keep them in for the rest of the journey.

'Only when we are no longer afraid

do we begin to live.'

- Dorothy Thompson -

# Excuse 2:
## 'This is so not me'

'Argue for your limitations and
sure enough, they're yours.'
- Richard Bach -

© Photo: Jeroen van Amelsvoort

# Facing the challenge with defiance.

'This is getting exciting,' I thought when hearing I was selected and told to be ready to leave within a few days. I could not wait to go, but at the same time I felt nervous about having to comply with the rules of the program. I was so used to doing things my way and taking responsibility for my own life. My freedom was my most precious possession, something I was not prepared to give up easily. I realized I was about to face two of my biggest fears: not having much to eat and having to submit to a group... I would have to surrender completely.

I started hiding useful items in my luggage, as a personal Act of Resistance. 'If you create your own rules within the given circumstances it will give you a greater feeling of control,' I reckoned. I had sewn a piece of dental floss inside my cap, and concealed some toothpicks and a tiny bottle of disinfecting tea tree oil in an invisible pocket of my beach towel. I made a bracelet by plaiting a few meters of very thin but strong rope: according to the survival expert no one would ever find out about that. In the seam of my trouser legs I hooked a few safety pins which might double for fishing hooks. I also poured some tiny fast growing bean sprout seeds in my bag: they would be a rich source of badly needed vitamins.

On the day of departure I bought tampons with cardboard applicator. My sister and I cut the wrappings and filled each applicator with a vitamin pill, a raisin, and a hazelnut. 'It might not seem like much but, believe me, you'll be so happy to have this,' my sister said wisely. Carefully we glued the paper wrappers back together, put them in their box and viewed the result: you would never know they had been opened. Hopefully the production team would not notice either... 'Aren't you worried you might get expelled from the program if they find out?' my sister asked. 'I can't imagine them doing that,' I answered. 'They've gone through so much trouble selecting me, I think I'll get away with just a warning if they find out about it.'
On our way to the airport we quickly stopped by at a friend's birthday party in Amsterdam. There was not enough time to stick around for the BBQ, so we just said our goodbyes. When we got back into the car, my friend came after me with a plate of food. 'Might be the last time you have something decent to eat,' she said with a wink.

## The big adventure

On the 19th of June 2005 I met the production team at the airport. They introduced me to the other candidates. 'Esther, this is Marnix.' I only briefly glanced at the 37 year-old Belgian man standing in front of me, expecting to shake another 16 pairs of hands, but to my astonishment Marnix and I were the only candidates present! 'You'll be flying to Singapore together where our team will be waiting for you,' we were told. A little confused we went through customs,

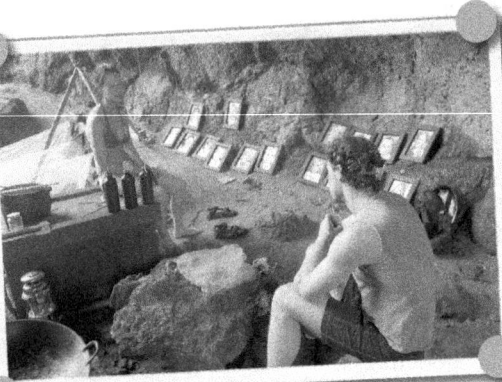

© Photo: Jeroen van Amelsvoort

realizing we were being given a special part in the show, each on a separate island or something like that. Why else would they have singled out a Belgian man and Dutch woman?

Marnix told me it had been a lifelong wish of his to join the program, but he had been rejected numerous times. Last year he was diagnosed with cancer and he had been fighting for his life. Luckily he had survived the disease, and having won his battle he auditioned once again for Survivor. 'I've looked death in the eye, and now I just want to enjoy life as much as I can. There is no challenge too big for me,' he wrote in his application, and here he was, 8 months later, sitting next to me at the airport, primed and ready for this great adventure.

His wife had been in tears waving her husband goodbye while he was walking through customs with this young blond woman. She was not going to see him for at least two whole months. I felt for her, but during our time together I discovered Marnix is a completely faithful house dad, whose family means the world to him.

At the gate I bumped into the father of a friend. 'What are you doing here?' he said. 'I shouldn't really say, but Marnix and I are on our way to Malaysia to join the Survivor TV Show!' I told him excitedly. 'Surviving on a deserted island?' he gasped, 'Wow! I've always wanted to do something like that, but to actually audition for such a program has always been too big a step,' he admitted. 'I've heard that one before,' laughed Marnix. 'But I can't tell you how happy I am to be given this chance, it will be such an incredible experience.' 'If you don't try, you'll never know,' I concluded.

When we arrived in Malaysia the production team was already waiting. They gave us a small backpack in which we had to place all our belongings while they carefully watched over us, afterwards we were told to stay in our hotel room. I found a small bar of soap in the bathroom and added this to the bag, as well as a pencil and a sheet of paper. I also packed two sugar bags. 'No idea if they will check us again tomorrow, but at least I have it for now,' I thought. A little later I tried to sneak out of my hotel room, but was immediately stopped by a Swedish security guard who had been flown in for this very purpose. He had been very well instructed and did not even tell me what time it was as we had to give up our watches on the first day.

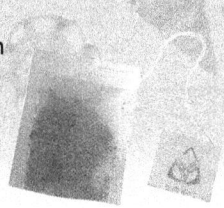

Ahead of us, in the mist, we saw a group of islands and we tried to guess which one we were heading for. Finally we arrived at a little rocky island and overheard the crew talking about a cave. 'They probably want us to do some kind of challenge and then they'll send us each to our own island,' I thought. But instead they dropped both of us in this cave, without telling us for how long we would be stranded there.

## The daily life of a cave dweller

Two days later we had established something of a daily routine: baking some 'bread' in the morning, fishing in the afternoon, and our evenings were spent preparing and eating what we had caught that day. I quickly learned how to fillet a cooked fish and became very skilled at removing every single piece of edible flesh from the bones. Mixed with some rice it was a delicious meal. We did not have toilet paper, tooth brushes or any other item of luxury, but what we did have was plenty of fresh water. I drank constantly in order to keep the feeling of hunger at bay. The cave's sharp rocky floor caused us a lot of problems: it was impossible to walk barefoot, but keeping our shoes on all the time gave us blisters. Once a day we had to be available for a compulsory interview, and the rest of our time we just spent relaxing so as not to waste any energy and to adjust to our situation.

29

*Our new home; the island of Harimau*

The camera crew followed us continually, hoping for some good shots and shocking comments, time and time again they asked us to have another look at the pictures of our fellow candidates. 'Could you tell us one more time what

you think of them?' they asked, and obediently we repeated what we had said before, wondering what the reason was for doing so. 'That man with the long white hair, he looks a bit like an old wise native American.' 'The guy with that happy smile, I think he's cool'. To keep ourselves occupied we had drawn a checkerboard on the back of one of the pictures, and

© *hraudiovisuals.com*

with some white and black shells we played a few games. The crew wanted to know which photo we had used as a board. 'I don't really know…,' I answered turning the board around. It was Nicole's photograph. 'Why did you choose Nicole's for that? Don't you like the look of her?' They were obviously trying to stir things up a little. 'Well, that's the picture that stood nearest to us, it doesn't mean anything,' I tried to explain. But they kept going on and on about it and, unwillingly, we got caught up in a heated discussion about Nicole. That's how Marnix and I learned that whatever we would do or say could be interpreted which ever way the camera crew chose to. During one of his daily interviews, Marnix was asked if he thought I was bossy. Marnix wasn't sure what they meant. 'Well, what did you think when you were cleaning the fish and Esther got involved? Don't you think she's a bit pushy?' Marnix got so angry about them trying to put words into his mouth that he decided to keep silent, but the interview had to continue and they did not release him until he had answered all questions. Deeply offended, his eyes dark with anger, he returned to the cave: 'You better prepare yourself, Esther, these guys are trying to create a dispute between us.' Much later we would joke about it: *'You don't even have the right to remain silent. Everything you say, or don't say, will be used against you by Survivor TV!'*

Someone who bore the brunt of our anger was Rudi, the reporter, who had been with us when we cooked our fish, so he must have contemplated all this. He had also been the one who went on and on about the 'checkerboard incident', as we called it. Marnix and I clearly felt we were up against the production team and this only strengthened our bond even more. We promised we would always stick together and, unknown to the annoying reporter, we started calling him 'Rudi the Rat'.

On the morning of the third day I woke up feeling weak and nauseous. Opening my eyes, or even the slightest movement, made me feel as if I was going to faint. I just did not have the strength to come out of my improvised bed.

Our fellow survivor candidates

'This is what I've been worried about,' I told Marnix. 'I simply need my food.' Marnix was concerned and fed me a piece of bread. When the camera crew arrived they could not hide their excitement at this unexpected event. 'We've got a sick person! Good shots!' I heard them radio back to their base. I hated having a camera aimed at me while feeling so bad. 'If this takes much longer I'll just go home,' I reminded myself. Fortunately, I started to feel much better after a while and have not felt so bad ever since. Despite the small amounts of food we received I actually felt quite good. Had I given up at that moment, I would never have discovered that I could get through it, and my fear of not having enough to eat would still be with me. I learned that a feeling of hunger is something which is determined by the mind, rather than the stomach, and the body is able to withstand a lot more than I had ever imagined. Marnix and I had our own theory for this: 'Firstly, you know you're not going to eat much when registering for a show like this, so you're probably tuned in somehow already. Secondly, your body will get used to small portions of food, and will send out less hunger signals. Finally, on a desert island you are not constantly surrounded by food, or even the smells, so less temptation.' We both thought this to be the most important factor. The camera crew had to have their lunch at a distance and, when visiting us, were not allowed to smoke or eat. Funnily enough, our noses became so sensitive, that we would notice immediately when a team member had eaten some chocolate, yummy!

I just don't want to be hampered by my own limitations
- Barbra Streisand -

One afternoon the camera crew, the photographer, even the interviewers had left us. Their presence must have been required somewhere else, we were completely alone on the island. Even the grumpy Swedish security guard was nowhere to be seen. Marnix and I floated about in the warm deep blue water and watched our inhospitable cave from a distance. The silence was beautiful, no people surrounding or watching us, for once we did not have to be careful of what we said, and how we said it. It felt unreal, to be completely free, a kind of freedom unknown to us, albeit temporary. It brought a smile to our faces, shouting out loud Martin Luther King's famous words: 'Free at last!' I felt incredibly happy.

## Survival strategies

*A white-tailed eagle majestically circling the skies above our cave.*

One afternoon Marnix came back from exploring the area around the cave. He could hardly contain himself: 'I've seen where the camera crew keep their lunchbox! I think they've left a bit of pasta salad in it,' he whispered excitedly. We thought of ways to take some of the salad out of the box unnoticed: 'You could fill up one of the aluminium drinking bottles, you carry one of those with you all the time anyway. I don't think that would raise any suspicion,' I said. Marnix went back and, while the crew was not looking, he stole some of their pasta. It was our first Act of Rebellion! That evening, when the crew had returned to their hotel, we feasted on five spoonfuls of pasta, and could not have been any happier.

The next day we tried again, and before breakfast we already had one full drinking bottle. When the crew left that evening, they forgot to take the lunchbox. We could not believe our luck! Quietly, so not to disturb the Swedish night guard, we sneaked towards it and opened the lid: three huge pieces of French bread! I thought I was dreaming. 'I'm not sure it's such a good idea to take anything out, it might be a trap,' Marnix said, suddenly uncertain, while licking his lips at the thought of a large slice of bread. 'I am not going to waste this opportunity. What if we slice a little off each piece, so there'll still be three chunks left, surely nobody will notice,' I suggested. The heat of the day had turned the bread moldy, but we decided to eat it anyway, and seeing Marnix munch on a stale musty crust made me realize feeling hungry makes you do strange things…

Stealing the crew's lunch unnoticed became a daily challenge. Not only did it boost our meager diet, but it also gave us a feeling of freedom, a way of coping with the rules forced upon us. The idea that they could not get us down easily created a lot of positive energy, and a firm bond developed between Marnix and me. We started thinking seriously about a strategic approach to our riotous actions: 'If we get to the lunchbox before lunchtime, the crew would not yet be aware of what's in it, so they'll never know what exactly is missing!' We decided. 'And after lunch, when it's only leftovers, we'll just take a bit of everything so it will still look as they left it.'

The first time I set out to loot the lunchbox, I was so scared I could feel my heart pounding. I nervously circled the box, while Marnix tried to distract the camera crew. Adrenaline rushed through my body while I opened and closed the lid of the lunchbox three times, before finally daring to take something out. Without thinking I grabbed a wrapped parcel, quickly hid it between the rocks, and ran back to the cave. It had not been a smart move: there had been three similar parcels in the box, now there were only two left, but there were three crew... Guess who missed out on his omelet sandwich? Rudi the Rat!

Marnix and I had a true banquet that evening. 'A gift from heaven!' said Marnix with his mouth full. 'Yeah, delicious, although it comes at a price! Of course, Rudi will have worked it out by now,' I said. 'But imagining his face, when he couldn't find his sandwich, that was priceless!' We laughed. The following evening we tried again, but our hearts sank when we noticed they had hidden the

' If you can't have fun with the problem, you will never solve it...'

33

lunchbox in a wooden trunk, fixed with a large padlock. 'Well, end of story,' I said, disappointed, and turned around. Marnix, however, did not give up that easily and he started to muddle with the lock. Suddenly I heard him yell: 'I've cracked the code!' I could not believe it and quickly went back. He showed me how he had opened the combination lock using the 6,3 and 1. 'You're my hero!' I really meant it, and jumped around him ecstatically. The magical number 631 was the key to some delicious treats and a lot of fun during our stay in the cave.

We did not want the camera crew to find out about our obsession with their lunchbox, so we had to think of a plan.

They needed new footage on a daily basis, and so far they had filmed us sunbathing, sleeping, fishing, and preparing dinner. 'If you're planning on doing something else, something different, will you please let us know?' the crew kept asking us eagerly. But to keep them on edge, we made sure we completed as many of our tasks while they were not around. When they arrived in the morning we would have baked our daily portion of bread; by the time they got out of their boat we were already sunbathing; we would go fishing while they were having lunch, and when they returned we would be enjoying our well earned siësta. By the end of the afternoon the crew would be desperate for some useful material, and Marnix and I would start a well timed activity. Once, Marnix climbed the rocks and shook a tree, waiting for its red fruits to drop. Another time I got a piece of driftwood and, using some charcoal, I wrote a message on it: 'Welcome to Harimau: Life is a Beach'. At such moments the crew would jump up and run after us like madmen, hoping to get their shot for the day. Not once did they notice one of us hurrying into the cave and taking their provisions.

Those treats remained the focus of our attention. We had so much fun, and enjoyed every crumb we could get our hands on. Instead of worrying about the awkwardness of living in a cave, the restrictions being put upon us, and about what might happen, we were focusing on the possibilities of making our situation as pleasant as possible.

We still did not know how much longer our stay was going to last. During one of the interviews I had said: 'I am definitely able to manage one week, two weeks will become difficult. I can't even imagine what three weeks would be like, and after four weeks I'll be dead. Despite using only a tiny amount everyday, our stock of rice and flour was shrinking at an alarming rate, and it was not being replaced. We thought this may be a signal that times were about to change, but we were not told anything by the crew. In the meantime the other candidates were living on an island not far away from us. They were busy getting to know each other, making friendships and taking up the Reward Challenges, in which they could compete for luxuries like extra food or even alcohol. They also had a challenge in which they could earn a status of immunity that would protect them from being voted off by the Tribal Council.

'Too many people are thinking of security instead of opportunity. They seem to be more afraid of life than death.'

- James F. Byrnes -

'We also want to participate in these challenges! It's not fair, we too should get a chance at winning some extra food,' we complained. By now we had settled into our cave and were actually having a really good time! Of course, we did not want the crew to discover this, as they might choose to restrict us even further, so Marnix and I had decided to voice a complaint every day. We also tried to act not too cheerful. 'I told them we would like to meet the other candidates,' I whispered to Marnix after one of my daily interviews. 'Okay,' answered Marnix, 'then I'll mention we're running out of food, and that it isn't acceptable...' 'We really enjoyed our collaboration; I suppose we felt we gained some control over our own situation.

'Why have you put *us* in this cave? What's the point?' we kept asking the production team. Once, Marnix put them in an awkward position by saying angrily: 'Listen, I didn't audition for *Temptation Island*! How do you think my

© hraudiovisuals.com

wife will feel, and my family and friends, when they see me on television, in a cave with another woman?' The reporters clearly felt uncomfortable and tried to put put Marnix at ease: 'You'll have to be patient, we are doing this for a reason, you'll see, it won't take much longer.'

During many sleepless nights, laid on the uncomfortable and hard rock floor, we filled the long dark hours speaking about all sorts of things. Marnix told me about overcoming his disease. 'Lance Armstrong is my hero. He really inspires me, he's showed me that you will need to fight and that there's always hope, no matter how little,' I heard him say in the dark. 'The thought of not seeing my children grow up....' He was holding back his tears. 'Anyway, you should read his book,' he ended.

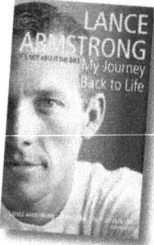

Under the starry sky, which we could see from a corner of the cave, we sang our favorite songs. Marnix told me about his life at home, and described in detail the delicious buns he and his children would fetch every Sunday morning from the local bakery. I told him everything about my travels, and discovered we shared a lust for life, and the skill to remain positive. I could not have wished for a better friend in that deserted cave. We were a real team, working well together and complementing each other.

By now we knew our cave inside out, we were familiar with every stone and recognized every single noise. 'I can tell the time by listening to the water rise or fall,' said Marnix at night, while we heard the tide coming in. We could also tell when it was about to become light, looking at the position of the stars. 'I have been to a desert island before, but never lived in a cave, and I have really come to appreciate the bareness of it,' I told Marnix. To our surprise

© Photo: Jeroen van Amelsvoort

we had started to feel very much at home.

We were completely at the production team's mercy. They invented the rules. However, this sounds worse than it was, since they had manufactured a small and easily manageable world where by design there was nothing to do. This forced us to take things as they came and we truly lived for the moment. We did not think about tomorrow or yesterday, about home, work or anything else. We had accepted our situation and were trying to make the best of it.

© *Photo: Jeroen van Amelsvoort*

## A sudden change

We had been in the cave for only a week, which had seemed like a lifetime, when suddenly our routine was rudely disturbed by Marnix calling out: 'Esther, you've got to see this!' I looked up and saw a small boat, carrying a big man, approaching over the shimmering sea. The boat carefully moored and moments later the Neanderthal-lookalike, with his wild grey hair and big bushy beard, stepped into our cave. 'I'm Douwe,' he introduced himself. 'I'm one of the other contestants.' Marnix and I were very excited to finally hear some news.

'Do you understand now why you were isolated?' the production team asked, eager to explain. 'You are the only two contestants who are in their thirties. The others are either younger or older, and we've divided them into two age groups. That's the reason why you're here: you have a special role.' It emerged that Douwe had been voted off by the older group, and he had been sent to deliver a letter to our island.

*'Dear Marnix and Esther, build a raft and try to get to the island of Mensirip before the thirtienth*

© *Photo: Jeroen van Amelsvoort*

*day. If you succeed both you and Douwe will be allowed to stay on the show, if not, you will be asked to leave Survivor."*

Enclosed was a map and a compass.
'Finally, our chance to join in!' Marnix said excitedly.
While we walked to higher grounds in order to get a good look of Mensirip, Douwe told us all about the other contestants and the tough challenges they had competed in. 'We had to hang off a huge wooden cross for as long as we could, which was incredibly hard. One of the guys is a bodybuilder and we all thought he would easily win but, despite his muscles and incredible strength, the challenge was won by a lanky guy who does a lot of mountain climbing. He was up there for nearly an hour!' Douwe said admiringly. He himself had come off the cross almost immediately, which was why he had been eliminated. 'It's a shame I haven't had the opportunity to show what I am capable of,' he said, his voice full of regret. 'I am an experienced sailor, and I have skills which could be essential in these circumstances.' Marnix and I looked at each other, we knew he was absolutely right. His sailing experience would be vital if we were to get safely to the other island.

MARNIX & ESTHER

This is day six of the expedition. If you succeed in reaching the island Mensirip before day thirteen, you will fully participate in the expedition. If you don't, then you're both out.

For days we were busy building a raft which would be sturdy enough to make it to Mensirip. We had enough wood, bamboo and rope to work with. Douwe was in charge of the design as Marnix and I did not have a clue of what a raft should look like. As there was not enough space for the three of us to work simultaneously, I decided to let the men do the job. 'I'll take care of the catering,' I joked, and went out fishing, baked some bread and cooked dinner, while the raft slowly but steadily took shape.

Before setting off on such a long journey, we needed to test the raft's performance in the water. It was quite scary to find out it only just carried the weight of three adults. The production team was, of course, hoping to shoot some very interesting material, and Rudi the Rat suggested we should sail towards the beach with the palm trees, which we had seen when we had arrived. 'That is very far, it will be quite a journey,' Marnix looked concerned. 'Think about what you'll find when you get there: you can eat as many coconuts as you like,' Rudi promised.
When we started paddling, we immediately became aware of the strong current. A fierce wind was blowing against us and, despite rowing as hard as we could,

we were not moving. We had no other option but to get into the water and start swimming. Big waves kept crashing over my head, it was exhausting. Rudi tried to encourage us from the safety of his boat: 'Do you see that rock right in front of you? If you go round that, you'll be at the beach, you're so close, keep going!' We struggled with the wind, waves and currents, being close to giving up, but time and time again Rudi promised us we were nearly there.

After what seemed like an eternity we reached the rock, Marnix looked around and said: 'Where's the beach?' Miles and miles of rocky coast stretched ahead of us, not a palm tree in sight. Rudi had already moved on, he had known this all along, and his only reason for pushing us onwards was to get some dramatic footage. I was so angry he had made us waste our precious energy, that I climbed on top of the raft, shouting: 'This is so mean, what a dirty trick! You KNEW all along, and we've been wasting our strengths for your petty filmshots! You jerk!' Marnix and Douwe could not believe what they were hearing, but they too were furious.
We swam back and fell down on the rocky beach in front of our cave, worn out. Nobody said a word and the crew filmed Marnix staring angrily into the camera. It was later shown on television with the narrator saying 'After these challenging events, Marnix was too exhausted for words.'

© Photo: Jeroen van Amelsvoort

The next day would be our eleventh on the island, we had to leave soon, and Marnix and Douwe put a few changes in place to improve our raft. We decided to finish our last portion of rice and keep some flour. 'We wouldn't have lasted much longer anyway,' said Douwe, looking at the empty cans of food. Marnix and I realized the lunchbox would not accompany us to our next location; if we wanted to treat ourselves one more time we should do it now.

© Photo: Jeroen van Amelsvoort

After the crew had eaten their lunch, we took a container of left-over pota-to-salad out of the trunk, and ate until we ached. Our stomachs had shrunk so much we could hardly finish the small portion…

Unfortunately we had to postpone our crossing due to bad weather. We were given some extra food in order to get through the extra day in our cave: a bit of rice and three small banana's which we fried in our last drop of oil; delicious! Quietly, Rudi the Rat left us some more fruit for a bit of extra energy. 'He must be feeling guilty,' we laughed. But it also indicated the production team was concerned about what lay ahead; it was going to be a tough crossing. Douwe was particularly worried about sharks: 'I saw a baby shark this morning, usually the mother isn't far away,' he told anyone who would listen.

The next morning, Marnix and I woke up full of adrenaline. The weather had improved. 'I feel as if going on a school trip.' I said to Marnix. 'Me too,' he replied, 'and finally we'll be meeting the others!'

We secured our luggage to the raft and left, joking and laughing, singing 'I am Sailing'. Douwe, however, was grumpy and irritated. He was dead serious about what lay ahead, and clearly did not appreciate our behavior. He reckoned Men-sirip was about four or five kilometers away and as a sailor he was very aware of the risks we were facing, his biggest worry being sharks.

When we set off the current was too strong to paddle in and, again, we had to get into the water and start swimming while pushing the raft: Douwe's worst nightmare. 'Surely they're not letting us get into the water if there's a real danger of sharks,' I thought. Then I noticed the camera crew were staying in their boats, even though they were wearing wet suits. Apparently they had been planning to film in the water. They usually filmed anything. Then why did they stay in their boat? 'Just don't think about it, and keep swimming' I told myself.

We got further and further away from our cave, and after a while we were surrounded by nothing but the blue sea. In the far distance we could see the contours of Mensirip, where new opportunities were waiting for us, but first we had to get there...

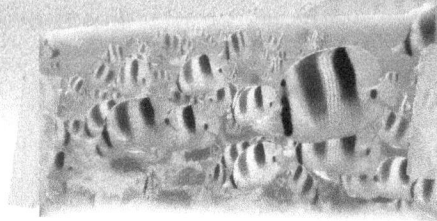

Being a contestant on the Survivor show has been a true privilege, I've learnt some important lessons and cherish the wonderful memories which I wouldn't have had if I had submitted to my fears/excuses:

- Marnix; he has become one of my dearest friends.
- Fish; it is now one of my favorite dishes
- The remote Marine Reserve in Malaysia; a place you would normally not be able to get to.
- Tranquility, Zen and Live for the Moment; I use my experiences in the cave frequently as a reference, in order to put things into perspective again.

I also found that physical restrictions only exist in my head. It's given me an enormous boost being able to overcome these constraints.

'Conventional wisdom says to know your limits. To know them you must find them first. Finding your limits generally involves getting in over your head and hoping you live long enough to benefit from the experience. That's the fun part'

Drew Marold

I love snorkeling, but since having been on the Survivor show, instead of just admiring the fish, I can't help thinking how lovely they might taste. I don't really like myself for it, but it's a thought that keeps popping up, as if edged in my mind.

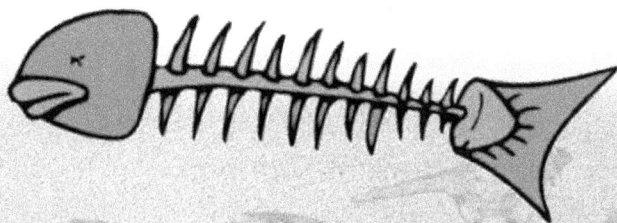

# Excuse 3:
## 'I have a career to think about'

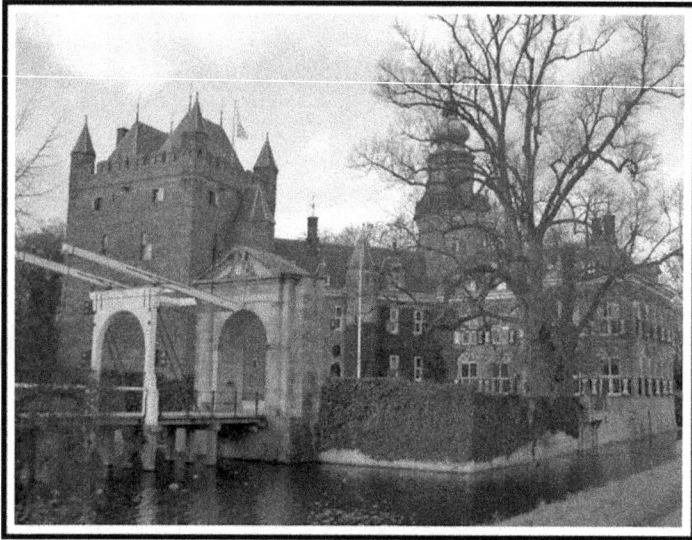
Nyenrode Business University in Breukelen, The Netherlands.

'Don't ask what you can do for the world.
Find out what makes you come alive,
and then go out and do it.
What the world needs
is people who have come alive.'
- Howard Thurman -

## Paths untrodden

'Congratulations! What would you like as a graduation gift?' My dad asked me proudly when I received my Bachelor's degree in Business Administration. I did not have to think for long: 'A backpack for my trip around the world,' I replied. 'Traveling? Shouldn't you get out there and start looking for a job?' Was my dad's surprised reaction. 'Or even apply for an MBA? I hear a lot of your fellow students are thinking about studying Economics and Communication,' he tried. 'No, I am going backpacking,' I said resolutely. 'If I started a job I would have money but no time to do anything with it. I might not have much money now but what I do have is plenty of time!' I explained. Realizing he did not have any arguments to bring against this logic, my dad eventually accepted my plan and drove me straight to an outdoor shop. After being properly advised on backpacks of all shapes and sizes, I

Graduation party with my best friends (1992).

chose a very cool model. 'Are you sure?' My dad asked me one last time before paying. 'Yes, this one is perfect, and guess what, it's also in my favorite color!' I smiled.

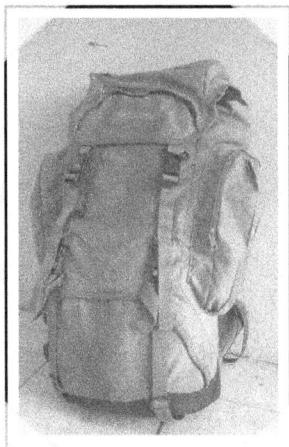

I would not start using the rucksack until much later, as a few days after graduating, I was contacted by one of my father's friends. He owned a board games distribution company, and I had done some promotional work for him before. This time he asked me if I would be interested in setting up a subsidiary company in the UK. I felt honored and boldly said 'yes'. My trip around the world would have to wait. Instead, I moved to London for three months, to assist the owner's brother with the start-up of the company. Not having much work experience, I found the project very challenging and I had to learn quickly as the games industry, the bureaucracy, and the cultural differences were all new to me.

Amir, my colleague, was a marine biologist who had only recently arrived from Israel and his English was not that good. Also, being the youngest he would

Our London office

never disagree with his older brother, which made it awkward for us to get relatively simple things organized. An example was registering with the Chamber of Commerce. In order to do so we needed a bank account, but the bank would not open an account unless we had a Chamber of Commerce registration. In the end Amir's brother had to come over himself to sort everything out. However tough, working with a tiny budget had its advantages: it forced us into being creative, we did learn a lot during our first months, and those few times we seriously got stuck we could always count on support from someone belonging to the owner's vast Jewish network.

Even though Amir did not have any business background, he had enough life experience to prevent me from making silly beginners-mistakes. Once we needed to hire someone for a game-promotion in Harrods, London's up-market department store. I had never done a job interview myself. I placed an add in the cheapest newspaper. When we received our first reactions I could not believe my eyes: re-used envelopes, with the previous address simply crossed out, and letters written on scraps of paper, full of spelling mistakes. Apparently, low market news- papers were read by low market people!

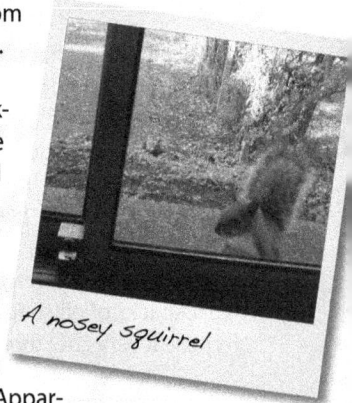
A nosey squirrel

All I could worry about was finding someone in time, so I invited one of the applicants for a job interview, a woman who seemed extremely motivated. She told me she loved games and she could start immediately. 'Great, then you're hired!' I said naively and, relieved, looked at Amir, who stood behind the lady, wildly gesturing. 'Uhm, I should actually discuss this with my colleague first, we'll let you know tomorrow,' I corrected myself.

As soon as she had gone out of the door, Amir asked me what I thought I was doing. 'Why? She needs a job, she is keen and she can start tomorrow...' I hesitated. 'Have you seen what she looked like?' he said. 'Er, I don't know, I suppose I haven't paid much attention,' I admitted. 'Her clothes looked worn and her teeth were loose in

The games event

her mouth,' Amir put his hands up in despair. 'We can't possibly send her to work in Harrods!' Thankfully, just in time, some Israeli friends introduced us to Tanya, a South African lady, well liked by Harrods and the shopping public. Our business started to grow as more and more people got interested in our games, and the orders were coming in.

Meanwhile, back in the Netherlands, the owner's wife had become jealous because of her husband spending so much time working away from home. 'While setting up business in London he has even less time for his family,' Amir

Harrods: Our first big customer!

explained his brother's situation. 'And because you are based over here, she sees you as part of the problem. Don't take this personally, but she doesn't want anything to do with you,' he added apologetically. I was not even allowed to record the voice mail message on our answering machine! It was an absurd situation.

Fortunately, my three month contract was coming to an end. A (family) friend of Amir's asked me if I wanted to join his telecom company. 'We have thought of a new concept,' Sammy explained. 'When business travelers make an international call from their hotel room, the charges are sky high. With our Interglobe phone card they'll call a toll-free phone number which allows them to make any calls, national or international, at a much cheaper rate!'

Trafalgar Square

I could not wait to make a fresh start and to be released from that ridiculous situation at the games company. Sammy noticed I was anxious about something and when he asked me what was up, I told him the whole story. He said I should not worry. 'I know that woman, she often acts like that, you shouldn't take it personally.' However, a few days before signing, Sammy suddenly cancelled our contract, saying he could not hire me. 'But why not? What's changed?' I asked, completely astonished. Sammy had told his wife about the situation with the jealous woman: 'My wife does not think it's a good idea to have someone like you working for us.' 'But that is so unfair!' I called out. 'I haven't done anything wrong, and besides, there is nothing going on between me and that man!'

No matter how hard I defended myself, Sammy was not going to change his mind. 'I know all that, but my wife clearly thinks differently, and I don't want any trouble at home, you've got to understand,' he concluded.

I was so taken aback that I did not know what to do. Getting angry, threatening him, or demanding he would stick to his word would not make things any better, so I decided to let it rest and move on, feeling incredibly sad for being so unfairly treated. First a jealous wife in the Netherlands, and now this. How could such an absurdity have such far reaching consequences? It taught me business is not always fair and honest, and sadly it was not the last time I would encounter such injustice.

Eventually Sammy offered me a role as the Benelux agent for Interglobe, working from Holland, and I decided to take the job, focusing on the opportunity, forgetting about any set backs.

## Thugs

A few weeks later I was at the airport again, full of energy and ready to launch Interglobe to the Benelux countries. I had blatantly written a letter to the editors at Playboy magazine, explaining our new phone concept for business travelers: 'This phone-card offers your readers a lot of advantages, would you be interested in doing a shared promotion?' To my surprise, they invited me to their offices to discuss the possibilities of a small advert on the gadgets page, and I we managed to come to a deal. All they needed was a professional photograph of the card and also the appliance that comes with it. 'Uhm, I've only just started, I'm afraid I don't have any promotional material at hand,' I said, feeling incredibly embarrassed. 'How much will it be to have the pictures taken?' I asked. 'A few hundred guilders,' was their reply. Whoops, that was a lot of money, money I did not have. Luckily, one of the editors came to my rescue: 'Listen, I know a photographer who might do the job in exchange of a bottle of whiskey, just give me the card and the appliance, and tomorrow you'll have your shots.' And indeed, the next day, he came back with some very professional looking photographs, and a small article was published in *Playboy*.

Not long after, I received a very strange phone call from a softly spoken man with a strange accent: 'Helloisthisestherjacobs?' I could barely make out what he was saying, but after confirming it was me he set out to explain: 'I'm from Merchant Trade Finance in Switzerland and we've taken over the Interglobe franchise for Europe. We understand you work for them and we would like to offer you a contract. Would it be possible for you to come to our offices in Geneva, at our expense of course?'

A 'business trip' to Geneva! This was so exciting, I could not wait to tell my friends and family. A few days later I was at Geneva Airport, 22 years young, naïve and overconfident, wearing my two

piece suit, waiting to be picked up by Amal, a big, dark African. I recognized his voice immediately from our phone call a few days earlier. Amal took me to a castle at the edge of Lake Geneva in which Merchant Trade Finance (or MTF) were located.

I was made to wait for hours before being led into a huge dark wooden paneled room. In the middle an imposing antique desk, at which a pale, tired looking, grey-haired man was sitting. He introduced himself as the CEO. After a cold welcome he leant back in his leather chair, put his feet on the desk, and did not say anything. Not feeling comfortable at all, I started rattling: 'I don't quite understand, you have invited me to become your Benelux agent, but I already have an exclusive contract with Interglobe. There must be a misunderstanding...' Before I could even finish my sentence, the CEO slapped his fist on the desk with a loud bang, and shouted angrily in French at Amal: 'I told you, this is not going to work!' After this, he left the room. In complete disbelief I stared at Amal, who had remained very calm throughout, and he said: 'Don't worry Esther, I'll get him back, let me do the talking, trust me.' I nodded; it felt good to have at least someone on my side in this weird situation. Amal disappeared and I heard them both whisper in the corridor, then they returned as if nothing had happened. Amal said: 'Esther, we would like to ask if you would be interested in becoming our agent for the Benelux. Here, take our contract, go to your hotel and read it through carefully. We'll meet again tomorrow morning when you can tell us what you think of it.' I was overwhelmed by the situation; I was tired, hungry and thirsty, and desperate to be alone in order to reflect on what had happened, so I accepted the pile of paper and without any further conversation Amal drove me to my hotel.

In my room I ordered a sandwich and started reading through the contract. To my amusement it was an exact copy of the Interglobe contract, in which they had replaced *Interglobe* by *MTF*. They had also altered a few sentences, using poor English, which meant some conditions could be interpreted in more than one way. Most striking was that MTF was only prepared to pay me half of the commission I received at Interglobe. The contract was not attractive for me at all, instead it was worse in every aspect!

When I woke up the next morning I felt refreshed after a good night's sleep; the strange meeting seemed like just a bad dream. But when Amal picked me up after breakfast, the bad vibes from the previous day returned. At the castle we walked straight to the CEO's office, nothing had changed; the mood was still as threatening and close as it had been the day before. 'So tell us, what do you think of the contract,' the CEO asked me, without even saying good morning. This annoyed me more than anything, I was not here to be treated as a little girl, I did know what I was talking about, and so I asked him who had set up the contract. A long silence followed. 'Why?' Amal finally asked. 'Well, it's full of spelling errors and a few strange changes have been made compared to my previous Interglobe contract,' I explained. Amal and the CEO exchanged a few irritated looks, and I decided to go for it: 'Interglobe pays me twice as much commission, so why would I be interested in signing up with you?'

I jumped when the CEO slammed his hand down on the desk again. 'Now, listen to me young lady, we have an exclusive European contract with Interglobe which includes the Benelux countries; you are either working on our terms and conditions or you're out!' He said angrily. 'But...there must be some kind of mistake...' I said hesitantly, 'Sammy himself assured me that...' This time it was Amal who rudely interrupted me, suggesting we should give Sammy a ring. After having briefly spoken to Sammy he handed the phone to me. I explained what was going on, but all Sammy said was: 'Just talk to them, I'm sure it will be alright.'

Meanwhile, the CEO had dug up a pile of papers from a drawer. 'Take a look at this,' he said, and I tried to read the sheet he was holding up. It was obviously their contract with Interglobe, but he kept waving it in front of my eyes, so I could not make any sense of it. I said to him: 'If it is indeed true that Sammy has assigned the Benelux to us both, then we better take this to court and let the judge decide who can have it.' I was playing it hard now. 'When was your contract signed? Mine dates back to January, when you weren't even in the picture yet, which means mine is legally binding,' I bluffed, opposing the arrogant CEO who gave Amal a puzzled glance, and then quickly put his papers back in his drawer. 'There won't be a court case,' he said. 'You don't have any evidence and you'll never get your hands on my contract.' Furiously he sat back in his chair, but his confidence had faded somewhat: he'd taken his feet off the desk...

Amal quickly reverted back into his role of Guardian Angel: 'Listen Esther, I'm sure we'll sort this out. Let's discuss things over lunch, we'll come to a solution, don't worry,' and he discreetly led me out of the office, away from his livid CEO.

I felt insecure and did not know what to do. I had never experienced anything like it. Was this how business was done? Whatever it was, it did not feel good. To my astonishment, Amal suddenly opened up when we sat down in the restaurant: 'Maybe Sammy has made an error of judgment, but it's obvious, he expects us to come to an agreement. We would really like to work with you as our Benelux agent, so what is *your* proposal?' he asked me.

'Well, I definitely don't want to lose out on any commission,' I said decisively. 'Yes, I accept that, but you'll have to understand we are currently not in a position to be able to pay that much. We have invested a lot of our funds into introducing the phone card in Europe, but what we are able to help you with is the start-up of your own company,' Amal continued. 'What would you say if we support you with five-thousand dollars? That would give you a kick start, wouldn't it?' I did not want to seem too eager, but I was in desperate need of some cash, and five-thousand dollars was an enormous amount of money to me. Amal must have noticed my hesitance and he quickly took out his check book, wrote the check and waved it in front of my face. Then he picked up the contract and asked me to sign it there and then.

The offer was tempting, I could use the money, and Amal seemed to have my best interest at heart, but I was tired of being cautious. In order to gain some time I looked at my watch, and was shocked to see the time. 'Oh my God, my plane leaves in an hour, I need to get to the airport!' I shouted. When I hurriedly got up, the spell was broken, and despite Amal with his contract and check, the only thing I wanted was to get out of there quick…

At the airport I thanked Amal as diplomatically as I could. 'I'll think about your offer, I'll give you a call at the end of this week.' Briskly I walked through the doors, leaving a perplexed Amal behind. Because of my late arrival at the gate I was upgraded to business class and welcomed on board with a glass of champagne. Leaning back in my seat, I proposed a toast to myself, I had escaped! A heavy load was lifted from my shoulders, only now I realized what pressure I had been under.

Back home I told my dad what had happened. 'That CEO was such an arrogant and rude character, but Amal was kind and tried to help me out' I said, but my dad shook his head wistfully, and said: 'It's the oldest trick in the book, the 'Good cop - Bad cop' routine, in which they try to confuse you and then get you to agree. You did not sign anything did you?' he suddenly sounded alarmed. Proudly, I told him it had not come to that. 'I cannot believe that two experienced business people like that have tried to play a trick on a young, enthusiastic, woman like you,' he said angrily.

On my father's advice I gave Sammy an ultimatum, after which we agreed I would work as an agent for MTF, under the same commission scheme as I had with Interglobe. This time my dad accompanied me to Geneva, just to be sure. I was happy with the new contract, although it still contained some strange wording and unusual sentences, but Amal assured me this was not important. 'It's about our intention to work together,' he said, and to my astonishment he pulled out the five-thousand dollar check. 'MTF would like to support you with your start-up costs.' My dad nodded approvingly, and to make things even better, on our return flight we were upgraded again to business class! This time my dad and I both toasted to my success.

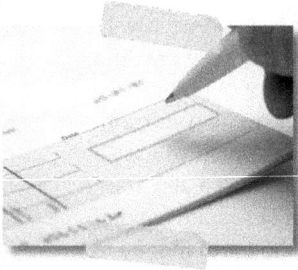

'What do you mean this check can't be cashed?' I asked the bank employee who called me a week later: the MTF check had bounced. I called Amal immediately, who explained there had been trouble with the NYSE, but everything was now back under control. 'Just send me the check and I'll make sure you'll get a new one,' he promised. Trusting as I was, I did send back the check and waited in anticipation, but the money never arrived and every time Amal had another excuse: 'I've sent it, how strange hasn't it arrived yet?' or: 'Money is a bit tight right now, but you'll have it by the end of next week.' I realized getting upset wouldn't lead to anything, instead I kept pressuring them, waiting for the money.

## A new challenge

Despite Amal's promise, I did not expect the Interglobe business to be very lucrative, but setting up a company was still high on my list. I needed to find a way of earning some proper money, or otherwise I had to start looking for a regular job. I got involved with a few network marketing agencies. 'Every conversation is a potential sale opportunity,' I was told, but quickly found out this was not appreciated by everyone. My client base consisted mainly of my friends and family, and some people even started avoiding me. I realized I had to stop, it was simply 'not done'. 'Why don't you go to Spain and work in the timeshare business?' a friend advised me. 'I'm sure you will be very good at it, your trip and accommodation will be paid for, and you could earn a lot of money this way.' I thought it was a very good idea and, looking forward to this new challenge, I registered with a timeshare agency. Everything was organized, I only needed to book my flight, when

I received another weird phone call which would change my plans completely: 'This is Philip Ochtman, my company is interested in buying Interglobe. I understand you work for MTF in Geneva?' I answered that I did not work *for* them, but I had attempted working *with* them. 'Would you be able to come to Paris to discuss a few things?' Philip asked me. I could not believe it, here I was, jumping from one adventure into the next, while most of my friends were in -what I considered- 'boring' jobs! First London and Geneva, and now I was off to Paris! There was one thing I could not help worrying about: what if this company was as bad as those crooks at MTF? In an instant I had made up my mind. 'If you send me a ticket, I will come to Paris.' Philip hesitated for a moment: 'Send you a ticket?' he repeated. 'Yes, so I can come and visit you, MTF usually pays for my tickets,' I said naively. Apparently it was not common practice to pay for tickets if you wanted to talk to someone, but in the end Philip agreed.

A few days later I arrived in Paris, and was picked up by Philip and Ed, his marketing manager. In the car they asked me if I would mind having our meeting in a motel, instead of going all the way back to the office. That was fine with me, and ten minutes later we sat around the table.
'What exactly is your relationship with Interglobe?' Ed asked me. 'And MTF?' Philip added immediately. They kept repeating the same questions again and again, I did not quite understand what was going on, but felt they were somehow testing me.
It all unfolded when they said: 'Listen, we'll be open with you, we're trying to get rid of MTF, but they have a contract with Interglobe, and we're trying to find ways of terminating that.' My face lit up, and I asked if I could see the contract. Ed and Philip exchanged a glance and then handed me a pile of pages, which I immediately recognized as the strangely worded contract, drawn up by Amal. 'This contract,' I said slowly, 'is full of loopholes.
It will be so easy to cancel it. 'I showed them a few sentences which were subject to multiple interpretations and therefore legally not binding. I also explained Sammy had given out an exclusive Benelux contract twice, which meant one of them simply could not be valid. 'How do you know all this?' Ed and Philip asked surprised, and I told them how MTF had tried to lure me into signing, and how I had spent a whole evening in the hotel comparing the MTF and Interglobe contracts, marking all the differences.

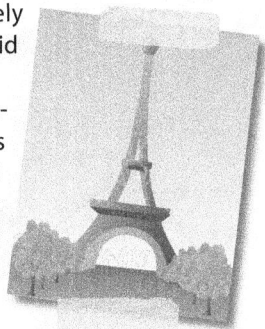

'OK, get in the car, let's go to the office!' Philip jumped up and in the car he explained why they had been so hesitant to invite me to their offices. 'We did not know what to make of you, we thought you might work for MTF, or even spy for them! But it's obvious you're one of us.' 'I suppose it's also in your interest if MTF would disappear,' Ed added. 'They're real crooks!' we agreed, and I knew I had found some genuine allies. Adrenaline was rushing through my veins. 'Justice, at last!' I called out loudly, and we all laughed.

In the few hours that remained before my return flight, we took a detailed look at the contract and thought up a plan to get back to MTF.

The next day Philip asked me if I would be interested in coming to Paris for a month, writing the marketing plan for the European launch of Interglobe. 'Why not?' I thought, I could still sell timeshares another day. By now, I knew the telecom business inside out and I felt I really had something to contribute. Living and working in Paris for a month would be such a valuable experience. I would earn a lot more than in London and was even offered accommodation! Above all, Ed and Philip seemed nice people to work with, at least a lot more pleasant than Amal and his CEO! It was a true opportunity.

A week later, I moved into a small apartment close to the quaint *Quartier Latin*. Philip and his brother owned a number of companies, and Interglobe was their latest purchase. Part of the marketing plan was a competitor analysis. Some American telecom companies offered similar services, but Interglobe was the first of it's kind in Europe. 'Your job is to assess the international rates at AT&T, MCI and other providers,' the two men requested, so I set up a scheme and started calling round. It was a very frustrating job, the customer-service reps I spoke to never seemed to understand what I was calling about. After a week I had enough. 'There are so many different rates!' I told Ed and Philip. 'If I make five calls to At&T, asking the same question, I get five different answers!' I grumbled. 'Hang in there, just keep trying,' they insisted.

Philip was very kind and attentive, and as I did not know anyone in Paris, he invited me to parties and picnics with his friends. Sometimes we went out for a meal together. Philip was born in India, his parents were Dutch and he had spent his entire youth living abroad, attending international schools. Usually we spoke in English, but every so often he would try his oldfashioned, broken Dutch, which I thought was funny. I liked him very much and we definitely clicked. I admired his business instinct, his calm intelligence and modesty. Compared to him I often felt like a puppy: too enthusiastic, too impatient, too naive and too loud.

Working with Ed and Philip taught me a lot. They both had so much business experience. Together we did the market research, designed a brochure, and wrote a business plan. Much sooner than expected, my time in Paris had come to an end.

WhenPhilipaskedmeifIwouldliketostayanothermonth,Ididnothavetothinklong. I moved in with him and his brother in their wooden summerhouse on a little island in the river Marne, south of Paris. Every morning we crossed the water in a small rowing boat, in order to reach the mainland where the car was parked. It was quite romantic, but sometimes the boat would fill up, leaving me balancing on the edge, clutching our leather briefcases, while Philip rowed us across, standing on top of the seats, trying to keep his feet dry.

Diving lessons in the Philippines.

Philip and I got to know each other very well while working together at Interglobe and our friendship developed into a romance. I would have liked to have stayed with him much longer, but I had arranged a two month trip through Asia

Safari in Nepal

55

with my best friend, so at the end of the second month in Paris, we had to say goodbye.

By the time I got back from a fantastic trip to Indonesia, the Philippines, Thailand, and Nepal, Philip had left Paris and had moved to London, his chosen location for the Interglobe head office. I was delighted when Philip asked me if I wanted to move in with him, and help to expand Interglobe further. Louise and Nitza, two girls hired by Sammy were still working in the London office. They had never been very nice to me. One day I gathered up my courage and asked them why. 'You've never, ever come to us for anything, you always went straight to Sammy,' they answered. 'But Sammy specifically asked me to come to him if I needed any help!' I defended myself, but my explanation was in vain, the damage was done, and me being with Philip only worsened the relationship. With Nitza and Louise being so bitchy, Philip took me under his wing. He let me work in his office and made sure contact with the ladies was kept to an absolute minimum. But such protection from the big boss gave, of course, rise to even more animosity.

Amal from MTF in Geneva however, had managed to wrap the girls around his finger, and they briefed him on any new development at Interglobe. When Amal heard I was going out with Philip he called me, and said: 'Now you can forget about your five thousand dollars!'

The job itself was exciting and challenging, but Louisa and Nitza's behavior continued. There was an ever-present tension in the office, and I felt I had to watch my step constantly. It put a strain on my relationship with Philip, and on my birthday I told him I thought it would be better if I would return to the Netherlands. In tears we said goodbye, both knowing this meant the end of our romance.

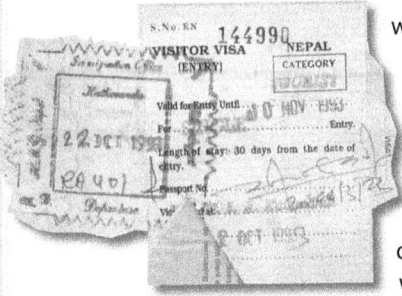

## Fruitgirl

I was heartbroken after leaving Philip. To cheer myself up I decided to stay with my dad for a while, who was now enjoying early retirement on the Caribbean island of Curaçao. The lovely weather, the relaxed pace of life, the people I met... It did me a world of good. I was having a wonderful time, and was in no hurry to go back home.

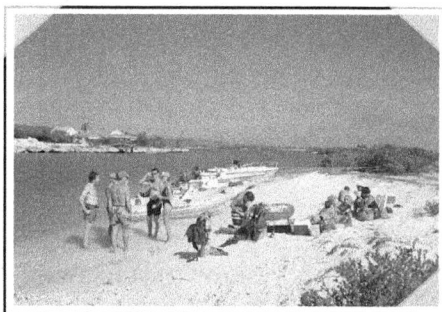

*The Curaçaoan good life.*

Every morning I walked to a little fruit stall just around the corner, and bought a delicious fruit smoothie. I got on really well with the owner, and he told me many times it was his dream to set up a franchise of healthy snacks. One day I said: 'We're wasting our time talking about this, let's just do it!' The next morning I loaded the car with yummy fruit salads, put on a cap with a huge pineapple printed on it, and set off for the many banks and trust companies on the island.

News traveled fast, and after work, during the happy hours in one of the many bars on the island clients promoted me enthusiastically to their business relations: 'Does the fruitgirl visit your offices yet?' It brought me a lot of new customers, and within a couple of weeks I was selling a hundred and fifty fruit salads per morning. Unexpectedly, the owner of the fruit stall passed away. However, despite my sadness, I decided to continue his business. I worked hard, going to the market early in the morning to buy fruit, then making the salads, and delivering them to my regular customers before lunchtime. I spent my

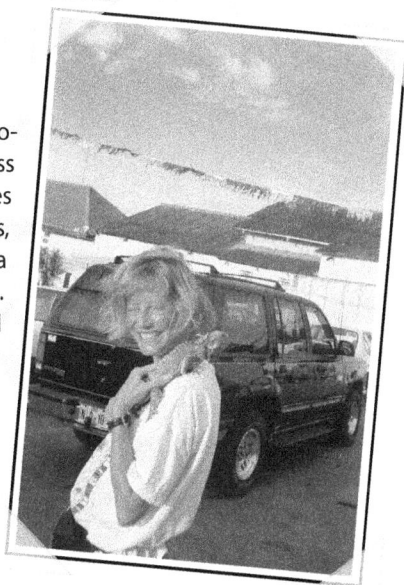

*'s'o clock in the morning:*

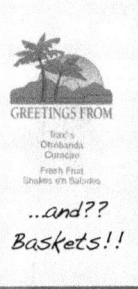

afternoons at the beach, diving, or exploring the island, contented and with my well-earned money in my pocket. The knowledge that I could make a living like this anywhere in the world, filled me with a sense of pride and security.

My newly acquired client network led to a few other jobs and projects, like creating a brochure for Hertz Car Rental, and for OHRA, a Dutch insurance company, researching new ways of advertising on the island.

GREETINGS FROM
Trax's
Otrobanda
Curaçao
Fresh Fruit
Shakes 'n Saladas

*...and??*
*Baskets!!*

*We love your spontaneity, drive, spirit, input, motivation, brains and know-how; you are a living advert for a good and healthy lifestyle, and we hope you'll always be 'our fruitgirl'.*

Although I was not consciously planning anything, I rolled from one interesting project into the next. I had often heard my customers complain about the expensive calling rates to the Netherlands. The local telecom company, who had a monopoly, charged a whopping ten guilders per minute (about $5.50). 'I might be able to provide you with an alternative,' I said, thinking about the Interglobe principle. After a little research, I found a company called Global Access. They supplied a call back number, which made it possible to call the Netherlands for only two guilders per minute (about $1). I quickly became an agent for them, and it was not long before I had signed up many clients, happy with the enormous savings on their telephone bills. I was paid on commission, and now received a good income every month without lifting a finger.

Curaçao is not far from the South American mainland, and I decided to cut my global travel plan into smaller trips, starting with the countries nearby. I saved up for tickets and traveled to far and remote areas, visiting the most unique places in the world. It was fascinating to see that many regions were still untouched by modernization, knowing however this situation

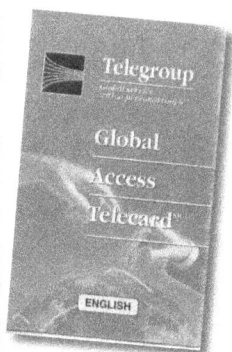

was changing rapidly due to globalization. I often went to the local markets and, while trying to communicate with the locals, realized that I was looking through my western eyes. There were so many things I did not understand, or simply did not see. It bothered me, and I knew I wanted to do something about it, but what?

# 'If you walk the footsteps of a stranger, you'll learn things you never knew'[1]

'I'm amazed at how you are able to turn whatever you come across into a commercial opportunity,' my father said one day. 'But isn't it time you started thinking about your future? Why don't you do that MBA?' he suggested. I gave it a good thought, it was true that I felt the need for putting my experiences into a certain context, and maybe an MBA would enable me to do so. It would certainly be the key to a good job and a flourishing career, but somewhere deep down I was not quite sure I wanted to give up my intuitive, independent lifestyle. 'You're absolutely right,' I decided after a while, 'A Masters might be exactly what I need just now.' My dad glowed with pride, he had never had the opportunity to study, but became CEO of a big company through sheer hard work and determination. His children receiving a thorough education was something which was very important to him.

I still could not help feeling apprehensive about doing an MBA, I thought it might be far too commercial, and specifically aimed at a career in the corporate world. During my travels, I had developed a huge interest for different cultures, and I found a study in the field of social sciences more appealing. When I heard the university of Florida offered a combination course in Latin American studies and Anthropology, I knew it would be perfect for me, and I decided to sign up. I was now earning about a thousand dollars a month with the Global Access scheme, which was just enough to pay for my studies.

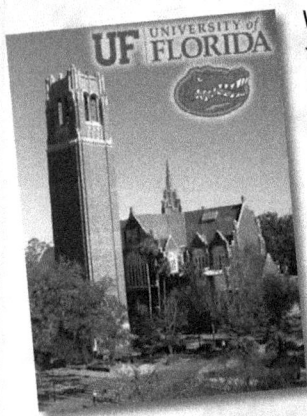

I did not know anyone else who studied Anthropology, it was entirely my own choice, and I enjoyed my studies enormously. One of my favorite subjects was *History and Religions of Latin America*, a topic close to my heart. I was also taught about various research methods, such as participant observation, when the researcher takes an active part in the group of people he or she is studying, which I preferred to the regular distant scientific approach. I was going to write my thesis on the use of medicinal plants in the developing world, and in order to do my research I spent three months in little villages in Belize and Guatemala, amongst the Maya peoples. I was hoping to learn more about their practice of herbal medicine, but was disappointed to find out it was a tradition still mastered by only a handful of people. 'The younger generations are simply not interested anymore,' an old wise shaman told me sadly. 'The church doesn't approve of our old traditions.

---

[1] Lyrics from *Circle of life*, the *Lion King* soundtrack

We now need to buy our medicines at a pharmacy, which is extremely expensive and it is a two days' walk from here,' sighed a Mayan woman in one of the villages, while all kinds of beautiful indigenous herbs were lusciously overgrowing her garden.

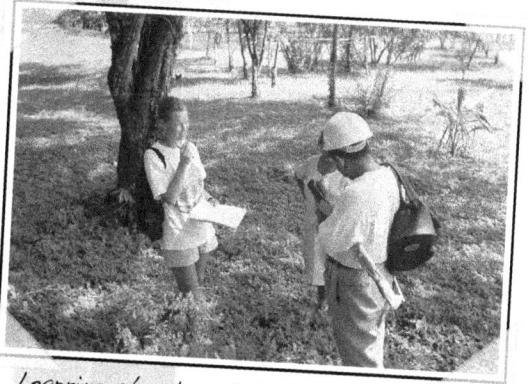

Learning about medicinal plants in Belize.

During my time in South America, I came across some very successful projects. One of them had been designed to make the population aware of the importance of the rainforest, its protection being crucial for them just as for the rest of the world. A huge amount of effort was put into employing local people, for example in the tourism industry, but also to protect the forest. 'The most renowned and skillful poachers turn out to be the best foresters,' one of the project leaders told me.

I also discovered some small, but very rewarding, projects and initiatives which had been started specifically to support a particular village, an orphanage, or a hospital. It showed me that the tiniest amount of money could go a long way, provided the locals were involved. If they had not been made to participate, the plan would be abandoned as soon as support from abroad would stop.

These projects showed me that it is possible to make a real difference in the lives of others, however small it might seem in the global scheme of things. With this in the back of my mind, I promised myself I would one day contribute, doing something charitable, in order to make that difference.

Just when I was about to write my thesis, the Curaçao phone company announced they were reducing their tariffs, and my extra income would be cut back dramatically. At the same time, my younger brother's home situation was about to change. He had been living with my dad's ex-girlfriend, but this was no longer possible. He had to find somewhere else to live. Impulsively, I decided to go back to the Netherlands and take care of him. With my dad's help we bought a house in the Amsterdam suburbs, and it was arranged that my mum and sister would look after my little brother when I would be traveling.

## Entrepreneurship

After having spent almost two years in the Caribbean, it was not easy adapting to life in the Netherlands. I arrived in the middle of a dark, cold winter, the days were short and temperatures freezing. The cold spell seemed to last forever, and people were skating on Amsterdam's frozen canals. My friends had such busy agenda's, that in order to meet up with them I had to plan well ahead. It was something I found extremely hard to get used to, it was so different from the easy going lifestyle I had been enjoying on Curaçao, where socializing was a lot less organized.

'I'm afraid this is the end of my carefree life and independent projects, it's time to find a regular job,' I complained to my masseur. 'The company my wife works for are looking to recruit new people, why don't you talk to them?' he advised. To tell you the truth, I had never thought of my masseur as a serious head hunter, but decided I would give it a go. *Roughmen* was an intermediate agency between cartoon artists and the advertisement industry. I gave them a call, and was invited for an interview. We had a very pleasant meeting, and afterwards the owner of the company said to my astonishment: 'For some reason I can't see you in a regular job, I simply don't think it's challenging enough for you. Would you be interested in leading a project for us instead? We are considering the possibility to extend our market to Germany, but we have no idea what the current situation is over there.'

Who could have thought the market research experience I gained on Curaçao would come in use so soon? After completing that first research project, I was asked by the owner's husband to do a similar project for his company, and he, in his turn, had a friend who had his own company as well. I became part of a network of entrepreneurs, who asked me to look into the possibilities of broadening the scope of their activities, not having time for this themselves.

It was impossible to explain in a few words what I did for a living, I was involved in so many different projects. I would often use the example of selling shoelaces in Timbuktu: 'Imagine you want to sell shoelaces, but you don't have a clue where to start, that's when you call me. I will find out everything you need to know for setting up a new business successfully,' I explained. 'Within a few days I can give you an overview of the entire shoelace market in Timbuktu,

© Vincent Mentzel

Esther Jacobs

JBN PROJECTS

P. Lautaanweg 12
1181 XG Amstelveen
The Netherlands

phone +31 (0)20 4451519
fax +31 (0)20 6409955
mobile +31 (0)6 54287328
e-mail ejacobs@

jbnprojects.nl

including the current prices, the most important players on the market, and people and organizations worth talking to.'

During a trip through Morocco, I came across this roadsign: 52 days (per camel!) to Timbuktu...

Without exception I was able to find written information on the topic in question, even for the most unusual business proposals, and I would always know or meet the right people who could help me out when I needed some assistance with a certain project. It gave me the courage to take on even the most extraordinary projects. One of these out-of-the-box assignments was a project for Undutchables, a recruitment agency for international jobseekers in the Netherlands. I looked into the possibilities of helping expats find a job in their native language. 'We can't rely on the quality of research done by students, and professional agencies are often too expensive and usually produce extensive reports, which are too big to read anyway, but you are very good at telling us exactly what we need, being an entrepreneur yourself,' I was complimented by Kluun, a famous Dutch writer, whose wife owned Undutchables. A few years later, I read his first novel *Love Life*, which is based on his experience of his wife being diagnosed with breast cancer. I was deeply moved by his account of their relationship and his wife's terminal illness, and although it had been a while since my neighbor predicted a doomsday scenario, this book was a reminder that you never know what lies around the corner. The best thing you can do is to make choices which are right for you. I had been through some unhappy times in my life as well, but it had made me into the person I was. I realized it was because of those kind of experiences, that I was living my life the way I was.

Not all projects turned out to be a success, and I sometimes got myself involved into schemes which were doomed to fail. Once, a group of very successful network marketers asked me to design an advantage card for their network members. These men used to carry suitcases full of cash, and used bodyguards for their protection. It did not feel good, but I would earn a lot of money with it. 'Obviously, this is dodgy as hell, but there's nothing wrong with the work itself,' I tried to convince myself, and accepted the offer. However, halfway into the job, the whole management was arrested and sentenced for fraudulent activities. It was a rude reminder of my Geneva experience. 'This is the last time I get involved in this kind of business,' I promised myself.

My masseur should have been a headhunter instead! He got me another job, this time introducing me to a small consultancy agency called ACG. Eddy Scheffer, ACG's Executive Director, asked me if I could lead a European research project for the meat industry. 'But...I am a vegetarian!' I stuttered. 'Shouldn't be a problem,' said Eddy, 'it might be a fun challenge, making sure our customers don't find out about that! And, if they ever offer a guided tour of the meat factory, just decline,' he advised with a smile. Eddy showed me the benefit of using catchy titles: Nice to meat you! Eddy put that on the cover of the meat industry report. When I was about to present the results to a group of high powered professionals, all of whom I had interviewed in the past months, Eddy announced me as follows: 'Here is Esther, and you might not know this yet, but she is a vegetarian.' It put my presentation in a completely different light...

The deregulation of the Dutch telecom market created an interesting commercial opportunity for me. Having worked for Interglobe, MTF and Global Access, I had gained a huge amount of knowledge about the foreign telecom markets, and this put me into an advantageous position. Together with a friend I created OptiTel, a company advising organizations on the consequences of the liberalization of the telecom industry. We even joined a business plan competition and won the first price!

By now, I was confident that I would always find a job if I needed to. At my brothers school there was a shortage of teachers in Economics, and I offered to help out. 'I always help my brother with his homework, I might as well help some other kids,' I said during a parent information evening. I received some strange looks, I could see the other people thinking: 'Is she a pupil or a parent?' Amazingly, the school took me up on my offer, and I ended up becoming an Economics teacher for one day a week, teaching my brothers class as well as two others. My brother was a lot more nervous than I was, that first lesson. At the end of class he ran up to my desk, and nervously said: 'That was not too bad was it?' I thought I best take it as a compliment. It was nice to be so closely involved in my brother's daily life. I had also negotiated proper consultancy fees, arguing I would not be able to accept any commercial projects while teaching. 'You are now the best paid teacher in the country,' the school management joked.

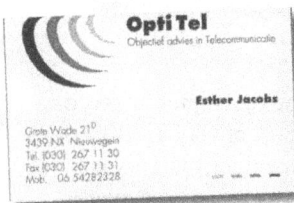

This weird roller coaster ride taught me the ins and outs of entrepreneurship. Instead of studying for an MBA I had been learning on the job. Who would have thought my unconventional resume would prove so valuable. I told my dad: 'my friends from university are making more money than I do, they are building a pension and are slowly rising on the career ladder. But at least I get to know a lot of different companies, markets and people.' To my surprise my dad added: 'more importantly, you're getting to know yourself. I was quite concerned about the choices you made when you just started, remember those people in Geneva?' he winked, 'but now I see you're a lot more streetwise and your sense for business has grown tremendously; you are flexible and able to adjust quickly in any situation...'

What we did not know was that it would not be long before I was going to need all the experience I had, in order to keep my head above water.

*'Everyone has talent. What's rare is the courage to follow it to the dark places it leads.'*
*- Erica Jong -*

Ever since I came back from skiing in January, it's been a madhouse over here. Can you believe it: after all that time of not knowing what to do, all of a sudden I am swamped! I started working two days a week for this small, international, fun consulting company based in Amersfoort. And at the same time I also became involved in this marketingproject, through one of my dad's friends. You can imagine I'm very busy at the moment: I'm launching a European advantage card, which offers deals on all kinds of things: hotels, restaurants, telecommunication, and insurances. I love the job, even though it's taking up a ridiculous amount of time, but hopefully I'll be earning an equally ridiculous amount of money once I'm finished with it! I also started work on a

A letter to a girlfriend.

# Excuse 4:
# 'I wouldn't know where to start'

'A journey of a
thousand miles
begins with a first step.'
- Old Chinese proverb -

# Birth of an idea

'Did you know that once the euro has been introduced, you won't be able to change your old foreign coins?' I was surprised when a friend told me this, a few years before the actual launch of the new currency in 2002. 'All left over change will become useless by then!' he said, and suggested we should set up a company to collect all this soon-to-be obsolete money. 'If necessary we could even drive around Europe, getting the best exchange rates' he added enthusiastically.

I thought about that big jar of coins I had at home, filled up to the rim with all kinds of foreign money. I expected to use these up one day while holidaying abroad. But for some reason that never happened and the jar was now so full it nearly over-flowed. It was inconceivable that this money would lose its value, and I could not imagine many people were aware of this; maybe my friend's idea was not so bad after all.

We tried to think of a strategy, but the longer we racked our brains, the more unrealistic our plan seemed to be. Would people be willing enough to look for their spare holiday coins and hand them over in return for only a few euro-cents? Surely, they would be put off by the idea of us making a profit! After some research I found that major banks only exchange foreign bills, but GWK Travelex would accept as little as four currency units, however charging an incredible twenty five percent commission; and even they were considering canceling the service as the exchange process was too elaborate and profits were low! In short, the idea of collecting foreign coins seemed interesting, but was not viable commercially. Still, it kept lingering in the back of my mind.

On my return to the Netherlands in 1996, in order to take care of my younger brother, I again picked up my resolution to do something charitable, using my South America experiences. I spent hours leafing through the job pages at the Médecins Sans Frontières offices but became a little disillusioned when I saw that every available vacancy, including the volunteer projects, seemed to require a medical background. 'I am a marketing consultant,' I told them, 'do you think I could be of any use to your organization?' They gave me the same answer as I would also get from all the other charities: 'You could hand out flyers at the shopping mall if you want...' but I felt that, with my experience, skills and education, I was better suited and qualified for a completely different kind of volunteer work.

As I began to lose my enthusiasm, I shared my experience with others and found that these stories were common and many people, although keen, struggled to find a way to be of any help and did not know where to start.

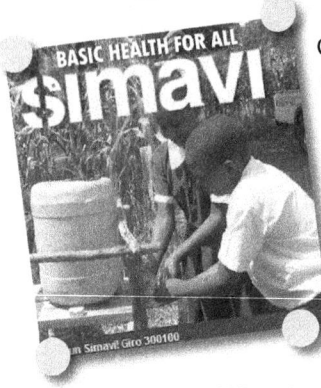

One day, a friendly old man rang my doorbell, he was a door-to-door charity collector asking for a small donation, and we got to talking: 'My wife and I have been collecting for Simavi for years' he said and his voice quivered. 'But now my wife has fallen ill, and I'm trying to find someone who can take over for her.' He looked me straight in the eye: 'Is that something you would consider?' I have to admit door-to-door collecting had never been high on my priority list, but even though I did not know what Simavi stood for, I simply could not refuse this good man; besides, I had been telling myself for a long time I should do something charitable, well, here was my chance.

Door-to-door collection was an amazing experience. Even on a dark, cold and rainy winter's evening, people were very happy to open the door to me and donated generously into the collection box. Not just one guilder (like I always did) but two or even five guilders! It did not seem anybody's concern what Simavi is dedicated to (I had learnt by now that they organize 'medical transport in Africa', but that was about all I knew). I met one lady who, clearly embarrassed, admitted the organization's ideals did not appeal to her and therefore she would not donate, but she was the only one who appeared to carefully consider her donations.

This experience taught me it actually does not matter what you are asking money or assistance for, the difference lies in who you are asking and how. Most people are very keen to be of any help, as long as it is made simple for them.

I collected over three hundred guilders in two evenings which was, according to a very happy Simavi coordinator, 'a highly respectable score!' Still, I did not feel I had made a huge difference in the scheme of things. I had dealt with much larger sums of money working on commercial projects, and I was convinced I could achieve a lot more.

A few weeks after the brainstorming session on how to collect the soon-to-be worthless foreign coins, my boyfriend and I were in southern India. We were having lunch on a beautiful beach which had a very relaxed atmosphere, allowing me to think quietly about my future plans. I was looking for a new project to earn myself some proper money, but on the other hand I still felt I should do something a bit more socially beneficial, not just for my own benefit. Suddenly it hit me: why not combine the two ideals? 'The problem with collecting coins commercially is how to get people to hand over their leftover change' I explained. 'But what if we collect the coins for charity instead for ourselves? That incentive might encourage people. And instead of door-to-door collections, we could just put the collection boxes in shops and banks, plus I am sure banks will be happy to exchange the coins for charity!'

I could not stop daydreaming about this simple but ingenious idea. The euro introduction was the perfect timing for this one-off project. Our plan would be straightforward and simple to explain and, not asking for any cash but collecting something that had already lost its value anyway, we would not compete with money being regularly donated to charity.' Exchanging the collected coins, we would raise an enormous sum for a variety of good causes, and I would be surprised if we would not make a small profit ourselves. I was so inspired by this plan, and could not wait to get started when we got back. My poor boyfriend did not hear me talk about much else during the rest of our holiday!

## How do you eat an elephant?

## One bite at a time.

Once back home in the Netherlands I immediately started putting the idea into action. Unfortunately, my friend could not join me, 'I have a busy career, a young family, and simply no time for another project,' he admitted regretfully. He did, however, like the charity version of his idea and encouraged me to carry on developing it further.

My to-do list seemed never ending. 'Where do I start?' I repeatedly asked myself, but discussing my plans with others helped me to focus, enabling me to identify my first steps. I thought the best approach would be creating a partnership between the charities, who would decide what the money would be used for. The shops, where the money would be collected, the banks who would exchange the coins, and an advertising agency taking care of the publicity.

These were four enormous projects, in addition to which a feasibility study needed to be carried out, and the non-profit foundation established.

Many different parties needed to be contacted, but they all seemed intertwined to such a degree that I couldn't separate the trees from the forest. I almost started to doubt I would ever succeed. However, being self-employed I had taught myself to think in terms of 'projects' instead of 'problems', and found that it is a lot easier when you divide a big, elaborate project into bite-size tasks. Therefore, I was able to reassure myself that by the time I got going the rest would fall into place.

One of my first priorities was to decide which charities would benefit from the money that would be raised. Once I had a charity onboard I could approach the shops, banks, and advertising agencies. I decided to propose my plans to three organizations, each with a different focus: children, the environment, and lastly an organization concentrating on international aid, as 'Something for Everybody' seemed appropriate.

Not being familiar with any charity, I randomly picked three well established names: Plan International, The World Wildlife Fund, and Médecins Sans Frontières. I struggled immediately, as it seemed impossible to arrange a meeting with any of them. Naively I had assumed they would jump at my fundraising ideas, but in reality they were approached frequently, and were in a position to be very selective about whom they invited. This was not made any easier by the fact that I was apprehensive about explaining my plan over the phone, in fear of them stealing my ideas. Nevertheless, I needed to give them some information in order to attract their interest.

My charity of choice would be determined by the percentage of donated funds that were actually going to be spent on the projects instead of on overhead costs. I had my first meeting with Plan International who promote child rights and fight child poverty. Before seeing them I had gone through their annual report thoroughly, which had raised questions on the cost percentage details. The meeting was nothing like I had imagined: instead of being very happy at seeing me and answering my questions, they were downright suspicious.

'Why have you come to us with your ideas? What do you want us to do exactly?' It would not be the first time I was welcomed by such hostility, as none of the charities seemed to have any procedure in place for a situation in which they were offered a project. However, once I had set out my ideas their initial apprehension turned into enthusiasm, and they were genuinely interested in how I was going to implement this plan. Unfortunately I did not have all the answers to their questions, this being the exact reason why I had approached them. 'Would you be interested in launching this project together?' I asked them. Quite rightly the charities did not jump at my plan, cautiously wondering who Esther Jacobs was and which other charities and shops would join in. 'Please come back when you have finalized your plans and found other partners,' was their friendly but definite answer, and I was back at square one. 'I need the charities to set up the organization and find other partners, but they don't want to join before everything is already in place!' I grumbled to my friends.

As a matter of fact, I actually did not have time at all to get engaged in a venture like this. I simply needed to look for commercial projects which would generate some income, as there were bills to be paid. A lot of my time was spent on taking up new assignments and writing many proposals, of which only a few resulted in a paid job. Still, the coin/charity scheme kept playing on my mind and I knew I should at least have one more go at it.

What kept me determined were the numerous positive reactions I received whenever I told anyone about the project, and I boldly decided to set up a foundation, which allowed me to at least tick off an item from my list, and this at least gave lots of positive energy. Finding a suitable name was a challenge: 'It should be easy to remember, have an international ring to it, and also say something about the nature of the scheme and charity,' I explained to friends while trying to come up with something good. We settled for Coins for Care, a catchy name which did not need any further clarification. A friendly attorney, who I had found through the yellow pages, helped me –free of charge- to set up the foundation, and I could not help but wonder how simple it was to start a new charity.

The next job on the list was finding a bank that was willing to exchange all foreign cash to euros. 'Don't expect the banks to cooperate just like that,' my friends warned me, but naively I was sure all banks would be very willing to help (after all it would be for charity) and I would simply pick the bank offering the best deal.

I could not have been more wrong: the banks were not interested at all in exchanging the collected coins. 'Firstly, our policy is not to trade any foreign currency,' a spokesperson explained patiently over the phone, 'it's a nasty job; there is simply too much work involved which is not worth the profit. Secondly, your timing is really bad; we will be up to our ears in exchanging our Dutch guilders to euros, let alone foreign money.'

If the banks did not want to help me out I would count and sort the money myself, I concluded, it could not be that difficult. I started looking up information on money counting machines and ended up at the manufacturer of ScanCoin. Unfortunately, these highly priced machines could only deal with a limited number of currencies, and jammed when processing large varieties of foreign coins.

Even if I had been able to pay for them I could not have purchased a ScanCoin, as all the machines, no matter how old, had been snapped up by the Dutch bank, the Royal Mint, and the other commercial banks to cope with the counting of all the soon-to-be-obsolete Dutch money: these were busy times for coin processors and they could not help me out.

I summarized the results of a year's hard work and concluded I had at least created the foundation, although my original plan had included four key components: charities, banks, shops and an advertising agency. Before deciding whether to join or not, the charities needed an outlined plan with some reputable partners and, most importantly, a solution for exchanging the for-

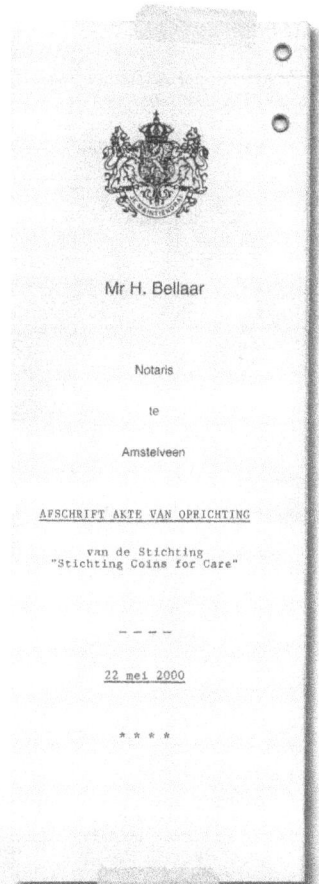

Mr H. Bellaar

Notaris

te

Amstelveen

AFSCHRIFT AKTE VAN OPRICHTING

van de Stichting
"Stichting Coins for Care"

– – – –

22 mei 2000

* * * *

SCAN COIN 4000
VALUE SORTER

□ SCAN COIN

eign cash currencies; and without the support of the charities and banks it would not make any sense to approach a big retail chain or an advertising agency. I had ended up in a road-block. Was this the end for Coins for Care?

*'If something needs to be perfect,*
*it won't have time to grow.'*
*- Coachingskalender -*

## Pushy or ambitious?

President Aristide looked up when an unfamiliar, scruffy looking, young blond walked into his spacious offices. It was 1996, he had only just returned from exile to Haiti and was preparing for a visit from Bill Clinton. The CIA had taken over security of his palace, and even the two Associated Press journalists interviewing him, could not hide their astonishment when I (because that blond girl was me) walked in just like that. We had separated only one hour ago, and they had not thought I would succeed in entering the palace without an introduction, press card or passport. Their interview with the president had come to an end, and they said: 'This is Esther, a backpacker all the way from the Netherlands.' We shook hands with the president and, after I had taken a picture of the three men together, I followed the two reporters through the long palace corridors back to the outside world.

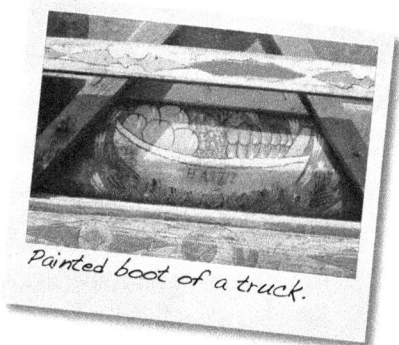

Painted boot of a truck.

Camera-assistant.

The day before, I had arrived at the Haitian airport; I had no plan, no reservation booked, not even a travel guide. I asked a taxi driver if he knew of any cheap hostels. He looked at me, bewildered, and said: 'There are no hostels here, we don't get any tourists because of the American boycott!'
I asked him how much it was to take me into Port-au-Prince, but I thought his asking price was much too high and decided to wait and see what would happen. About fifteen minutes later the same taxi driver came by again: 'Just get in, I know some people who might be able to help you.' I got in the car which

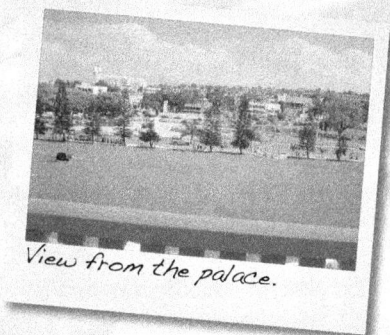

View from the palace.

75

Many people leave the rural areas for town.

stopped a few moments later in front of two cursing American journalists. They did not pay me any attention as they had just found out not all of their expensive equipment had arrived, and what had was badly damaged. While they were frantically trying to recover their belongings, the taxi driver inquired hesitantly if they could give me a ride into town. They glanced around and nodded briefly. I was just left standing there, feeling a bit lost, but finally they invited me to take a seat in their taxi van. When we drove off they asked me where I was heading. 'I don't know,' I answered, and they gave me a puzzled look. 'But what are you doing here then?' I explained I had bought a ticket which allowed me to travel the Caribbean for a month, and I had thought Haiti might be an interesting destination. Silence fell in the car. 'Interesting' was clearly not a legitimate explanation for being in one of the worlds poorest countries, which had been in a state of civil war for years, was heavily boycotted by the US, and completely ignored by tourists. After introducing themselves, Chris and Fernando invited me to join them in their hotel. They offered me one of their spare rooms, which had been reserved for a few colleagues arriving at a later stage, and I ended up in the most luxurious hotel of Haiti, in a beautiful room with a stunning view across Port-au-Prince.

As I did not have any plans, Chris and Fernando asked me if I would be interested in joining them on their visit to the presidential palace for an interview with president Aristide. It was a chance of a lifetime. The next morning we set off for the palace, which had received a fresh layer of paint in honor of Clinton's visit. The majestic building, virgin white, stood out in huge contrast to the impoverished, dirty town surrounding it. Waste collection seemed unheard of and the rubbish from the richer parts of town was simply dumped in the poor slums. President Clinton would arrive by helicopter and, to leave nothing to chance, the road over which he would fly was newly tarred. His impression of Haiti would be a far cry from reality.

Just before arriving at the palace Chris and Fernando received a phone call, and they were told the rooms they had booked in another hotel for the rest of their crew, were not available after all. Time was running out as rooms were going quickly, now journalists from all over the world were beginning to pour in, to await Clinton's visit. Seeing their dilemma, I

The Voodoo party

offered to go to the hotel and sort the rooms out, after which I would come back in order to join them for the interview. Obviously relieved they said: 'Make sure you'll be back within half an hour, otherwise we won't be able to get you in.' Then we approached the first security post and a dark suited CIA officer checked our car. We were allowed through, under the condition that the driver and I would be back within five

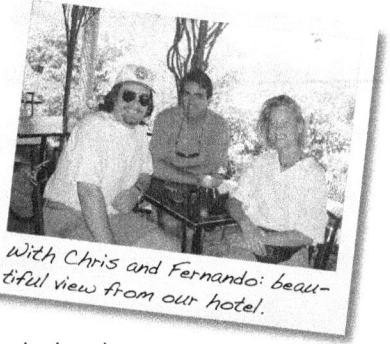

With Chris and Fernando: beautiful view from our hotel.

minutes. Chris and Fernando instructed me on the hotel rooms but remained doubtful I would be able to resolve the situation, as their own people back in the US had not been very successful so far. I am sure they did not expect to see me back soon.

It was only after the interview, while walking back through the heavily secured palace, that I was able to tell Chris and Fernando what had happened. 'How on earth did you get through security?' They asked me. 'And did you manage to get the hotel rooms back?'
I started with the hotel part and told them how I had convinced the owner that I had been sent specifically to correct the errors made by the hotel, and that I had been instructed not to leave until the rooms had been reconfirmed. Apparently, I had made such a resolute impression that he had been very quick to rectify the situation, and the driver and I had hurried back to the palace.

The same CIA agent from earlier was not going to let us in again: 'Lady, you're not on the guest list and you don't have a press card. I can't let you go through,' he said firmly. 'But you just saw me with the Associated Press journalists? I just needed to get something organized back at the hotel, and now they're waiting for me to carry out the interview,' I insisted. The officer repeated he needed to see a press card, but he appeared a little less stringent and I persistently repeated my argument. After a few minutes the good man realized I was not going to give up and he said, warily: 'Miss, if I were to let you through, you'll be stopped by my colleagues at the next post anyway, there's not point really, is there?' but I eagerly maintained I wanted to give it a try.

To my excitement, I was allowed to pass to the next checkpoint where I was asked the same questions. 'Your name is not on our list, you don't have a press card, not even a passport. Sorry, but we can't allow you in.' I told the guard I was with the Associated Press, that we had an arranged meeting with president Aristide, and that my two colleagues were already inside. Finally, I convinced him it was fine; why else had his colleague let me go through? Reasoning thus

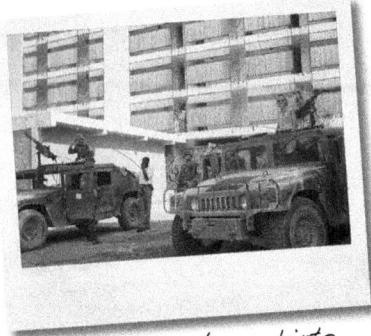

*On our way we bumped into some US soldiers. In the spur of the moment I asked them if I could have a look inside their tank, and they said yes!*

helped me to get past the next two check-points as well. There was only one last post left before the tightly protected presidential wing.

This time the officers were not going to move easily and said, stern-faced: 'Miss, we can't let you in, unless your presence is essential for the interview.' I gave them my biggest smile and stated: 'my presence is essential for the interview.'

This proved to be sufficient, and I was escorted by one of the security officers to the president's office, where Chris and Fernando were just finishing their interview with president Aristide. I took a picture of the three of them, but unfortunately have no picture of myself at this point.

Only much later I realized how lucky I was in not having to walk through the metal detectors, as I always carry a knife in my rucksack, which I use for peeling and cutting fruit!

Back at the hotel, Chris, Fernando, and I had a good laugh about our adventures at the palace. That evening, at a party for all the journalists and other foreigners, I noticed I was being pointed out and people were talking about me.

There were only a few women, I was by far the youngest and I thought that was what drew the attention. But then I caught what was being said about me: 'She's the one who got through Presidential security!'

Before I knew it, I was surrounded by a bunch of CIA officers, who boastfully said: 'We should apologize for our Haitian colleagues. They've never seen a blond girl, that's why they let you pass.'

They were so full of themselves; incredibly loud and arrogant. A little overwhelmed I pointd out to them: 'But you let me pass as well! And you,...and also you,..!'

## By word of mouth

I was being pushed from pillar to post trying to find a solution for processing the money. It might have just been easier to get rid of me, or maybe it was well meant, however, I was put in contact with a lot of different people, which prevented me from just giving up when things got tough. Another advantage was that having to pitch my ideas many times made me more fluent and convincing and, although there still was no direct answer to my problems, the reactions I received were always positive and enthusiastic. I was strengthened in my belief that I was doing the right thing which helped me to remain upbeat.

Various money transporters such as Brinks, not being able to help out, recommended Coin Co International, a small UK based family firm specializing in the conversion of foreign coins. In hindsight this recommendation proved to be the turning point.

*'It's better to have a good idea generating enthusiasm, than a brilliant idea which inspires no one.'*

## Heaps of Money

John Baker, owner of Coin Co, confirmed by phone that his company sorted and processed foreign money.
'Currency from countries all over the world!' he said proudly. He was very interested in my story and invited me to come round and see for myself how they worked.
I decided to combine my visit to Coin Co with a stay at Amir and Tanya's, owners of The Games Company, in order to keep costs at a minimum.
John was a big, jovial man with a friendly face. With his deep voice, beard, and roaring laugh he reminded me a bit of Santa! His wife Doreen was lovely too, and nothing like the ruthless business woman I had expected to meet.
They showed me around their company: from the outside a nondescript, large warehouse on an industrial estate on the outskirts of London. Inside were rows

and rows of shelves, stacked with bags and crates full of coins from all over the world. It made me slightly nervous having such large quantities of cash around me. 'Don't worry, you'll get used to it soon enough,' John said, sensing my reaction.

'After a few days you don't see it as money anymore.'

People at long tables were busily sorting out the coins.

'An experienced person will do about 40 kilo's a day,' explained John, 'whereas a beginner won't do more than 10.' Some employees were well passed their retirement age, there were people with slight disabilities, and there were people in wheelchairs, but everybody was clearly enjoying their work, and they showed me proudly what they were doing. 'A lot of pensioners love doing this job,' said John. 'We're also very popular with coin-collectors. But do you know who suits this job best?' John gave me a wry smile: 'Managers suffering from executive burnout!'

'Coin Co started as a hobby when the airline John worked for went bust,' said Doreen. 'They had this big box of foreign coins and nobody seemed to be interested in it, so John asked if he could take it home.' The whole family had got involved in sorting the money, and every time they went on holiday they took some coins with them. I smiled at the idea of John, Doreen, and the kids sitting around the kitchen table, sifting through a big pile of coins.

Coin Co was a unique company and did not have any direct competitors in Europe, which was why their client base kept increasing: Airlines gathering huge amounts of change through tax-free sales, British charities collecting foreign coins, and even the Royal Mail who got rid of their exotic currencies in this manner.

'But our most unusual customer must be the parking authorities of some big cities in West Germany.' John grinned 'A lot of their Polish and East German customers have found that some Polish coins are of a similar size to the German Marks, and they use them for paying at the parking meters, which means they are virtually parking for free!' The parking authorities had come to John in

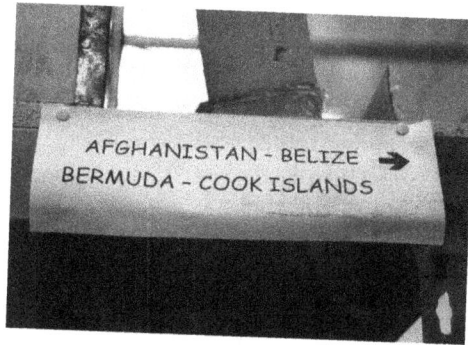

order to get at least some earnings out of these Polish Zloty's, even though they were only worth a fraction of the Mark.

According to John, dealing with these amounts of coinage had its own problems and was not as simple as it seemed: 'You can't just load up a truck with money,' he said, 'the sheer weight would break the axle!' There goes the idea of traveling through Europe, picking up coins along the way,' I thought.

'Besides, no insurance will be prepared to cover the risk, they'll regard it as high-risk money transport.' This had never even crossed my mind, I had been so busy telling everyone the coins would be worthless and had compared it to scrap metal instead…''And also,' John continued, 'when you arrive at the Spanish border, for example, with a car full of Peseta's, they won't let you through! You see, in some countries exporting coins is forbidden by law, although they hardly ever do checks on that. But, when you try to import them back into the country, they'll say: sorry, we can't accept your money, you shouldn't have taken it out of the country in the first place.'

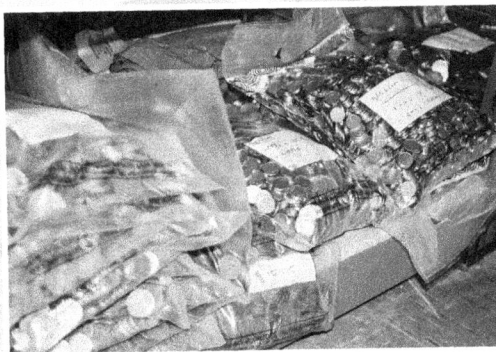

Coin Co now held over 20 years of experience with coin conversion and had partners worldwide. Doreen explained to me that even if Central Banks were not interested in the loose change, local banks would, avoiding having to buy from their federal counterparts. They assured me that even obsolete currencies would bring in a bit of money through Coin Co's contacts with commercial banks, coin collectors, and scrap metal dealers.

John and Doreen's story made me realize I should not even attempt to process huge amounts of foreign coins myself. I had been convinced it was a job waiting to be done by a specialist. After a year of investigating, Coin Co seemed not only the best option, it actually was the only option I had. John

---

**189 currencies separated into their own jar**

Het bedrijf Coins for Care 25 januari 2007

Elke 24 uur ligt een gewicht van 5 ton vreemd geld klaar voor verscheping naar banken op het continent. "Het leek allemaal zo eenvoudig toen ik Coins for Care lanceerde", vertelt Esther Jacobs, initiatiefneemster van de actie, de telefoon vanuit Nederland. Ik dacht: iedereen heeft thuis wel buitenlands geld liggen. Maar er was geen bank in Nederland die het wilde wisselen, dat is aanvankelijk niet. " Dan een manier bedenken om munten bij hun eigen banken te krijgen. "Anderhalf jaar zat ik in gesprek geweest met bedrijven, maar geen kon de hoeveelheid bolwerken. Ik ga via noodte ik van ...

**Engels bedrijf sorteert munten voor Coins voor Care**

# It takes months before you are any good at this job

Door Dick Hofland
**London**

Coins for Care is een Nederlandse actie voor het goede doel, maar de Engelsen doen het werk. Zij sorteren de munten die in Nederland zijn opgehaald, met de hand. Dat is zo arbeidsintensief dat het bedrijf 10 procent van de opbrengst in rekening ... Voor al het ...

In een nauwelijks beveiligde hal op het industrieterrein van Burgess Hill, zo'n zestig kilometer ten zuiden van Londen, raapt John Baker een cent van de grond. "Die is ook hier niets meer waard," zegt hij, terwijl hij plastic zakken met guldens en knaken in een stelling legt.

# No security required for 'left-over' coins

**Coins for Care**
*VERVOLG VAN PAGINA 1*

John Baker vond met zijn Coin Co het klassieke gat in de markt. Het bedrijf moest eigen transport, scheepscontainers, op- en overslag organiseren en werd een belangrijke connectie tussen de wereldbanken. In Ierland, Canada en Duitsland werden bijkantoren geopend en langzaam vonden den liefdadigheidsinstellingen hun weg. "We geven goede doelen een gunstige wisselkoers, omdat zij meeliften op de infrastructuur die we al hebben opgezet voor de commerciële bedrijven."

Met de komst van de euro ziet CCI een kwart van haar markt verdwijnen. Maar het contract dat het bedrijf met Esther Jacobs van Coins for Care en geestverwanten kon sluiten, betekende een eenmalige grote opdracht en een goede reclame voor de toekomst. Baker: "We proberen in deze hoogtijdagen alles eruit te halen wat erin zit. Onze capaciteit is met 300 procent gegroeid en nu behoorlijk overspannen, want we vechten tegen de tijd; binnen een jaar houden de eerste Europese banken op hun oude geld te wisselen. Coins for Care was één van onze eerste opdrachtgevers, we den ...

die voor het einde van het jaar een eindresultaat kunnen presenteren. Voor alle Europese initiatieven tezamen hopen we zo'n 50 miljoen euro op te halen." Koekblikken, enveloppen, tonnen, zakken, bunkers vol geldstukken munten liggen opgestapeld in de Engelse pakhuizen. De beveiliging is echter bescheiden. "Wij hoeven ons niet te wapenen tegen inbrekers en overvallers – wat moeten die nou met een vracht munten die grotendeels niet langer in omloop zijn?" Het kantoor, de magazijnen en transportwagens zijn bewust niet aangekleed met herkenbare logo's en adres. "Niemand weet ...

wat we hier doen. Op deze manier houden we ook de overheadkosten laag en kunnen we minder commissie over de geldtransacties vragen."

Als alle campagnes ten einde zijn, moet CCI weer inkrimpen. "Maar werk blijft er genoeg", meent John Baker optimistisch. "In Duitsland wordt een grootscheepse inzameling van buitenlandse munten voorbereid voor de WK in 2006. Dan komen mensen van over de hele wereld naar Europa. En wie weet, op een dag, waagt Engeland de overstap naar de euro. Dan kan ons bedrijf een tweede grote slag slaan."

*Esther Gotink*

en Doreen emphasized they would be happy to work with Coins for Care: 'The Euro replacing a dozen currencies will reduce our workload with about 25 percent. Working with Coins for Care will increase our reputation and attract new clients,' John reckoned. He offered to sort and exchange the money collected by Coins for Care, and added they would even be prepared to pick up the currency from the Netherlands using their special trucks.

I went home feeling incredibly happy. Finally I had met someone who had showed me it was possible to convert all these coins, and even better, who was willing to help me in doing so! John send me a draft contract in which it was stated that Coins for Care would sell the collected currencies to Coin Co for a set amount, per country, per coin. Enclosed was a list with the offered counter value for every currency's coins and notes, which was denoted in a percentage of the nominal value, the 'true' value of the money. After a few negotiations by phone, we agreed on 98 percent for the Dutch Guilder and 92 percent for the other European currencies. I only became aware afterwards that Coin Co had

## COIN CO INTERNATIONAL

Group Currency Details

15/06/00

Page 2 of 5

*Group* €uro Project rates     *Comments* Special rates for "JBN Projects" - €uro charity fundraiser

| Country | €uro Rate | Coin Ratio | Coin Rate | Note Ratio | Note Rate |
|---|---|---|---|---|---|
| Estonia | 15.636 | 15 | 17.981 | 8 | 16.887 |
| Ethiopia | 7.733 | 20 | 9.28 | 10 | 8.506 |
| Europe | 1 | 4 | 1.04 | 2 | 1.02 |
| Falkland Islands | 0.63 | 20 | 0.756 | 10 | 0.693 |
| Fiji | 1.995 | 20 | 2.394 | 10 | 2.194 |
| Finland | 5.945 | 8 | 6.421 | 4 | 6.183 |
| France | 6.559 | 8 | 7.084 | 4 | 6.821 |
| French Pacific Isl. | 124.267 | 20 | 149.12 | 10 | 136.694 |
| Gambia | 12.09 | 20 | 14.508 | 10 | 13.299 |
| Germany | 1.955 | 8 | 2.111 | 4 | 2.033 |

not been very sharp as their tariffs were way below their processing cost price...

When launching the Coins for Care project, one of my aims was to encourage cooperation between charities. It would be a waste of energy if identical programs would be initiated, encountering the same difficulties with coin conversion. That is why I decided to sign an exclusive deal with Coin Co, so they would refer any party with identical plans to Coins for Care.

My year long investigation into the world of foreign currencies had brought me another, albeit unexpected, advantage, which I was not immediately aware of: my extensive talks to various organizations had turned me into a true coinage-expert. It was beyond any doubt that the 'Who is Esther Jacobs'-question had been answered adequately.

| Country | Euro Rate | Euro Ratio | Coin Rate | Euro Ratio | Note Rate |
|---|---|---|---|---|---|
| Japan | | | | | 111.759 |
| Jersey | | | | | 0.662 |
| Jordan | | | | | 0.746 |
| Kazakhs | | | | | 149.673 |
| Kenya | | | | | 81.736 |
| Kiribati | | | | | 1.775 |
| Korea, S | | | | | 1168.165 |
| Kuwait | | | | | 0.321 |
| Kyrgyzst | | | | | 45.818 |
| Laos | | | | | 7974.186 |
| Latvia | | | | | 0.616 |
| Lebanon | | | | | 1588.567 |
| Lesotho | | | | | 7.374 |
| Liberia | | | | | 1.048 |
| Libya | | | | | 0.525 |
| Lithuania | | | | | 4.119 |
| Luxembx | | | | | 41.953 |
| Macao | | | | | 8.379 |
| Macedonia | 60.192 | 20 | 72.23 | 10 | 66.211 |
| Madagascar | 6056.947 | 20 | 7268.336 | 10 | 6662.642 |
| Madeira | 200.482 | 8 | 216.521 | 4 | 208.501 |
| Malawi | 52.456 | 20 | 62.947 | 10 | 57.702 |
| Malaysia | 3.624 | 20 | 4.349 | 10 | 3.986 |
| Maldives | 11.179 | 20 | 13.415 | 10 | 12.297 |
| Malta | 0.41 | 20 | 0.492 | 10 | 0.451 |
| Mauritania | 230.336 | 20 | 276.403 | 10 | 253.37 |
| Mauritius | 24.738 | 20 | 29.686 | 10 | 27.212 |
| Mexico | 9.409 | 20 | 11.291 | 10 | 10.35 |
| Moldovia | 12.051 | 20 | 14.461 | 10 | 13.256 |
| Monaco | 6.559 | 8 | 7.084 | 4 | 6.821 |
| Mongolia | 971.896 | 20 | 1166.275 | 10 | 1069.086 |
| Morocco | 9.949 | 20 | 11.939 | 10 | 10.944 |
| Mozambique | 15357.025 | 20 | 18428.43 | 10 | 16892.728 |
| Namibia | 6.704 | 20 | 8.045 | 10 | 7.374 |
| Nepal | 67.217 | 20 | 80.66 | 10 | 73.939 |
| Netherlands | 2.203 | 4 | 2.291 | 2 | 2.247 |
| Netherlands Antilles | 1.697 | 20 | 2.036 | 10 | 1.867 |
| New Caledonia | 124.267 | 20 | 149.12 | 10 | 136.694 |
| New Zealand | 2.029 | 20 | 2.435 | 10 | 2.232 |
| Nicaragua | 11.905 | 20 | 14.286 | 10 | 13.096 |
| Nigeria | 98.246 | 20 | 117.895 | 10 | 108.071 |
| Norway | 8.202 | 10 | 9.121 | 5 | 8.707 |
| Oman | 0.367 | 20 | 0.44 | 10 | 0.404 |

I had noticed it was more credible referring to 'us' instead of 'me' when speaking about Coins for Care. Even though I still worked on my own, using the plural form would make it seem as if I had the backing of a big organization, and made me sound a lot more trustworthy. The Coin for Care plans were now clear and concise. I had developed a short and powerful elevator pitch which I could present within 30 seconds, and as time went by I learned to have a prepared answer for any possible situation. 'I'll show the charities and shops I know what I'm talking about, even though they've never heard of me, nor Coins for Care,' I thought. My thorough preparation would prove invaluable in the talks I would have with various big organizations.

*'Whatever you can do or dream,*
*you can begin it.*
*Boldness has genius,*
*power and magic in it.'*
*- Goethe -*

# Excuse 5: 'I cannot do this alone'

*'Do not wait for leaders;*
*do it alone, person to*
*person.'*
*- Mother Theresa -*

## Think Big!

It had been my wish to turn Coins for Care into a European wide project. I realized this was ambitious, and therefore I had contacted three international charities. So far, I had managed to find a solution to process the collected money, and now I was waiting for the charities to decide whether to join or not. In the meanwhile I planned to generate some publicity for Coins for Care.

While many people were opposed to the Euro, I thought Coins for Care could give the introduction campaign a charitable spin, so I contacted the European Central Bank (ECB): 'Some positive publicity might get the general public more interested,' I said, but my letters, e-mails, and phone calls were politely rejected, time and time again: 'You've come through to the wrong department, we cannot help you with this,'Sorry, this plan is not part of the marketing campaign,'We'll keep your request on file, and we'll contact you if we are interested.' I was sent from pillar to post, nobody was willing to take responsibility for deciding whether or not my idea would fit into their mega-project of introducing a new currency.

*'Don't put all your eggs in one basket.'*
*- Old Dutch saying -*

I kept on pressuring the Central Bank, but at the same time I also started looking for other options. I contacted Publicis, an advertising agency, who were immediately interested in my idea. Coincidently, their head office was preparing a proposal for the ECB. 'We're hoping to run the Euro campaign,' the Publicis team told me. 'We think the Coins for Care project would fit in perfectly!' If they would indeed win the *contract* for the Euro campaign, Publicis' profits

would be huge, so I carefully negotiated two percent of all earnings for my efforts of organizing the collection. To my relief Publicis thought it was a realistic offer, and agreed.

I was in seventh heaven! Finally something was about to happen. I started dreaming about the money we could make: if we would collect five-million, I would receive one hundred thousand Euro's! Imagine we would raise twenty-million, or even more!
Publicis had asked me to join their management team in Frankfurt, where they were preparing their proposal to the ECB. I did not need to be asked twice! I hastily put together a presentation, and got on the plane to Germany. I felt confident that my role as the sole initiator of the project was coming to an end; I would not be on my own anymore. Publicis had been so enthusiastic, they had even paid for my flight, and I was convinced they thought my ideas were feasible. I felt incredibly happy, and even a little bit important...
When I arrived at the hotel and discovered I was expected to pay myself for the two-hundred-a-night hotel room they had booked for me, I could not help but feeling a twinge of disappointment. 'Oh well, don't worry about it,' I told myself, 'Think about the two percent commission.' That night I had dinner with all the Publicis hotshots, and was given the chance to explain the Coins for Care concept in great detail. They were impressed: 'Your idea is so straightforward and simple, it's bound to become a success.' They were so excited about my plan, and unanimously decided they would include it into their proposal to the ECB.

Once back in the Netherlands, a mutual agreement between Publicis and Coins for Care was drawn up. I honestly had thought that things would start happening much faster, now I had found a partner in Publicis, but these expectations were unfounded. It would still be a long time before the ECB would finally decide which agency to contract, and until then Publicis was reluctant to sign any agreement. It was a very frustrating time for everybody involved. I found it hard to accept I did not have any control over the process, and simply had to wait. But January 1st, the day of the Euro introduction, was approaching fast. 'There is still so much to be done,' I moaned impatiently, desperate to get moving. Deep down I knew it wouldn't make any sense to start doing things on my own accord, and I should really leave it to Publicis and the ECB, but weeks turned into months and, as time ticked by, I grew increasingly restless.

You can imagine my excitement, when the news finally came that Publicis had won the contract: Coins for Care would officially be part of the Euro campaign! With Publicis as a partner, and with the support of the ECB, we would be able to organize a European coin collection!

I thought the waiting was over, but hopes of a speedy development quickly disappeared. The first months after the assignment were completely taken up by contract meetings. Despite Coins for Care being regarded as an integral part of the campaign by both Publicis and the ECB, it was merely one of the many hundred items on their agenda. It was a peculiar state of affairs: Publicis and the ECB being involved in busy negotiations, while I was waiting at home,

anxious to get started! Raymond van Buuren, managing director of Publicis, kept me updated constantly, despite his busy schedule. We got along really well, and he personally was a fervent supporter of the Coins for Care initiative, but his position at Publicis prevented him from doing anything that could speed up the wait. As a gesture of goodwill and commitment, Raymond introduced me to his wife, a children's book illustrator. She could help me with creating a logo. It was an absurd situation, the director of a huge advertising agency, *which has* thousands of designers on the payroll, referring me to his wife for a logo design!

European Central Bank (ECB)

As time went on, I was tempted to turn the pressure up on Raymond or Publicis, but knew it would probably not make much difference. 'Everybody is doing what they can, we're just stuck in the slow bureaucratic ECB mill,' I tried to calm myself. I was so sick and tired of this waiting game, I felt completely powerless, it nearly drove me insane; I would rather start all over again than have to wait any longer. 'Sorry Esther, I can't promise you anything, I'm afraid this could last for a while,' Raymond sighed defeated, and I realized I was seriously facing the possibility of our partnership still being months away, or worse, not happening after all. That would be a disaster.

Even though I did not want to burn any bridges behind me, I knew it would be wise to go out there and D take matters into my own hands. I was going to conduct an independent publicity campaign; anything was better than having to wait any longer. 'If an opportunity opens up, you are always welcome to join us again,' promised Raymond, when I informed him of my decision.

**'Why wait when you can create.'**

## Who is Esther Jacobs?

My first priority was to contact the three charities I was hoping to work with. I notified Plan International, the World Wildlife Fund, and Médecins Sans Frontières that the money processing was now in place. 'Our next step will be contacting a number of retailers, and get them to commit to placing collection boxes in their stores,' I explained, adding it would probably be more successful if we would approach the retailers jointly. The charities, however, thought it was better to wait a while.

Instead, I tried my luck with the stores, and managed to arrange a few meetings. These all developed according to a certain pattern: a marketing manager would first listen to my story when he would ask: 'Who is Esther Jacobs?' The following question would be: 'Which other retailers and charities are already involved?' After a mere fifteen minutes I would be out in the street again.

It was a chicken-or-egg dilemma: the shops wanted to know which charities were involved before committing themselves, and the charities were waiting for the retailers to confirm, before making their decision on whether to become involved. My confidence was fading. I knew I needed partners to make Coins for Care a success, but I did not like being dependent on them, being made to wait, stuck in a dead-end street.

I was determined to make it work. I knew it was possible and I felt I was very close to a breakthrough, I just needed to take one all important last step. The big question was how to get through to the general public and persuade them to hand in their old coins to charity?

*'Do not wait; the time will never be "just right".*
*Start where you stand, and work with whatever*
*tools you may have at your command,*
*and better tools will be found as you go along.'*
*- Napoleon Hill -*

## Care for Coins

My strategy was to talk to as many people as possible, expanding my network of business contacts. I received some very useful tips and advice, and reactions to my plans were, without exception, all positive. It helped me to remain passionate and I was confirmed in my thinking that the idea was achievable, even though it had not taken off yet.

Good ideas can appear in different places at the same time, and as Coins for Care generated more publicity, I was contacted by several people who had similar plans for collecting obsolete coins for charity. Coins for Care was open to working with other parties, as long as they could add value, such as taking care of publicity or logistics, or have a specific knowledge or skill. But none of the people who came to me had anything like this, nor the sharp enthusiasm I was looking for. They had faced rejection a number of times, and had not always been treated respectfully. It had left them bitter and disappointed, and some of them had even developed a very negative attitude towards certain charities, claiming they had gone off with their idea. Their only motivation for offering to help out Coins for Care was to be compensated for their own failed attempts.

Initially I had been hoping to make a nice profit out of the charity scheme myself, but I became increasingly uncomfortable with the idea. There were so many people looking to benefit through Coins for Care, and I felt it was a very unpleasant ambition. Suddenly I understood I would never succeed if I kept regarding the project as a way of making money for myself. This had been the exact reason why it had not worked out for all the others: 'The only way to turn this project into a success, is to do it completely selflessly,' I concluded.

The first time I realized this was when I explained to a fellow fortune hunter, that I could not promise him any pay: 'If everybody involved asks for a piece of the pie, there won't be much left for the charities.' It was staggering to see the confusion in his eyes, when I excitingly told him how I had decided not to earn anything myself. 'And I don't think it's right for anybody to make money out of this project,' I told the man. We will show it is possible to organize a charitable event in which all money goes to the charities.' I could see it clearly now, and got more and more passionate. 'So, can I count you in? When would you like to start?' But he politely declined my offer, and quickly left with his tail between his legs.

My newly found theory was based on the fact that if you were committed to working for charity, you should be willing to do it voluntarily, without expecting any compensation. It was astonishing to see what a clearing effect this had on all parties who had offered their help. It surely separated the wheat from the chaff, and I was left with people and businesses who had one clear selfless drive: supporting charity.
My friends and acquaintances reacted differently to my sudden move from a commercial to a purely charitable project. Some spontaneously offered their help, whereas others were slightly suspicious, thinking there must be more to it than meets the eye.

I happily realized I was finally doing something I had always wanted to do; bringing good to others, and I was actually enjoying it! The positive reactions from the charities and the public, my own determination to make this plan into a huge success, and the general enthusiasm for the scheme lit a fire deep inside

*'Everyone is your best friend when you are successful. Make sure that the people you surround yourself with are also the people that you are not afraid of failing with'*
*- Paula Abdul -*

me, which was burning stronger by the minute; the fiercer the opposition, the bigger this untamable blaze. Instead of money, my motivational force had become to follow my intuition, to make this project a success, supporting the charities, and thus fulfilling a long cherished dream.

" I guess you could say we're a 'faith-based' company. Everyone worships the dollar around here."

## Power to the donor!

So far, the charities I had approached had not been terribly helpful; they had not even given permission to use their name yet. Only Médecins Sans Frontières (MSF) had committed to participating in the scheme, and had promised to contribute five-thousand guilders to our starting up costs. Plan International and the World Wildlife Fund (WWF) were still biding their time. Disappointed by the lack of response, I began to doubt if I had made the right choices.

I had chosen MSF, WWF, and International Plan simply because they had been the first three to come to mind which, I admit, was not a particular good reason. They were three large organizations, whereas it had originally been my plan to also sponsor much smaller initiatives. So, I started exploring the charity industry and found there were many more interesting organizations, also focusing on supporting children, the environment, and healthcare. They did not always have the means to start a particular charity project, and were hardly ever included in national programs or lottery schemes. Surprisingly, those smaller organizations were usually much more closely involved with their target groups, they motivated people working for them, and were a lot more efficient due to their limited means.

'Is it actually appropriate, that it's me who decides where the money goes to?' I started wondering. 'Wouldn't it be a lot more fair if the donors themselves choose what their gift is being spent on?' After tossing around the idea for a while, I decided to open up Coins for Care to all charities. 'Everyone can donate to their favorite good cause!' I said enthusiastically, 'And the money will be divided equally over all organizations chosen by the public!'

## Unexpected help

Now it was clear that no profits could be made by helping Coins for Care, fewer people and companies were interested in getting involved. It was a natural selection process: Coins for Care was now attracting the *right* people.

One of those people was Ted Bos, (owner of a small communication agency), who became one of the first Coins for Care enthusiasts. Ted was energetic, friendly, and very creative, and had his heart in the right place. He worked and lived in a beautifully renovated coach house on an estate at the Veluwe National Park. I met him when he was in the midst of starting up a telecom company. We had a very pleasant meeting, and when I was about to leave, he suddenly asked: 'What do you enjoy in life? Are you involved in any other projects?'

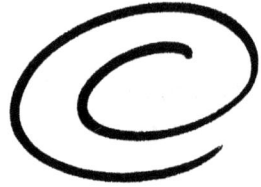

**Coins·for·Care**

**uw buitenlands (munt)geld voor het goede doel**

*Your foreign coins for charity*

I told him about Coins for Care, which was then still at its early stages. 'What a marvelous idea, I really would like to get involved,' said Ted, 'Is there anything I can help you with?' he added to my surprise. I answered I had already somebody working on a logo, and that I was in the process of waiting for Publicis to become my partner. I could not really think of anything he could help me with at that time, but Ted was persistent: 'Would you mind if I sent you a draft for a logo design, no obligations of course?' It was an offer too good to refuse.

A few days later, Ted presented a beautifully designed, professional logo. It appealed to me straight away; I thought it was perfect. 'The spiral, which represents a rolling coin, consists of the two C's in *Coins* and *Care*, the bigger C embracing the smaller letter,' explained Ted, 'and the flow of the line symbolizes motion and progress.' He had also given special thought to the colors: red, representing action and attention, and sky blue, symbolizing care and responsibility.

I could not believe my eyes, I absolutely loved the design. 'I've also taken the liberty of designing a house style and letterhead,' said Ted, with a big smile. I was speechless at so much initiative. 'It's absolutely great,' I told Ted, 'and I really would like to use this, but will need to talk to the Publicis director's wife, who is also designing a logo for us.' Fortunately she reacted wonderfully, and encouraged me to continue working with Ted.

Ted even managed to persuade a publisher to print our letterhead for free. He also had great ideas for a business card: we took pictures of me running around with a butterfly net, as if I was catching coins, and these were printed on the business cards. The distinct cards were an instant success! Ted became Coins for Care's creative force, and he introduced me to many people whose priority it was to put time and energy into something they believed in, rather than making money.

During one of the many conversations I had with Ted, I reached an important decision. 'So, you still want to organize this collection throughout the whole of Europe?' he asked me one day. 'Yes,...I actually do,' I answered hesitantly. Waiting for a decision by Publicis and the ECB, however, had wasted valuable time and expanding our activities throughout Europe had in fact become an unrealistic aim. We simply did not have enough time left until the Euro introduction. Ted did not need to say more. It was tough, but I had to let go of my European plans, and confine our activities to the Netherlands. 'I've got my hands full anyway, trying to get things organized over here, let alone in other European countries,' I admitted eventually. 'A wise decision,' said Ted, 'let's go for it.'

*'Don't wait for someone to take you under their wing.*
*Find a good wing and climb up underneath it.'*
*- Frank C. Bucaro -*

## CollectePlan

The Ministry of Finance had created a special team to manage the introduction of the Euro. I called to inform them about Coins for Care, and
to see if they could offer some free publicity. 'Information on the Euro
introduction is so serious and official; by attaching a positive, charitable
message, we bring the Euro closer to the people.' I said enthusiastically.
The Euro-team spokesperson listened carefully, but answered: 'Did you
know there is already an organization called Collecteplan, who are arrang-
ing a door-to-door collection in January 2000?' 'Collecteplan?' I asked, surprised. I had never heard of them. 'Yes, it's a joint venture of 20 collecting
charities,' he explained. 'You'd better contact them first,' was his advice.

Collecteplan's initial reaction was reserved, when I called them to see if we
could work together. It was only after they understood I had been referred
by the Dutch ministry that they agreed to meet me.
When I arrived at their office, I was surprised to find there
were no fewer than five Collecteplan people attending
the meeting. They acted a little aloof and the atmosphere was
tense and distant. I was, however, determined to make the best
of it, and started talking animatedly about Coins for Care, and
what we had achieved so far. Nothing was said, but every so often I noticed
a few meaningful glances being exchanged. When it was their turn to tell me
about their plan, they said: 'We are organizing a giant door-to-door collection,
but its still early days. Our committee consists of temporary members, and we
still need to give structure to it.' They told me they were not even convinced
that they could go ahead and actually realize their project. The only thing they
were certain of was that they were only going to collect Dutch coins.

Their lack of any finalized plans, was a much better scenario than I could have
hoped for. I was so excited about having found a possible partner, that I overwhelmed them with all my newly acquired knowledge. I completely ignored
the alarming silence at the other side of the table, and explained about the processing of coins, the potentially enormous amount of money, and our possible
partnership. I rattled on about how Coins for Care
could process all the foreign currencies, and how
we both would benefit from my sponsorship
network. Coin Co would take care of the processing, and I would be dealing with the major
part of the publicity. In the spur of the moment
failed to recognize that the other party was not
sharing in my enthusiasm.

At the end of the meeting one of the men made a sneering remark: 'You'd be lucky if we'd let you assist us with our publicity.' He could not wait to end our meeting: 'We'll call you in a few weeks time when our plan has taken shape,' he said, and I was directed to the door. I thought their reticence was due to the fact they did not know where to place me. 'Once they realize my intentions are good, and they see what I've already been able to achieve, they'll understand we should be partners,' I encouraged myself.

I was looking forward to working with Collecteplan. They were a professional organization, with experience in collecting money for charities. Besides, I did not have the intention of setting up this whole action by myself, I would like to contribute positively, but did not feel it necessary to reinvent the wheel.

Following our meeting I wrote a proposal for a joint collection strategy. Collecteplan would organize the planned door-to-door collections and Coins for Care would place the money boxes in stores and banks. Collecteplan had experience in sorting and processing Dutch coins, so I suggested they deal with that. Coins for Care would take care of the foreign coins, for which Collecteplan did not have the processing tools in place.

Our first meeting had clearly indicated that both organizations were completely different; Collecteplan consisted of a powerful group of 20 charities which needed to be taken into consideration, while Coins for Care could adapt and move a lot faster due to its flexibility. That's why I suggested our common focus should be mostly public relations. And with the processing being organized efficiently both parties would still be able to sail their own course. 'Let's make sure not one coin will be left lying in the kitchen drawer!' I ended enthusiastically.

In the following weeks and months I did not hear back from Collecteplan. Had my enthusiasm and style been too overpowering? My phone calls remained unanswered. I was very disappointed, and felt Collecteplan was not taking me seriously. So, I stubbornly decided to show them they were making a huge mistake, and that Coins for Care was definitely worth working with.

**HOOGVLiET**

BLOKKER

Blokker B.V.
Postbus 94072
1090 GB Amsterdam
van der Madeweg 13-15
1099 BS Amsterdam
Telefoon : 020 5683462
Telefax : 020 5683463
Aantal pagina's (inclusief deze): 1

Dear Miss Jacobs,

Following our telephone converstation not interested in the Coins-for-Care project.

Yours sincerely,

Blokker Ltd.

# He that cannot keep a penny...

We still had not found a retailer who would allow us to use their premises for the coin collection. It worried me; if we were not able to place the money boxes, our scheme would fail. Not having had much luck with the national retailers, we decided to approach the smaller regional supermarkets.

I was invited by the Hoogvliet food stores. With about forty supermarkets in the southwest of the country, they were a well known name in this area. The manager was a nice man who listened attentively to the Coins for Care pitch, which I knew inside out by now. When I had finished I sort of expected the usual -reaction, but to my surprise, the manager said: 'I think it's a very good idea, you can count us in!' Completely overwhelmed I thanked him, and confessed we did not have any details yet on how the collection was going to take place, but he reassured me, saying it would all be fine. I was walking on air, finally I had met someone who clearly had confidence in my idea!

I had started my journey at the top end, contacting the European Central Bank, but eventually ended up at a regional retailer. 'What would have happened if I'd done it the other way around?' I wondered. It definitely would have saved a lot of effort and frustration, but the experience had been worthwhile; It had resulted in a polished pitch, and I had built up a useful contact network. Now, it felt good to be taking control, continuing on my own, not being dependent on anyone.

I was hoping Hoogvliet would be the first of many retailers to get involved. I informed all other stores that we had our first confirmation, but, contrary to my expectations, it did not generate any reaction. Apparently Hoogvliet was not significant enough to interest the other supermarket chains in joining.

Looking back at what I had achieved. I proudly realized I had managed to get this far on my own. Without any help...
Sometimes it is better to just get on with it, instead of waiting and depending on others. If you take the first step, others will follow.

*'Don't wait for extraordinary opportunities.*
*Seize common occasions and make them great.*
*Weak men wait for opportunities;*
*strong men make them.'*
*- Orison Swett Marden -*

## The Euro; the new currency for twelve countries

De euro is de nieuwe munt van twaalf landen van de Europese Unie. Die landen zijn: Ierland, Ierland, Nederland, Griekenland, Finland, Luxemburg, Oostenrijk, Frankrijk, België, Italië, Portugal en Spanje (makkelijk onthouden: DING FLOF BIPSI.

De euro bestaat al sinds 1 januari 1999. Toen is bepaald dat de euro precies 2.20371 gulden waard is. Die waarde verandert niet meer.

U wordt niet rijker of armer door de euro. Uw guldens (of bijvoorbeeld uw Duitse marken) blijven precies evenveel waard, ook al heet de munt van twaalf Europese landen voortaan euro. Sinds 1 januari 1999 loopt u al geen koersrisico meer wanneer u guldens omwisselt tegen muntten uit een ander land dat meedoet aan de euro. Wel moet u bij de bank meestal nog transactiekosten betalen voor het wisselen. Vanaf 1 januari 2002 hoeft u helemaal niet meer te wisselen. U kunt dan in de twaalf landen die meedoen gewoon met dezelfde euromunten en eurobankbiljetten betalen. Dat scheelt moeite en kosten.

## Important moments for the introduction

### September 2001
Actie Nationale Eurocollecte/ ... voor meer dan honderd ... . Voor buitenlands muntgeld ... eer nodig hebt, staat een ... klaar in veel winkels en bij ... filialen. Papiergeld uit de ... kunt u nog tot 1 april 2002 bij ... omwisselen voor euro's.

### Oktober 2001
... peciale Spaarweken van de ... u spaargeld alvast storten op ... kening. Vooral als u bijvoor- ...

Hiermee kan een gratis eurokit afgehaald, met één exemplaar Nederlandse euromunt. Waar eurokit: € 3,88 ofwel ƒ 8,55.

U zult de euro nu steeds ... komen. Benzinestations en a... worden omgebouwd en u ku... acceptgiro's in euro's ontva...

### 14 t/m 31 december 200
In deze periode kunt u tege... van de afhaalcoupon uw g... len bij ABN AMRO, Fortis I Rabobank, Postbank, GWK of COMBI.

Ook kunt u vanaf 14 c banken en bij verschillen... voor ƒ 25,- pakketten met kopen ... wisse...

# Excuse 6:
## 'I don't have any money'

'He who is poor, needs to be creative.'
- Dutch saying -

© Jeroen Oerlemans

## Coins in Cyberspace

Sometimes you will find an answer to your problems, when you are least expecting it.

One warm spring evening, I met up with my old friends from university at a sorority dinner. It was June 2000 and the internet industry was booming; dot.com companies were sprouting up everywhere. 'Anything you promote on the internet becomes an instant success,' said one of my friends, a trend watcher, now living

Rent-A-Bitch ☺

in New York. All girls in our group were active in a particular industry like finance, logistics, strategics, or marketing, and we held a huge amount of skills and knowledge between us. Spontaneously, someone suggested we should set up our own consultancy, offering our joint services on a freelance basis. She even came up with a name: *Rent-a-Bitch*! We thought it was hilarious. 'The name itself will generate a lot of publicity immediately, and possibly even attract a few customers,' laughed one of the girls, who was an internet expert. As the evening wore on, and more drinks were consumed, we really got into the idea. We had so much fun talking about it: 'Internet will be the key to our success!' we cheered each other, and in the end someone even registered an internet domain, just in case we would seriously follow up on our *Rent-a-Bitch* plan.

I did not sleep much that night. Excited, not being able to stop thinking about how we should benefit from the power of the internet, I decided Coins for Care needed a website. It would be great for the promotion of our scheme, and give the organization a lot more credibility. 'How exactly do you design a website?' I asked myself in the dark.

The next morning I was presenting a strategic workshop at Ernst and Young Consulting. Two of my study friends who had also been at the dinner party, were working in the same office, and I exitedly told them about my plan: 'I'm going to set up a website for Coins for Care!'

Coincidentally, Mark Spronk, one of the partners at Ernst & Young, overheard what we were talking about, and said: 'Why don't you ask us if we can build this site for you?' Confused, I replied '...but I did not say I would pay for it.' 'Neither did I,' he answered with a smile, and then offered to assist with building a website for Coins for Care. I could not believe my luck, I was going to have a website and a reliable sponsor!

Ernst & Young asked freelancer Robin Stolle to build a site, using Ted's logo; Robin also built a voting tool, which allowed people to choose their favorite charity. I was taking care of the text, while Ernst & Young organized free hosting with one phone call to their netprovider Netpresence.

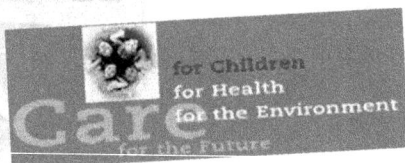

This way of getting things organized had opened my eyes: charities would usually have to pay for these services using collected money, but why such a detour? From now on, I would try to get everything in kind, directly through sponsorship.

Even with the website finished, Robin remained so enthusiastic, that he promised to take care of the maintenance in his spare time. It was a wonderful offer, and I really enjoyed someone else being involved in the project with whom I could exchange ideas, and delegate part of the work to.

Nobody could have known what the Coins for Care website would set in motion. Once it was up and running we 'existed'; I was no longer *the girl with a nice story*, but was now regarded as representing a serious organization. Ernst & Young being our sponsor made us reliable and added credibility, which we had been lacking until then.

I would now start my pitches announcing that we did not have any overhead costs. It became an important argument in persuading businesses to become sponsors. When I explained we were not being paid, received sponsorship for nearly everything, and all money would be for charity, they were usually quick to commit. The concept was a huge success in the business industry, and hopefully it would work with the public as well.

Aug
2000

## Front-page news

Robin and I had decided to run a one month trial on our website, so friends and family could try out the feedback option, and test the voting tool. Closer to the official launch date, we were hoping to generate as much publicity as possible, by interesting magazines and newspapers in publishing our story. Hopefully, this would open a lot of new doors for us.

Not hampered by any knowledge or experience, I put together an early press release, announcing the launch of our site, and explaining what the Coins for Care program entailed. I spent a couple of hours in front of the magazine rack in the supermarket, collecting the editorial addresses from the most influential magazines. Unfortunately, the Coins for Care letterheads were not ready yet, so instead I copied the logo by hand, which took a lot of time, but was worth the effort. With a bag full of envelopes I finally went to the letterbox, and posted them out into the big wide world, silently hoping for a lot of reactions. And then I waited, and waited, and waited...

On August 8, 2000, the day of our website launch, my heart made a little jump when I picked up my newspaper: 'Mega-collection of old coins' it said in big chocolate letters on the front page. I let a sigh of relief, someone had read my press release! But when I looked closer, I shockingly realized the article was about Collecteplan. Without going in too much detail the article announced their mega door-to-door collection on the day of the Euro introduction. I was astonished to find that Collecteplan had continued planning their project, without including or even informing me!

My disappointment only grew when my friends started calling me, congratulating me with the publicity. 'Straight onto the front page!' It was tough having to explain it was not my collection scheme. 'Are you going ahead with Coins for Care, now you have such a big competitor?' they asked me. I got onto the phone and called the secretary of Collecteplan, who I had met at our first meeting. She clearly felt uncomfortable with the whole situation. 'I think the plan was leaked to the press,' she sounded slightly panicky, 'it was definitely not our intention to have it published yet, we are not prepared for it at all!

"Coins-for-Care: Your foreign coins for charity."

Coins·for·Care
uw buitenlands (munt)geld
voor het goede doel

Telegraaf, August 8th, 2000

# Mega-collection 'old' coins.

Millions of coins now sitting in piggybanks and coin pots, will become obsolete with the introduction of the euro.

There is still so much to finalize, and most of our staff are on holiday at the moment,' she added despondently, promising to call me as soon as she had more news, and to stay in touch this time.

To keep the damage to a minimum, that morning Robin and I opened up the Coins for Care website to the public. I sent out a quickly improvised press release, and to my surprise, received some reactions straight away. It was the summer and news was slack, and the announcement of two collections during the Euro introduction, was obviously a welcome distraction. My first encounter with the press was a challenging one. Instead of being able to quietly set out my pitch, I was overwhelmed by questions about 'a possible feud between Coins for Care and Collecteplan'.

'Promising cooperation...' I taught myself to answer diplomatically. I would have liked to answer that Collecteplan had let me down badly, but instinctively I felt I should not upset anybody. I expected us to pick up negotiations again, after all this commotion in the press. So, I decided to keep the door ajar. Collecteplan did not name Coins for Care in their reactions to the press, but they spoke about being approached by *many organizations interested in a possible joint operation*. In the end a number of articles were published in the newspapers, announcing there was another organization which was planning to collect coins.

As a result of these articles in the press, Coins for Care became widely known to the Dutch public, and our website received thousands of hits in just a few days time. As more and more people learnt about the planned collection scheme, they started to enter their favorite charities, and the first votes were coming in.

Not long after, I was called by Viva, a weekly women's magazine, who asked me if I would like to feature in their September edition with an interview and picture. 'We think your story is perfect for our Open Stage pages, for which we interview people who have achieved something special in

Amersfoortse Courant, 9 august 2000

their lives,' the editor explained. I felt very proud, and was so honored they had thought of me, I did not know what to say. The editor must have mistaken my hesitation for suspicion, because she added: 'Uhm, well, to be honest, the person we had in mind has cancelled the interview, and it's difficult to find someone interesting at such a short notice. But, of course, we think you have a great story to tell as well! So, I hope you would like to go ahead...?'

Whether I was a substitute for someone far more interesting or not, it did not matter, it was a great chance to reach an even bigger audience. 'I would love to do it,' was my answer.

The picture would be such a determining factor in how the article would be perceived; a little nervous I showed up for the photo shoot:
It was at Harold Pereira's studio, a famous photographer who had done a lot of work for *Viva*. He lived in a beautiful penthouse with a view over Zandvoort, a well known Dutch beach resort. The photographer was very talkative, and deeply interested in all the Coins for Care details; it was probably his way of putting someone at ease, and it worked well for me.
I felt I was calming down talking about something I had a great passion for. Suddenly I thought of something, and carefully asked if I could use the *Viva* pictures for the Coins for Care publicity. But his answer was no: 'I can't do that, these pictures are Viva's, and can't be used for anything else,' he said resolutely. But he must have been infected by my enthusiasm, because a little later he proposed: 'You know what, I'll shoot some extra photo's which you can use for Coins for Care.' I had found another sponsor!

## Hunt for the Obsolete Coin

A true money box war is awaiting us once the euro is introduced at the beginning of 2002. The Dutch are thought to be keeping tens of millions of old coins which will become useless after the introduction of the euro. Several charities are on the hunt, to collect this money, which is usually a leftover from foreign holidays. A few big organizations like the Cancer-fund, the Arthritis-fund, Jantje Beton, de Heart-foundation, and the Salvation Army have joined forces in CollectPlan, and are planning a huge coin-collection.
The introduction of the euro offers a unique chance of collecting a huge amount for charity. How the money will be collected, processed and exchanged is still being looked into.

A second party interested in the obsolete load of coins announced itself yesterday, when the Amsterdam marketing consultant Esther Jacobs launched Coins-for-Care. A few years ago she already looked into the viability of collecting old coins commercially, but this appeared to be too costly. 'That's when I thought of collecting for charity instead,' says Jacobs. She expects the coins to be collected centrally and all participating charities will receive a share of the profit. Donors can choose the charity of their choice at "http://www.coinsforcare.nl" www.coinsforcare.nl.

**Costs**
'This is a workable solution for everyone,' says Jacobs. 'The collection costs will not exceed 2 percent of the total of collected money. This is something which is not achievable if charities operate on their own account, let alone managing to organize enough collectors. I truly hope CollectPlan and other organizations will decide to join Coins for Care. Els Hekstra, a spokesperson for CollectPlan says they were slightly surprised by Coins for Care: 'We knew they had similar plans, and we had even spoken a couple of times, but we need to find out for ourselves first what the best way is for collecting coins, while taking into account what is best for our charities. Our organizations would not have a say in the allocation of profits when they would join Coins for Care. It might not be a decisive factor, but we still need to make a decision on that.

## Collecteplan 2

Early September I was invited by Collecteplan to, again, discuss the possibility of working together. When I walked into the meeting room I immediately felt a tense atmosphere. I was met by a group of people of whom I only recognized one person: his name was Raymond van Haeften, he had ended our first meeting with a derogatory remark, and it would not be the last time I would have to deal with him.

While I was explaining how Coins for Care was developing, the room was silent and a few people were taking notes. There was no sign of encouragement, nor did anyone seem impressed with our achievements so far.

When I had finished my talk, I was asked a few prepared questions, clearly aimed at identifying our weaknesses and belittling me. 'Why did you get involved in this? Shouldn't you be doing something useful, and let the experts deal with this kind of work?' they asked, obviously meaning themselves. 'Why did you chose an English name? Don't you think that's a bit strange? It's a Dutch scheme, after all.'

'Can we see the Coin Co contract for the exchange of foreign coins? Would you be willing to give up its exclusivity?'

I explained that they could, of course, see the contract, and that if we would work together, the same profitable conditions would apply to them. 'Why have you opened up to all charities? Have you done any checks on these organizations?' 'Why is the public allowed to decide how the

*Viva 38, 2000*

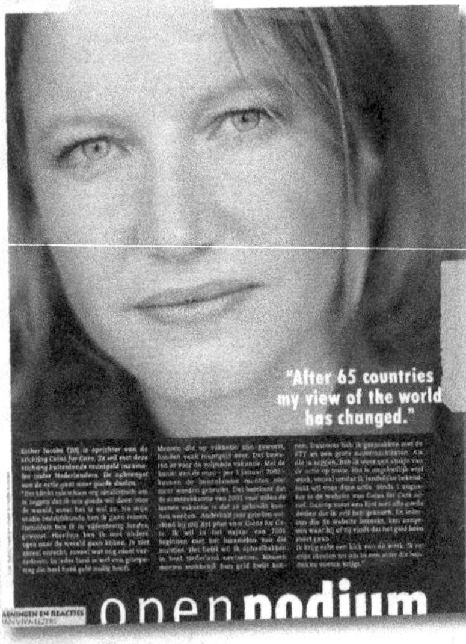

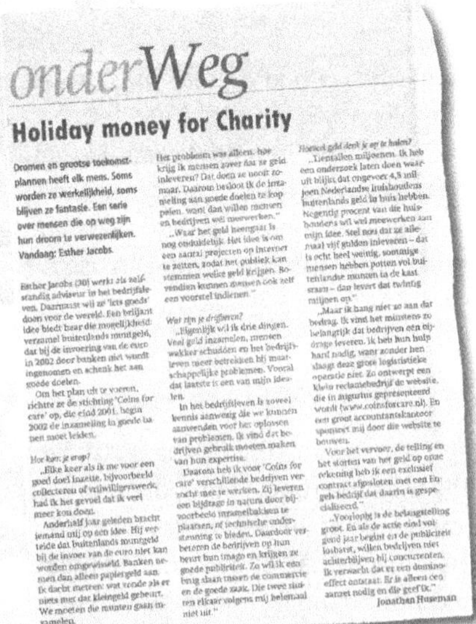

"After 65 countries my view of the world has changed."

**onen podium**

## onderWeg
### Holiday money for Charity

*Trouw, July 14th 2000*

GELD & GOED / AGENDA   23/8

# Coins for Care will start in Amstelveen

'Voel mensen vragen mij nu al waar ze hun muntjes kunnen inleveren'

*Amstelveens Weekblad, Aug 23rd 2000*
*Money & Business / Agenda*

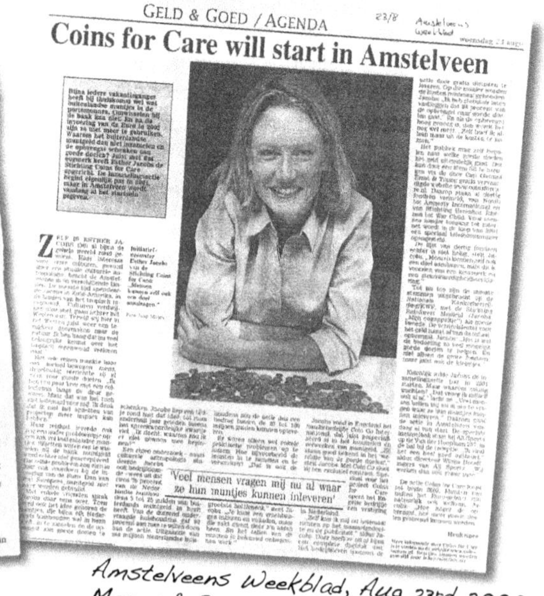

money is divided, that's a bit unusual and unnecessary, isn't it?' 'Why do you object to having our projects running separately alongside each other?'

So there I was, trying to be as open and positive as I could, I really wanted us to join forces. I thought me being a newcomer in this charity world, was the reason for this. I figured this attitude would only be temporary, easily overcome by being open and sharing the information I had.
I emphasized again the advantages of working together: 'Our position will be much stronger, it doesn't make sense if we have two separate schemes, it will only confuse the public. Why not show that we can work together, instead of wasting energy on being each other's competitor? We should focus on the collection of as many coins as possible! Also, if we'd unite, we'll have less costs, which means more money for charity, surely that must be our goal?' I looked around hopefully, but Collecteplan told me they were about to finalize their own plans. 'And, we've decided to include the collection of foreign coins as well,' they said shamelessly. They were also involved in negotiations with the Dutch Olympic Committee (NOC), who were planning a coin collection at the traditional parties at sport clubs and societies across the country.
'Well, I definitely think it's best to join forces, so we can all benefit from each strong points,' I insisted. But Collecteplan did not want to discuss this any further; they first wanted to talk to NOC.

I was confused; I just could not see why Collecteplan was so opposed to working with Coins for Care. I understood that an established organization should always be careful with whom they partner; me being new to the industry might have been a risk, but that still did not fully explain their attitude.

They could at least have shared what their fears were, but they seemed to have already dismissed the whole idea of working together.
I also thought it was weird that they did not seem to be interested in the processes Coins for Care already had put in place, like the handling of foreign coins. This must have been a totally new concept to them as well, and if I was in their position, I would have wanted to know exactly what the other party had organized already, before reinventing the wheel.
Stubbornly, I decided to put everything on paper, determined to disarm Collecteplan's objections, one by one.

## Coins on TV

TV-shows often get their ideas from publications in magazines and newspapers, and after publication of the Viva

*from an interview in a regional newspaper:*

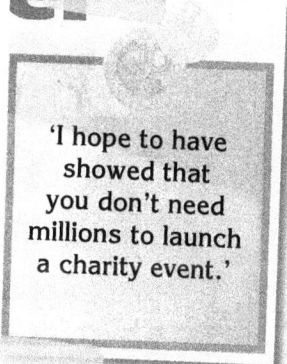

'I hope to have showed that you don't need millions to launch a charity event.'

*RTL Morning Show*

*Current Affairs*

*RTL Live*

*Spott*

article, I was invited to a number of news desks and daytime programs. I had never watched much television, and a particular show or its famous presenter I had not even heard of. This caused a few painful, but hilarious moments when they called me for an interview.

I remember being very nervous when I drove to the TVstudios for the first time. Everything was so new to me; the lady who took care of me during the whole event, the make-up artists, who blow-dried and styled my hair until I was a completely different person... I just let it happen and went with the flow, being overwhelmed by the attention, the bright lights, the exact timings, and the dynamic pace of a TV-show.

I knew the Coins for Care pitch inside out; it was one of my strengths, I could talk knowledgeably about anything related to the topic, and tried to squeeze as much information as possible into the allocated three minutes. After a few interviews I could anticipate what kind of questions would be asked, and I learned how to steer the conversation, ensuring that all important aspects were being mentioned. I became very good at explaining my idea in a clear and concise manner, and the TV crew was always very content with my pitch. Of course there were a few amusing 'bloopers': during one of my first television performances at a daytime show, I was not aware that the program was coming to an end, and I interrupted the presenter who was in the middle of rounding off: 'I also brought a collection box for you and your team...'

In another show I made a mistake while listing a few currencies which would be suitable for collection: 'German Marks, Spanish *Francs* and French *Pesetas*...!' Unfortunately there was no time left to set this straight, and I felt I was making history as a 'dumb blonde'.

The *Viva*-article and the enormous publicity around my TV appearances attracted more and more supporters to Coins for Care. People started calling me at home, and I received letters and e-mails with enthusiastic reactions, tips, and incredible offers of help: a grandma asking me if we were also taking coins from Zimbabwe; A widow offering me her late husband's antique coin collection; the caretaker of the public toilets at a major

Mevrouw Ester Jacobs ✧ Coins for Care ✧ 1 december 2001

Dear Miss Jacobs,

A few coins, as I don't mind sending a postal package. My apologies if you have to pick it up from your local post-office; I am so old that I still remember parcels being delivered to the door. For: Medecins sans Frontieres (my French is somewhat rusty)

Kind regards, Theo.

trainstation donating a bucket full of foreign coins, and also offering to place one of our collection boxes on his premises; the Dutch Railways lost-and-found department calling me they had boxes full of coins, could we please pick them up. There was even a young man asking where I had bought that nice leather jacket I were wearing on television, 'I would like to buy it for my girlfriend.' Some offers would come in useful at a much later stage, like the packaging specialist Beumer offering to provide tailor-made cardboard boxes, or the young fashion designer who had designed a dress out of foreign coins, donating his creation to be used for PR purposes. These were only a few examples of many heartfelt reactions. Proudly I realized I had successfully managed to transfer my enthusiasm to others, turning Coins for Care into a friendly, easily approachable organization, to which people were keen to contribute and do something positive for charity.

© © Photo: Bas Wilders
© Design: Maurice Spapens, Dutch Design.

## Getting the best seats for free

©Maurice Spapens,
Dutch Design.

With all this media attention, Coins for Care became an attractive partner for companies interested in helping charities. When we were still fairly unknown, there had been reservations, but now they could not wait to be part of our growing success. It was amazing to see how doors opened up to us, now we had become an established name.

By this time Capgemini had taken over Ernst & Young Consulting, and the new management had plans to set up a sponsoring scheme for their employees. Lucas Stassen, a tall, intelligent man with a winning smile, had been hired as the PR-man and we got together a couple of times to brainstorm about joint publicity. Lucas introduced me to Paul Kok Consultants (PKC), who were specialists in communication: 'Coincidentally, we are currently looking into the best way of sponsoring a charity' they told me, and straight away offered to take care of all our press related matters. They also offered to organize a huge press conference at the launch of the scheme. 'That might be the perfect occasion for using that sexy dress made out of coins,' suggested Lucas.

© Marco Okhuizen

'Focusing your life solely on making a buck shows a certain poverty of ambition. It asks too little of yourself. Because it's only when you hitch your wagon to something larger than yourself that you realize your true potential.'
- Barack Obama -

Through PKC I learned about services I did not even know existed: for instance, there was a company who specialized in collecting all publications about Coins for Care, and then digitalizing them so Robin could put them on our website. There was also a 'one woman' company -*Assistant-To*- who took care of the preparation and sending of press releases.

In our case this type of sponsoring in kind was priceless. Not only did we have access to knowledge and skills we could not have afforded, but we also had a few extra pairs of well-trained hands! A kind of virtual back office was taking shape: one phone call or e-mail to PKC, would set in motion an invaluable process of organizing, e-mailing and scanning.

I learnt that people are always willing to help out when asked by someone they know and trust. If you are creative, and are successful in building a network of people, you will be able to find a solution for anything. When we were in need of a certain service or product, I would now call a company directly and request if they could provide their product or services free of charge. Their first reaction would usually be negative: 'Sorry, we can't start doing that, if we did and word got out, all charities will be knocking on our door.' But I would respond that Coins for Care was a joint venture between more than eighty charities: 'So this is your chance to help out many important charities in one go!'
It was such a simple concept, and most businesses were more than happy to assist. They were often asked to make a donation, but had never come across such a clear, and practical request for their own specialized product or service. This is how I managed to organize a printer, screwdrivers, sticker sheets for the collection boxes, and a lot more. I probably should have stuck to the big, expensive items, as it was a very time consuming way of acquiring our office

'Happiness lies not in the mere possession of money;
it lies in the joy of achievement, in the thrill of creative effort'
- Franklin D. Roosevelt -

110

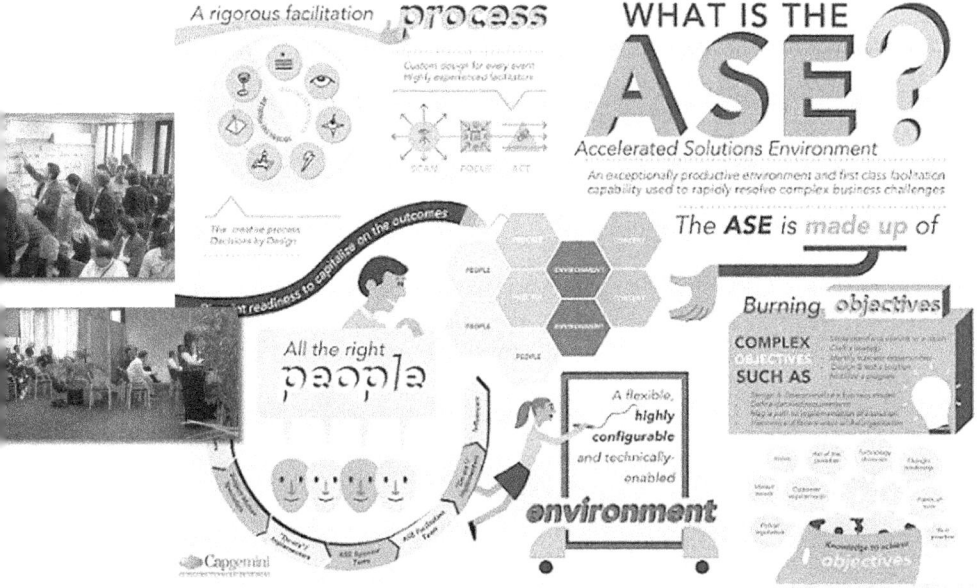

The Accelerated Solutions Environment of CapGemini

supplies, but it became my personal challenge to get everything sponsored, even the least important items, like pens.

I was lucky enough to be able to earn good money working as a freelance marketing consultant. Just before I had started Coins for Care, I got involved with the Accelerated Solutions Environment (ASE) at Capgemini. This was a three day corporate event, where management and staff of large firms were being coached to find strategic solutions for complicated problems. I was one of the consultants and could sometimes earn a few thousand guilders per week. These were tough assignments, however, working for six days solidly, with an unhealthy three or four hours sleep a night. I could not maintain this schedule full time, but I worked just enough to be able to live comfortably, and the rest of my time I dedicated to Coins for Care. Of course, I was sometimes concerned about my meager financial position, but over the years I had learnt to trust that I would always be able to find work, if I needed to. And letting go of these worries about money allowed me to focus on doing something fulfilling, something close to my heart.

'We make a living by what we get,
but we make a life by what we give'
- Winston Churchill -

# Excuse 7:
## 'I've already tried that.'

'Many of life's failures are by people
who did not realize how close they were
to success when they gave up.'
- Thomas Edison -

Sept
2000

# A stab in the back

One day I received a call from John, owner of Coin Co, the coin-processing company in England.

He asked me if I knew Jaap Zeekant and Raymond van Haeften. I told him I did and explained how I had met these two gentlemen at Collecteplan. 'Why do you want to know?' I asked John suspiciously. 'Well, they are sitting here in my office and have just spent the last half hour telling me how big and important their organization is compared to Coins for Care. To be honest, I think they are trying to prevent me from doing business with you and instead team up exclusively with them. Did you know anything about this?'

I was speechless, why would Collecteplan choose to do that? I had even offered them the option of using the contract I already had in place with Coin Co. Their behavior was down-

John during an interview at Coin Co

right rude and showed nothing but contempt for all I had achieved. It was a stab in the back. I felt anger rising within me but was also deeply concerned. What if they would successfully persuade John to join them? I certainly did not have the funds to file a lawsuit against Coin Co, and without their support it would be unlikely for any charity to be even remotely interested in my plans. I knew I was in a vulnerable position and I needed to think of a plan fast. The fact that John had contacted me to tell me what was going on gave me confidence and, knowing I could trust him, I explained the situation. 'I think it's better if you'd refer these guys to me. They're welcome to exploit the contract that's already in place,' I told him. Fortunately John agreed, hung up the phone and went back to his visitors.

I hoped with all my heart that he would stick to his word, but I still had concerns about Collecteplan. What if they would double cross me? I decided it was best to wait and see what would develop; it may well be a matter of time before Collecteplan would tell me about their visit to Coin Co; there was no need to worry just yet.

After a few days, when I still had not heard anything from Collecteplan, I phoned Jaap Zeekant. We talked about this and that, but he never mentioned Coin Co. 'So, how was England?' I suddenly let drop. Jaap was quiet for a moment, and when he finally spoke he sounded extremely defensive: 'We thought it was

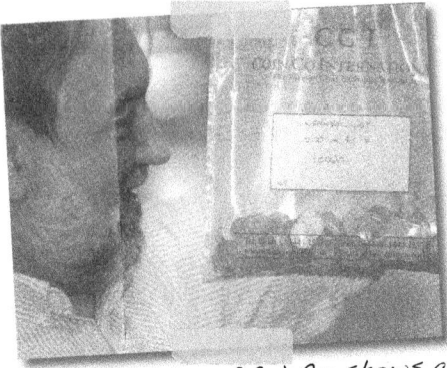

John Baker of CoinCo shows a
sealbag of Dutch coins.

important to find out for ourselves what kind of company Coin Co is. If we want to do business with you, we need to be sure you can deal with the enormity of the order,' he said. 'So why didn't you call me?' I asked. 'I could have brought the two of you together,' but he did not answer.

There was no point in telling Jaap how disrespectful I thought their actions had been. Instead, I told him about John's confidential phone-call: 'He called me while you were in his office,' I said. 'He was wondering if I knew anything about your visit and when I told him we were still in early discussion stages, John thought it was very rude of you to go behind my back. I have to agree with him that this is not how business is conducted.' Jaap mumbled something about 'a free market' and 'it had been worth trying' and then hung up.

I was shocked, I had never expected these kind of games to be played, especially not by a potential business partner striving for the same goal. At least it had been made clear that Coin Co was perfectly well equipped to process millions of foreign coins, and that in the future they should only be contacted through me. Collecteplan might now finally realize it would be worth working together after all.

> All our dreams can come true,
> if we have the courage to pursue them.
> - Walt Disney -

## Good cause or Bad cause?

The number of charities interested in joining our campaign was increasing fast. By September 2000, we had already signed up thirty organizations, and in the following month we registered a further fifty, while the applications continued to flood in!

We welcomed any charity, as long as they had a reasonable number of supporters. I thought a large following was a good benchmark for measuring whether a charity was trustworthy or not, but as time went on I began to wonder if

A slum in Brazil

it was correct to rely on the judgement of these individuals, or whether we ourselves should have a screening system in place, to ensure all charities registered were legitimate.

I heard stories, which moved heart and soul; 75 year old Nell from the Hague had visited the slums of Brazil, while on holiday in South America. She was overwhelmed by the extreme poverty and the sheer desperation of the local people and felt she had to do something. Determined to tell the people back home what she had experienced, she visited family and friends, armed with a photo-album to illustrate her stories. Within a few months she had collected about five-thousand Euros for the improvement of general living conditions in the slums.

After a second trip to Brazil, during which she visited a hospital for HIV-infected children, her fundraising activities became a lot more serious. Nell started to organize regular meetings at the Dutch Lions Clubs and gathered an impressive forty-thousand Euros for 'her' Brazilian kids.

Riet from Brabant was deeply affected by what she had witnessed while on holiday in Romania, and adopted a complete orphanage. She also organized a huge money- and goods-collection, involving the local media and retailers. She even managed to persuade truck-drivers to take the goods to Eastern Europe free of charge.

These dedicated people had set up large fundraising schemes on their own, and had inadvertently become local celebrities. Averse to making money, their success was due to pure enthusiasm. I intuitively felt I could trust them, and I was more than willing to support their organizations.

Occasionally I met people whose plans were clearly too good to be true. Once I was contacted by a 'foundation for boosting the economy of Bali'. Despite not being able to set out their objectives, they asked for funding which would allow the board of chairs to go on a 'research trip' to the Indonesian island.

Sometimes there was not even as much as a cover story and I had people simply requesting money, saying they would take good care of it, and make sure it would be 'spent fairly'.

As I did not have the time to check every charity in great detail, I looked for ways of finding out whether they were genuine or not. I discovered there was a national watchdog foundation, the Central Bureau of Fundraising (CBF), which registered and reviewed all fundraising charities.

Only a small number of all Dutch charities were members of the CBF scheme. The CBF's chief director told me that registration was voluntary, and the charities had to pay for inspections needed to acquire the CBF quality label.

'So, when a charity carries your logo, it means they don't have any excessive overhead costs?' I asked him. 'Well, one of the codes of conduct which needs to be adhered to, is that the fundraising costs do not exceed twenty-five percent of pledges raised,' was the directors answer. 'So at least three out of every four cents is being spent on charitable purposes?' I summarized. 'Well, of course, we do not have a full insight into the charity's operating costs,' admitted the director, 'but we do keep account of what they spent on fundraising campaigns and ensure these costs do not rise above twenty-five percent. If the fundraiser complies to this we will give out our quality label which proves their status to the public.'

I was not sure I fully understood. 'But what about the other seventy-five percent, what is that being spent on?' I asked. 'As I said, we don't have an insight in the organizational costs, or what is spend on overhead, housing, projects and so on,' he replied.

'So you're saying there is no guarantee that a charity carrying your logo doesn't spend the other seventy-five percent on overhead costs as well, without even one dime ending up at a good cause?' I asked in disbelief.

'Well, theoretically it's possible, but I think it's safe to say the cost-percentage will be much lower than that,' he answered.

I was completely astonished: not only was the CBF the sole 'quality control' body, but the charity sector was not even obliged to submit an annual balance sheet at the Chamber of Commerce, like any other organization!

As there was no alternative, we decided all charities who were interested in joining us should at least have a CBF 'quality label' or a 'Certificate of No Objection,' although the latter was even less stringent. It would not give us any guarantees but it was some sort of concession to Collecteplan, who thought we had too many unknown charities joining us.

As a gesture of good will I requested a "Certificate of No Objection" for Coins for Care as well. To set an example, and to stay one step ahead of any criticism.

*Bend at the knees if you want to jump high...*

Oct 2000

## Shopping

In the fall of 2000 I contacted Hoogvliet food stores, the Dutch supermarket chain with forty stores in the southwest of the country. Months earlier I had met the managing director who had been very enthusiastic about my plans and agreed to participate in the coin collection scheme. When I called him to finalize our plans, however, I was told that, sadly, he was on sick leave following a heart attack, and there was no one else who was aware of our agreement.

It was a huge disappointment, but I had no other choice than to move on. With renewed energy I focussed on finding locations for our money-boxes. I sent out a reminder to all retailers and approached Distrifood, a national retail-magazine.

The Body Shop, renowned for taking social responsibility, seemed the perfect store for placing a money-box. My first invitation did not spark any reaction, but shortly after sending out the reminder I received a phone-call from Annemarie Kornman, marketing manager of The Body Shop Benelux. 'I

Coins for Care: 'Besprekingen met Albert Heijn lopen'

## Looking for supermarkets to collect left-over coins for charity

door Peter Garstenveld

E. Jacobs (Coins for Care)

*Distrifood, 26 aug 2000*

117

received your mail regarding the money collection. Unfortunately I haven't had the time to look into it yet and the coming two weeks I'll be on a vacation. I will look at your proposal when I get back,' she said cheerfully. At least it was not a rejection, but two more weeks seemed a very long time. 'When do you think you know whether you'll join or not? We need to know soon, so we can order the right number of collection boxes,' I bluffed. The reply was better than I could have hoped for: 'Of course we're in! I just won't be able to discuss the details straightaway, I hope that's okay with you,' said Annemarie. I was over the moon and only just remembered to ask if I could announce that they were joining our scheme. Annemarie said this was absolutely fine; we had our first big name!

A couple of weeks later we had a meeting, which appeared to be a real turning point for me personally. So far, I had not done much business within the retail industry, and I had not learnt about its dealings through trial and error, as with the processing of coins. I prepared myself as well as I could: I wrote detailed proposals and thought of adequate answers to any question possible; I knew I was not going to get a second chance.

My story was simple: 'We'll take care of all logistics. The only thing we require from our partners is the use of a corner in their stores where we can place our money-boxes. Our volunteers will empty the boxes on a regular basis, and the coins will be transported to CoinCo, who manage the sorting process.' It was going to be a hell of a job, but I thought the operation itself would be pretty straightforward. I did not see any reason why the stores would object to this plan. When I sat down with Annemarie and her colleague Marieke, however, it became painfully obvious that my approach was far from realistic. 'How are you going to get these boxes to each of our shops?' Marieke asked, at which point I realized I had not thought of the logistics at all. Fortunately Annemarie came up with a solution. 'Why don't you just drop them all off at our central distribution center?' This inspired me to ask all retailers to distribute the boxes to their own stores from their central warehouse. It would make a substantial difference in the amount of work I had to do. I made a mental note to contact a logistics company and ask them to sponsor the transport to the distribution centers.

'So, when will the collection start exactly?' was the next obvious question. 'Somewhere towards the end of 2001 until early 2002,' I answered. So far, this had been a sufficient answer, but Annemarie explained that it was incredibly important for retailers to know the exact time and dates. She looked at me encouragingly, and I said: 'Well, let's say from the first of September 2001 until the first of March 2002.' And just like that the offical dates were set! While September was not too long after the summer vacation, it would give people plenty of time to sort out their coins and hand them in.

Annemarie told me that the Body Shop Benelux had fifty shops in the Netherlands, and another twenty in neighboring Belgium, who were also keen to join our scheme. It was a tempting offer, but I thought it was wiser to focus on Holland first.
I learnt a lot that day, and I am eternally grateful for Annemarie and Marieke spending so much of their valuable time thinking along with me.

As our name became more and more recognized due to increased publicity, we received reactions from all sorts of organizations, spontaneously offering to place a money-box. *Vertrekpunt*, a travel-agent with twenty branches nationwide, contacted us. *Het Huis*, optician with a hundred and twenty stores all over Holland, had heard about our project and was keen to be part of our initiative. A friend of mine worked for *De Harense Smit*, a large retailer in electrical home appliances, and told me they were also very interested in participating. When Ben & Jerry confirmed their Dutch stores would cooperate I was sent a large box of their delicious ice-cream.

· 3312 EV Dordrecht · The Neth
· www.benjerry.nl · K.v.K. Rot

Coins for Care was gaining recognition. We now had allocated collection-points in various parts of the country and the number was ever increasing. I was hoping to reel in some of the larger retailers, like Shell, Albert Heijn (the Dutch Publix) and C&A, who would give us even stronger coverage. Unfortunately, not long after sending out the reminder we received a second rejection from Albert Heijn, the international food retailer based in The Netherlands: they were not interested.

My to-do lists seemed never ending. There was so much to be done: comparing and listing all retailers, updating details of connected charities, writing strategic business plans, maintaining our website, trying to keep the free publicity going, searching for sponsorship, constantly trying to improve the logistics of our operation, and negotiating with Collecteplan, the large shopping chains, and charities. In the meantime I had to fit in some commercial projects to earn a living. I realized Coins for Care had outgrown me, it had become too large to manage on my own.

## The Politics of Charity

I needed to reach out to as many charities as possible and let them know about the prospect of joining us on a free, no obligation basis. However, it was easier said than done; in the Netherlands there was no such thing as a listing of all Dutch charities or other type of database where I could find their contact details.

The CBF advised me to get in touch with the Dutch Association of Fundraising Organizations (I'll use the original Dutch abbreviation: VFI) who looked after the interest of a 120 charities. I thought this was such good idea; a perfect opportunity to build up recognition within the charity industry. I would soon find out that this would prove to be a foolish assumption.

Gosse Bosma was VFI's young manager. Dressed in a well fitted suit and smart tie, he appeared friendly and courteous, but I thought he was somehow distant, even calculated. I could feel his blue piercing eyes while I told him about Coins for Care. When I had finished, he looked at me for a moment and asked: 'So, what can we do for you?'
I explained -again- my wish to invite all CBF registered charities to join Coins for Care and share our proceeds, and I asked if he could provide me with a list of all VFI members, so I could contact them.
'We don't give out addresses,' said Gosse firmly.
'If you can't give out any addresses, maybe you could make an announcement in your newsletter?' I suggested.
'It's not going to happen,' was Gosse's short reply.
'But don't you think your members should be made aware of our money collection?' I asked surprised.

I did not understand why he should be so blunt. Surely the VFI had its members' interests at heart, so why not offer them the opportunity to join a unique collection scheme?
Eventually it became clear why Gosse was being so uncooperative.
'We're already working together with Collecteplan,' he said curtly.
I could not believe what he was saying: 'Collecteplan only accepts charities that hold door-to-door collections; that means that only twenty of your members are eligible for their program! What about the other hundred non-collection VFI charities; would it not be a good thing for them if they could share our proceeds? Look, I'm not asking the VFI to choose sides, I only want to make your members aware that they can join our scheme!'
I was not getting anywhere. Gosse opened the door, a clear sign our meeting had come to an end. 'Sorry, I cannot help you,' he said.

It was only a glimpse of the politics being played within the charitable sector as a whole, and it would not be until many years later that I fully understood why the VFI put its relationship with Collecteplan above the interest of its affiliated charities.

Thankfully the CBF was so kind to give me access to their address-database. It meant I could finally start inviting 200 Dutch charities to join the Coins for Care scheme.

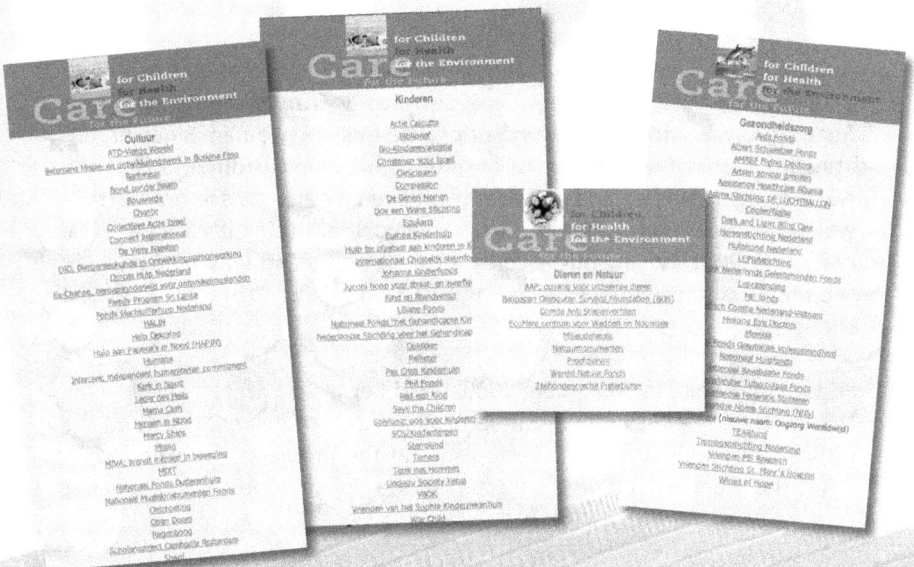

Not long after our mailing, we received our first applications. Some charities requested a meeting in person before committing to us, and I traveled across the country visiting all kinds of organizations. It was something I enjoyed very much, but in the end I received more invitations than I could physically deal with. I simply did not have the time to meet all requests. Fortunately there had been so much publicity that the necessity to inform every party personally had become less urgent.

Registering the charities and dealing with their information requests took up a large chunk of my time. I had to verify their CBF record, and they had to provide a written summary of their activities which I could publish on our website. I also wanted them to sign a declaration stating that any money received through Coins for Care should be spent on projects, and not used for covering overhead costs. 'There should be complete transparency in how the money is being distributed,' I had to explain many times.

## Collecteplan 3

'Four and a half million euro?' Anita could not believe what I had just told her. 'Yes, Collecteplan have 4.5 million euro at their disposal for setting up this project. A big part of that money will be wasted on the processing. It would be much easier for them to partner with us; we already have a contract with Coin Co, a specialist in foreign currency exchange. They are just trying to reinvent the wheel,' I said.

Anita van Leeuwen was one of the people who had spontaneously offered a helping hand with Coins for Care. She was 34, proud mother of a gorgeous two year old girl, and a no-nonsense businesswoman. Since graduating from law school she had been running her own customer satisfaction research agency, and had been deeply touched by the Coins for Care article which had been published in the Viva magazine. 'I think it's a great idea, collecting all those worthless coins. I can't understand why nobody ever thought about it before,' she said. 'But I also think it's a complex logistical challenge.'

When I met Anita in September 2000, I told her what I had achieved so far. Despite trying to be positive and up beat, I could not help reflecting on the recent developments with Collecteplan and the problems we were facing. 'I just don't understand why Collecteplan are being so obstructive when it comes to working with us!' I sighed.

I told Anita how Jaap and Raymond had gone behind my back, visiting Coin Co; how they had manipulated the press, how they refused to take me seriously, and how I was being treated without any respect. I guess I wanted to be sure Anita knew what she was getting herself into, but despite my warnings she became increasingly enthusiastic for helping me out.

One of Anita's first tasks was to read and record all of our paperwork, so she would be aware of the current situation. She was a calm, sensible woman, oozing authority who clearly enjoyed a good challenge, and I was very happy to have found a partner who thought along with me, sharing my ideas. At the next meeting we had with Collecteplan, Anita confirmed herself as a valuable ally.

Jaap and Raymond were appointed by Collecteplan as our official contacts. They both held impressive careers in the charity world. Jaap as a member of the board of directors at the Dutch Burns Foundation, and Raymond as a fundraiser at the Dutch Cancer Foundation (KWF). Their achievements included establishing the Fundraising Institute, setting up a behavioral code for the entire charity sector, as well as launching the trade journal 'Funds'. The huge door-to-door collection during the introduction of the euro had been their brainchild, and they had presented it to Collecteplan. Having taken a huge risk by giving up their jobs and starting their own agency, they were determined to turn this large project into a success, whilst continuing to work as independent consultants in the charity sector.

It was understandable who were not happy with us. Here we were, two young women who thought they could start a campaign on a whim, claiming we could launch it a lot cheaper and quicker, completely bypassing their knowledge and experience. We decided to take the humble approach, and be compliant with their wishes, so not to give them any reason to object. Anita soon got fed up with this, but I remained convinced it was the right thing to do; we needed to get together in the interest of all charities, the public, and other parties involved.

When Anita introduced herself as a legal expert, Jaap and Raymond looked worried. Assuming I had brought along one of my friends, Jaap asked: 'So, how long have you known each other?' His face turned into a surprised grin when Anita told them how we had met only a few weeks ago, when she had contacted me after reading the Viva article. 'I thought it would be fun to be able to contribute to a good cause like this.'
This put Jaap and Raymond in their place, and for a moment they did not know how to react. Anita was quick to come to the point: 'Esther has told me that

you have been talking for a while now, regarding a possible cooperation. As a preparation for this meeting we have, I believe for the third time, rewritten our proposal, but we have not received any reaction yet. It would be great if we could discuss this now.'

Jaap and Raymond skillfully avoided her question by focussing on the latest developments. Proudly they told us they had added another interested party to their list: the national Service Clubs, which included the Lions, the Rotary and the Round Table. After approaching several banks with an idea for a corporate collection campaign, these clubs had been referred to Collecteplan, and things had developed quickly from then. Recently, the Service Clubs and Collecteplan, had publicly announced their partnership with the Dutch Olympic Committee, and had even come up with a name: National EuroCollecte Foundation.

'I've got to say, this idea shows a lot of similarities with our plan to place collection boxes in shops,' Anita said. All the more reason to work together, I thought. 'Why don't we arrange a meeting with all parties concerned to discuss the possibility of teaming up?' I suggested. 'Perhaps we can come to a common list of action points?'

Jaap and Raymond were reluctant and said they wanted to discuss this with the ServiceClubs and the Dutch Olympic Committee first, before deciding if they should work with Coins for Care. I did not see the logic in this, but there was not a lot we could do, and so our third meeting with Collecteplan ended, again without any firm commitments. Anita was shocked at such lack of determination. 'Welcome to the world of charity!' I laughed.

> 'Fail, fail again, fail better...'
> - Samuel Beckett -

## The big breakthrough

'Don't laugh, not yet, don't say anything!' I hushed at my friend Carola while we hurriedly made our way out of the Shell head offices, stumbling over our own feet with excitement, desperately trying to suppress our giggles. As soon as we were out of sight we burst out in hysterical laughter, dancing around out of sheer relief and happiness, yelling: 'Yes, we did it, they're in!'

Carola had given up her marketing job to travel around the world. After returning home, she had not wanted to go straight back into the rat-race, but instead had been keen to do something useful. The Coins for Care idea had seemed attractive: 'I like the fact that the scheme offers help to more than one charity, against minimal costs and with the involvement of the public,' she said. I was happy to have an extra pair of hands for a few months and had suggested she'd join me at the fourth meeting I had with Shell.

'If you have built castles in the air, your work need not be lost; that is where they should be. Now put the foundations under them.'
- Henry David Thoreau -

The meeting was at the Shell head offices, and we were met by the CEO and four other gentlemen. I had expected having to give a brief summary about Coins for Care and what we stood for, but to our surprise the CEO got straight to the point: 'We can only join with the gas stations along the motorway. The other Shell gas stations are franchised.'
I glanced at Carola to see if I'd heard correctly what he'd just said. Shell had already decided to commit! The look on Carola's face told me she was surprised too.
'That's great, it would be fantastic if you join us, it doesn't matter really with how many stations, but of course we would prefer it if all stations were in,' I pushed gently. The CEO leant back in his chair and gave me an encouraging smile: 'So, why don't you convince me?'
Carola and I were only too happy to do so: 'Well, most people are not aware which Shell stations are franchises. Imagine what people would think when they get their gas at Shell, expecting to get rid of their change, and then they find out they can't!' I said. 'Surely Shell does not want to create such a confusing situation for its customers?' Carola was quick to add.
Clearly amused by our eagerness to convince, it didn't take the CEO long to decide that all Shell petrol stations would participate. We could not believe our luck!

I felt so happy: 'You see, she who perseveres wins!' I called out to Carola. With the Body Shop and Shell on our side we could finally show all other retailers that we were serious about Coins for Care.

We had made it. Two years ago, the coin collection campaign had been nothing more than an idea but now, after numerous problems and disappointments, it was finally working out. Coins for Care was now widely known and we were taken seriously by both the corporate world and the public. I felt we had reached a turning point; it would all be a lot easier from now on. Collecteplan could no longer ignore us.

'Quit now, you'll never make it.
If you disregard this advice, you'll be halfway there.'
- David Zucker -

*ViaShell magazine; available at all Dutch gas stations*

## SHELL NEWS,

### HOLIDAY COINS FOR CHARITIES

Shell in Nederland ondersteunt het project *Coins for Care*. Omdat veel buitenlands muntgeld als gevolg van de invoering van de euro na januari 2002 niet meer te gebruiken zal zijn en banken dit geld niet omwisselen, zullen er veel francs, marken en peseta's overblijven. Stichting Coins for Care heeft een grootschalig initiatief opgezet om al die buitenlandse munten in te zamelen. De opbrengst zal gaan naar zo veel mogelijk goede doelen.

Shell plaatst vanaf september dit jaar inzamelbakken op haar eigen stations in Nederland. Verder zal ze de overige Shell-stations vragen om ook mee te doen. 'Wij dragen dit initiatief een warm hart toe. Het idee is eenvoudig, maar krachtig. Bovendien kunnen wij door het plaatsen van inzamelbakken onze klanten helpen in één keer circa tachtig goede doelen te steunen,' aldus marketingmanager Dirk Baak.

Door de medewerking van Shell krijgt de inzamelingsactie nationale spreiding en is er voor iedereen in Nederland een mogelijkheid in de buurt om muntgeld in te leveren. Daarnaast bereikt Coins for Care hiermee een aanvullende doelgroep. Shell ziet de medewerking aan deze inzamelingsactie als een goede manier om haar maatschappelijke betrokkenheid te tonen en ook 'een duit in het zakje te doen'.

Als pilot worden in februari al inzamelbakken geplaatst in de Shell-kantoren in Den Haag en Capelle aan den IJssel, waarin medewerkers van Shell hun buitenlands muntgeld kunnen doen. 'Zo kunnen we het logistieke traject van tevoren goed testen en de Shell-medewerk[...] te grote inzamelingsactie die later dat jaar zal volgen', [...]eenister van Coins for Care.

[...]ting die speciaal is opgericht om straks - als de euro [...]enlands muntgeld te verzamelen, dat nu nog in het [...] Nederlandse huishoudens. Hiertoe worden van sep[...] 2002 door heel Nederland op verschillende plekken [...]ting Coins for Care is onafhankelijk en objectief en [...]rijfsleven. De kosten van de actie zijn daardoor [...]oede doelen is Coins for Care het grootste samen[...]oelen in de Nederlandse geschiedenis ooit. Het [...] bepalen hoe de opbrengst over de goede doelen [...]it te brengen op *www.coinsforcare.nl*

## WORTHLESS COINS FOR CHARITIES

Hoeveel buitenlands geld heeft u deze zomer overgehouden? Liggen er nog veel muntjes uit Frankrijk, Spanje of Duitsland in de keukenlade? Straks, als de euro is ingevoerd, is dat vreemde kleingeld niks meer waard. Geen nood. Coins for Care en Nationale Eurocollecte gaan de munten inzamelen voor goede doelen.

*Whether your name is Frank, Mark or Penny...*

O nder andere bij Shell komen met ingang van september speciale inzamelbakken te staan. Marketingmanager Dirk Baak (foto boven) is enthousiast. 'Shell draagt het initiatief een warm hart toe. Door het plaatsen van de bakken stellen we onze klanten in de gelegenheid een heleboel goede doelen te steunen,' zegt hij zelf ziet de medewerking aan de actie als een goede manier om een 'maatschappelijke duit in het zakje te doen'.

Volgens Esther Jacobs van stichting Coins for Care is het de bedoeling om in een half jaar tijd zo'n vijftig miljoen gulden aan buitenlands geld op te halen. De verwachte opbrengst is onder meer geschat op basis van gegevens van banken over de hoeveelheid buitenlands geld in de Nederlandse huishoudens. 'Uiteindelijk zal de opbrengst worden verdeeld over meer dan honderd goede doelen', zegt Esther Jacobs die tweeëneenhalf jaar geleden het idee voor Coins for Care kreeg. Zij maakte Shell maar ook Albert Heijn, de Hema en de Grenswisselkantoren warm om inzamelbakken te plaatsen.

Aan het begin van deze zomer besloten Coins for Care en de stichting Nationale Eurocollecte nauw te gaan samenwerken.

Vanaf 15 oktober plaatsen daarom ook 5700 bankfilialen inzamelbakken, gaan sportclubs vreemde valuta sparen en komt er nog een huis-aan-huis-collecte van 14 tot 26 januari volgend jaar. 'Er is geen ontkomen aan', lacht Esther, 'op 1 maart 2002 kan er haast geen vreemd Europees muntgeld meer in potjes of keukenlades liggen. Overigens zijn ook Nederlands geld en niet-Europese munten zeer welkom'.

Coins for Care en Nationale Eurocollecte ver-tegenwoordigen een breed scala aan goede doelen. Grote en kleine organisaties die zich inzetten voor onder andere gezondheidszorg, natuur en milieu, en kinderen komen in het rijtje voor. Dat betekent dat er altijd wel een goed doel is wat je iemand aanspreekt. 'Het aardige is', zegt Esther, 'dat het Nederlandse publiek zijn voorkeur kan aangeven over hoe de opbrengst over de goede doelen wordt verdeeld. Dat kan door een stem uit te brengen op de website *www.coinsforcare.nl* : Er is ook een telefoonnummer opengesteld 0900-9594 (22ct p/m). Als op 1 maart volgend jaar de inzamelactie is afgelopen, begint het grote sorteer- en telwerk. Deze omvangrijke klus is uitbesteed aan de Engelse firma Coin Co International, die het ingezamelde geld niet alleen sorteert en telt maar ook terugsluist naar het land van herkomst. De goede doelen krijgen dan de werkelijke waarde van het geld uitgekeerd in euro's. 'Ik denk dat we eind oktober de eerste tussenstand bekend kunnen maken. Een half jaar later weten we precies met hoeveel geld we de goede doelen kunnen verblijden.'

Verzamel dus uw buitenlandse (munt) geld, gooi dit vanaf 1 september bij Shell in een inzamelbak en steun meer dan 100 goede doelen! *

**Esther Jacobs**

Foto: GEROLD FERRIÈRE

20

127

Excuse 8:
'I am not being taken seriously...'

'Treat others as you would want to be treated.
For they have been planting the wind,
and their fruit will be the storm.'
-Religious principle-

## Pinstriped suits

While the Dutch banks were united in their wish to join a charity project at the introduction of the euro, it was up to the Dutch Bankers' Association (NVB) to decide on behalf of all banks whether they would join EuroCollecte, the ServiceClubs or another charity project. Encouraged by our latest success at Shell, Carola and I decided to contact the NVB, and introduce Coins for Care as a potential partner.

We moved heaven and earth to arrange a meeting in the NVB's impressive headquarters, which were built like a fort, in central Amsterdam. Carola and I had both opted for a dark grey suit, expecting to be the youngest, and probably the only two women around the table. We wanted to come across as serious candidates for a potential business partnership, and didn't want to be perceived as two young girls with just a good idea.

We introduced ourselves to the NVB members (who were, indeed, all older men dressed in striped suits) and we explained the progress of our project, mentioning who we had on board so far, and emphasizing we were keen to work together with CollectePlan, the Service Clubs and other parties.

Our listeners nodded approvingly. 'That's good to know, we strongly support partnerships and we would like to prevent solitary actions in this case,' said one of them.

It was clear that the NVB had close links with CollectePlan and were striving for some sort of cooperation with Coins for Care. I had to be honest, however, and described how communications with CollectePlan had come to a standstill, and I asked the NVB if they could break the deadlock by putting pressure on CollectePlan, forcing a decision.

Despite our plea, they were reluctant to do so. We were unable to come to a solution, and kept going round in circles.

## Bold at Quote's

Disappointed by our fruitless meeting at the NVB, Carola and I decided to grab something to eat. When we sat down I noticed the sign on the building at the other side of the street. Coincidentally the lunchroom was situated opposite the offices of the business magazine Quote. I grinned at Carola, suddenly feeling incredibly rebellious: 'Shall we...?'

At a bakery we bought some pastries and, still wearing our business suits, we stepped into the lobby of the Quote building where we announced ourselves at the reception desk. 'We don't have an appointment, but we need to see Mr Jort Kelder urgently.' Jort Kelder was the chief editor at Quote and a well known public figure in the Netherlands. We didn't explain ourselves any further and waited to see what would happen. The arrogant receptionists made a few calls and started to whisper amongst themselves, looking at us suspiciously.

After fifteen minutes we were led into a big office space, which was buzzing with people. Jort Kelder sat in a corner at the back, in deep conversation with another man. Even though he must have personally given permission for letting us through, he acted as if we were disturbing him. Carola and I hesitated for a moment, but then I produced a big smile and presented both Jort and his friend with a pastry. 'While you're enjoying this delicacy we would like five minutes of your attention to introduce you to an important and fun project.'

For a moment the two men dropped their bored pretense and smiled, but then fell back into their role: 'Alright, but you got to do it while sitting on my lap!' was Jort's macho reply.

Nothing could have prepared us for this: the country's most infamous editor seemed to be in a mischievous mood. Carola and I wished we could walk out as if nothing had happened. Ignoring his remark we hastily delivered our pitch, and explained we were looking for some further publicity for Coins for Care. Not waiting for a response, we thanked both men for their time, gave them our business cards and made sure we got out of the building.

Outside we burst out laughing, but felt incredibly embarrassed that we had allowed ourselves to be treated like little girls.

Carola was annoyed: 'Even in our business suits we're not taken seriously!' We decided from now on to focus on content. 'We just need to keep going, one day people will see they have judged us wrongly.'

**Zapp**

Coins for Care: Charities benefit from Euro

" It hurts me deeply when I see how some charities spend their money"

## Coins for Care

### CHARITIES BENEFIT FROM EURO

It hurts me deeply when I see how some charities spend their money.

I don't know if our visit had anything to do with it, but a few weeks later I was approached by Quote magazine for an interview... Millions of people read the magazine, so I was honored. The photographer insisted on a serious picture...

Carola and me traveling through Peru proved a good base for our friendship.

# Sewage pipes for charity

It was time to act upon our promises; we now had the support of a number of retailers, and more and more charities were still joining us. Our first priority was to find a simple and, if possible, free solution for collecting the money. Conventional collection boxes were too expensive as well as too small for the amount of money we were expecting to raise. They were also prone to theft as it was easy to remove them. What we needed was a big strong container, clearly distinguishable, which would draw the public's attention instantly.

I contacted Wavin, a producer specialized in plastics, who I remembered as a keen charity sponsor from my university days. They were immediately prepared to help, and told me they might have a type of box which we could use. I was invited to have a look around in their showroom. Unfortunately none of their products was suitable for our purposes. We did see a type of mailbox, however, which came close to what we were looking for, but that type was already being used by the Royal Mail. Wavin assured us they would look for an alternative, but we knew the production and design of a completely new product would take too long and be too expensive, so we had to start looking further afield.

I was getting desperate; despite having an enthusiastic sponsor, we still did not have a solution, and time was running out. Carola suggested I should approach an advertising company who specialized in branding solutions. 'These guys are so creative, they always have the most innovative ideas,' she told me. 'We don't need branding or advertising material, we need collection boxes!' I protested, but immediately realized I was making the same mistake as other people had made about me. First impressions aren't always right, and I had to seriously look into all options that were available to me.

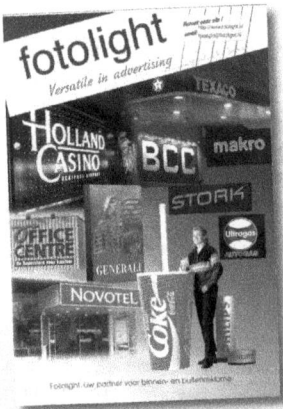

Fotolight was a small, dynamic company. Their workshop was scattered with all kinds of advertising displays, panels, and columns. We were met by Tim van Iersel, the owner, a friendly, practical man. We told him we didn't have a budget, but had seen a suitable mailbox at Wavin.

'I'm sure we can do something similar out of sewage pipes,' Tim said.

Seeing the astonished looks on our faces, he laughed and explained how he could make a proper collection box out of a large plastic sewage pipe. He drew a sketch for a box of about one meter high, and said: 'Look, on the top we place a see-through cover with a coin slot, so you can see how much money has been collected. The pipes will need to be closed at the bottom; Wavin do special caps for that, you will have to ask for the special glue.' He went on to say he would provide the necessary stickers explaining the Coins for Care action. It was nearly too good to be true. 'I got some pipe at the back, I can do a prototype if you want? It will be finished within a couple of days,' was our hero's promise and all of a sudden the world seemed our oyster.

My contact at Wavin agreed to deliver the products we required, but couldn't help laughing: 'Sewage pipes for charity?' I didn't care; at last we were going to have our own collection boxes!

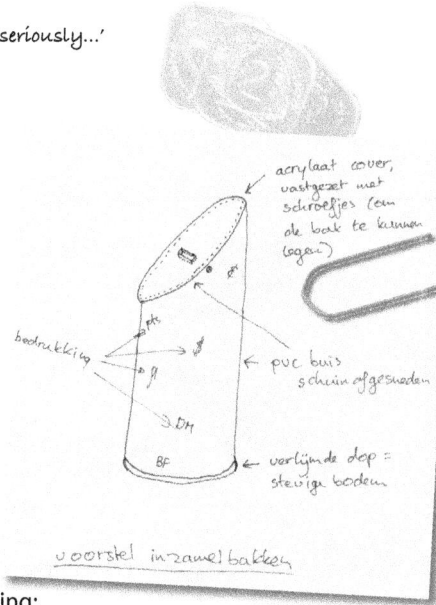

## Unite with Northsea FM Radio

One day Carola announced she had found a new job and was going to leave Coins for Care. Her last contribution was introducing me to Northsea FM, a well know radio station in The Netherlands. We needed to generate an awful lot of publicity if we wanted to launch our project nationally, and this popular radio station happened to be right in the middle of a publicity campaign following their name change from Radio Northsea. It was a win-win situation: 'If

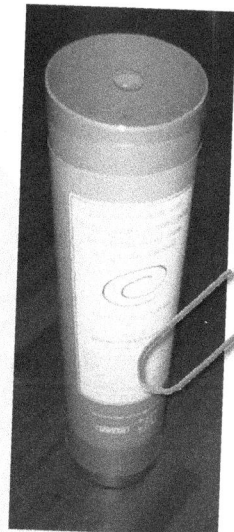

Donate your foreign coins and support over 100 certified charities!

Coins·for·Care

Kijk op
www.coinsforcare.nl
en stem zelf mee, of bel
0900-9594
voor meer info.

you become our exclusive radio-partner, we make sure you'll be the first to get updated on the sums raised and other fun Coins for Care news.' I offered.

'And what else do we get in return for the huge amount of free publicity you'll receive?' Northsea FM asked. We immediately offered to place the Northsea FM logo on our four thousand collection boxes.

Everyone was happy with this deal, and the ideas kept coming in: 'We could organize a weekly Coins for Care news report, and have people requesting a song for Coins for Care,' suggested one of the marketing guys.

From March 2001 onwards, Northsea FM was our official radio partner, ensuring a great deal of attention for Coins for Care. Sylvana Simons, one of the anchor presenters, updated the listeners every Friday evening about both the public and the corporate campaigns.

## Negotiations

Anita had been an enormous help with structuring our proposals to CollectePlan, who had now created a separate entity called EuroCollecte. My enthusiastic spontaneous notes had been turned into professionally structured business proposals, which had made it painfully obvious that EuroCollecte were using arguments at random, so as not to work with us. Every time we met they would have another objection, which was never detailed in writing. And none of our adjustments made them change their mind. ZThe only response we got was still more criticism.

EuroCollecte's main objection had been the involvement of a large number of unknown charities. After we decided that only CBF certified charities could participate, their next protest had been against the role of the public vote on how the money would be divided. Their latest criticism had been aimed at Coins for Care's commitment not to spend more than two percent of the proceeds on expenses.
When we suggested a joint organization, EuroCollecte's ambition was to have as little contact as possible. When we proposed peaceful coexistence, they would bring up arguments for a closer cooperation. Anita and I wrote one proposal after another but got involved in the same tired old discussions, over and over again: 'Why can't we just exist alongside each other?' EuroCollecte kept asking, at which we would repeat the advantages of working together: A clear

134

message to the public, central coordination of publicity and logistics, lower costs due to the prevention of overlap and duplicating work, and last but not least: working together as a national unit would secure the involvement of the banks and the government.

When EuroCollecte could no longer ignore the advantages of working together, the disagreements shifted to the practicalities of our cooperation. Anita had formulated a basic principle for our alliance: 'Both parties should have an equal interest in the success of the activities of the other. They should benefit equally from the success, as well as the profits of their partner.' With this principle in mind, we suggested an exchange of funds between ten and fifty percent, ten percent indicating a symbolic cooperation, with both parties still profiting from their own fundraising actions. The fifty percent option would represent a complete team effort, and any funds raised would be equally divided. EuroCollecte aimed to keep this percentage as low as possible, so we were expecting a ten percent exchange.

By December we had finally come to an agreement. 'EuroCollecte opts for a fifty percent rule,' Jaap had announced unexpectedly. 'But last time you told me you did not want more that ten percent,' I reminded him. Jaap shook his head. 'It's got to be fifty, no less,' he said adamantly. I did not really care about the percentage, I was just happy we had finally cut a deal.

'We've done it, they're in, finally!' I told Anita, who could not attend the meeting. 'Something tells me we're not quite there yet,' she said thoughtfully, 'but I hope you're right and that it really is a done deal.' 'Don't worry, I'm sure we're there, we've even confirmed a percentage, so no more endless negotiations,' I said optimistically.

All that was left to do was working out the details of our agreement with EuroCollecte. At our next meeting Anita and I were welcomed by a new member of the board. Klaas van de Poll was a pale man with a pair of dark piercing eyes, who introduced himself as the managing director of the Dutch Cancer Foundation, and board member of CollectePlan and EuroCollecte. To our astonishment he started the conversation with that same old question: 'Why should we work together? Surely, both projects can exist happily alongside each other?' he suggested. We couldn't believe what we just heard.
'I beg your pardon, but I really don't think we need to revisit that discussion. We have already agreed on working together and we have come here to discuss the conditions,' Anita replied.

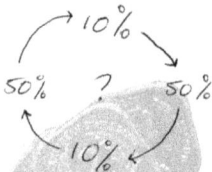

'Nothing has been decided yet,' said Klaas bluntly. Anita and I referred to the many meetings we had had with Jaap and Raymond, the EuroCollecte management. 'During our last conversation we even agreed on a percentage split of the funds to be raised,' I added.

'Jaap en Raymond have acted purely in their personal capacity. They do not represent EuroCollecte; I do,' said Klaas, without even blinking.

We were both completely taken aback, but then Anita reacted much fiercer than I would ever have dared. 'If that is the case, then we're out of the door now! We'll see what the government and the Dutch Banking Association have got to say about this. They're the ones who have referred us to you, we've spent the last nine months negotiating with your organization, we have written numerous proposals, and now you're acting as if it was all a big game? Nobody will ever take you seriously again!'

It was a brilliant outburst by Anita, and Klaas realized he had gone way too far, but he kept insisting on starting the negotiations all over again. Instead of the agreed fifty percent he went back to the minimal ten: we had returned to the 'peaceful coexistence' level.

> *'Men are respectable only as they respect.'*
> *- Ralph Waldo Emerson -*

After this meeting Anita took me apart. 'Esther, do you really want to continue with this? These people do not want to work with you, that much is clear by now,' she warned me. I knew she was right, but I reminded her that working together was in the interest of all charities. 'Think about all the money being wasted on organizing everything twice, while it could be done centrally! I cannot allow that to happen,' I said to Anita. 'I know EuroCollecte wishes to get rid of Coins for Care, so they can tell the banks and government they have tried everything, but we were not interested in working with them. I am also fed up with these silly, never ending, frustrating discussions. It makes me sick to think about the time we have wasted so far, but I refuse to give up! You can call me stubborn, but giving up would be too easy on them. We just need stay put and see what happens next.'

I AM GRATEFUL FOR ALL SKEPTICS; WITHOUT THEM I WOULD NOT HAVE CONTINUED.

At the end of January I was invited by another of the EuroCollecte board members. I had met Arno Wamsteker before, at the very first EuroCollecte meeting back in

April 2000. He was a quiet, friendly natured man, who appeared trustworthy and seemed truly open to the idea of working together. I found him an easy person to talk to, and outlined to him everything I had achieved so far with Coins for Care, while he listened carefully, taking a few notes. At the end of our meeting I felt I had his support, and I went as far as even confiding in him, expanding on the troubles we had been having with the other members of the board.

'I have the feeling I am not being taken seriously,' I said. I will never forget Arno's reply, which was meant to make me feel better, but typified how I was being perceived at EuroCollecte despite what I had achieved so far on a professional level: 'Of course I'm taking you seriously, I've got a daughter your age.'

Arno's extensive report of our conversation was sent to the board. It was a positive account, recommending a close cooperation with Coins for Care. I was disappointed though by his concluding summary: 'Esther Jacobs leaves a trustful impression, but can't guarantee the success of the Coins for Care action. I am, however, convinced that working together in the field of collecting foreign coins with either Coins for Care and/or the Postcode Lottery is essential for achieving the estimated amount of 23 million euros.'

So now all of a sudden they might partner up with the Postcode Lottery? Nobody had ever mentioned that, not even Arno. It seemed we found ourselves in a never ending story.

## An eye for an eye,...

My initial aspiration to turn Coins for Care into a commercial success had changed. My main motivation was now to do it on a non profit basis purely for a good cause. It had been difficult to get this project off the ground, and it had become a personal challenge to show my critics I was able to be successful. The more I was belittled as 'the little girl' the bigger my determination to raise above myself, instead of being defeated, my critics gave me the boost to continue and show them what I can achieve.

**Dutch households have as much as 300 million guilders lying about in foreign coins.**

With the growing interest from the press, the corporate world and the public, opposition within EuroCollecte had also increased. It was obvious that our low cost action, our high exposure and participation of the public was seen as a threat by the established industry.

I felt we were way past the wait-to-see-which-way-the-cat-jumps stage, I felt I had honestly tried everything. I had hung in there for much longer than was reasonable, and now I was done with it. These negotiations were not going anywhere and took too much valuable energy, energy which I needed to focus on extending my campaign. I did not see another option but to give up all further attempts of agreeing to a partnership, and decided to go my own way with Coins for Care.

Not long after, a great opportunity came up: I was asked to present Coins for Care at an annual congress, organized by the Alliance of Fundraisers. 'It will be a unique chance to announce your plans to the representatives of the entire charity industry,' were the encouraging words of the organization.

Jaap and Raymond, the founders of the Alliance, had started this event years ago, and this year they had outsourced the organization. When they heard that I had been invited to speak, they were furious. It was too late to cancel me; all invitations had already been sent.

> *'It is great to be a blonde. With low expectations*
> *it's very easy to surprise people.'*
> *- Pamela Anderson -*

Blissfully unaware of the stir I had caused, I started listing all the participating retailers. The retail chains who had not replied yet I put under a header *in negotiation*. The result was striking, it was an impressive list which added to the strength and credibility of the presentation.

It was a presentation from the heart, I outlined what my motivations had been for setting up the campaign, why I didn't want to be paid for my work, and how we operated on a non-cost basis by negotiating sponsorship for everything. I emphasized that all charities were invited to participate, and that we were particularly looking forward to reaching an agreement with EuroCollecte. The audience was excited, I couldn't have hoped for more enthusiastic reactions.

Then it was Raymond and Jaap's turn, they presented their intention of working together with the Service Clubs, the banks, and the Dutch Olympic Committee. Their pitch was good, however, while they visibly enjoyed the spotlight, their performance was dry and business like. Jaap referred a couple of times to Coins for Care but Raymond completely ignored me.

Following these two presentations, the audience was given the opportunity to fire some questions, but Jaap and Raymond were not in the mood: 'That's not necessary, I believe our presentation was clear enough. We don't have anything to add,' they said, and hurried off the stage.

The audience insisted, and the organization invited Jaap, Raymond and myself back onto the stage. The first question was to be expected: 'Why don't EuroCollecte and Coins for Care work together?'

Adrenalin was rushing through my veins; I knew this was an important moment and intuitively decided to let Jaap and Raymond answer first. Raymond reluctantly took the microphone: 'We are in negotiations, and we'd rather not comment at this stage,' he said, forcing a strained smile.

Even now, many years later while I am writing this, my stomach still knots up with tension thinking back to how I walked up to the mike, my hands trembling, my throat dry. I spoke as calmly as I could: 'I would like to say something about that; we have been in talks for nearly a year now. Coins for Care has made numerous proposals to find any possible way of working together, but we are still waiting for a reply from EuroCollecte. So, just like the audience, I too would like to know why we are not working together yet.'

Every person in the audience looked expectantly at both gentlemen on the stage who had stepped away from the microphone and were discussing what to do next. Raymond was furious, he turned away from me and stared angrily in the distance, leaving Jaap to resolve this. For a moment they reminded me of Amal and his irritable boss I had met in Geneva.

Jaap put on his friendliest smile, and walked up the stage: 'Yes indeed, we have met a couple of times with Esther, but..., well, Coins for Care does not have the CBF certificate, so you never know who you're really dealing with,' he said.

It took a moment before I realized what a vile and unfair remark he had just made. But before I could even react, a few people in the audience stood up: 'Jaap and Raymond, this is not fair! Esther has just delivered a very good presentation, solid argumentation, proving to us that Coins for Care is an effectively managed organization. She's explained she is operating on a non profit basis. You cannot just dismiss all that!'

People were nodding approvingly and there was even some booing in Jaap and Raymonds direction.

When I confirmed we had already applied for a *Declaration of No Objection* at the CBF, Jaap shouted: 'But they don't have it yet, and until such time there is no way we can get together!' After this outburst a shock went through the audience. Sensing this and trying to soften the impact of what he just said, Jaap added he had not been aware of the story behind Coins for Care. 'Now I have learnt more about it I don't think it is such a bad idea, we may have to reconsider it.'

*'I was not aware'* said the man with whom I'd had countless meetings and intense negotiations over the past months... Now I knew for sure they never had any intention to react to our proposals.

I had tried to respect their point of view, but it was now obvious that they had just kept me on a string, and that all our efforts had been a total waste of time. The sad thing was that Jaap and Raymond could not even come up with a good excuse. I could no longer contain myself and took the microphone: 'What a shame you couldn't be honest during our meetings, then I would have known what the score was, instead of having to create new proposals time and time again,' I hissed through clenched teeth. 'And by the way, if the CBF logo is so critical to you, why don't you have one yourself?' I snapped at Jaap. The mood was about to change into an uncontrollable shouting match and the organization had to intervene and end the question round prematurely.

### *'My intent will be evident in the results'*
### *- Thurgood Marshall -*

Trembling with anger, I made my way to a quiet corner of the room, feeling stupid for letting myself go like that. Immediately I was surrounded by many people who wished to compliment me on my presentation. 'Jaap and Raymond are known for their arrogance, and we really enjoyed your performance, standing up for yourself like that!' they said. 'What an embarrassing defeat for both gentlemen!' someone else laughed. Charity representatives congratulated me, showing their support, announcing they would be happy to join the Coins for Care scheme. Some of them admitted they had had their doubts, but these had all been removed by my passionate performance. 'You've absolutely convinced us with your enthusiasm and your impressive list of retailers and sponsors.'

When I was on my way home, very tired, but very contented, I updated Anita on what had happened that afternoon. I realized this had been a turning point for Coins for Care. We had gone into the lion's den and had come out stronger. We'd even made important alliances and the lion had not been happy with that!

EuroCollecte would announce their final decision on Valentine's Day. Jaap did not think it necessary for me and Anita to attend the board meeting. 'We've got all the information we require,' he snapped. Eagerly we awaited their phone call, it was a key moment. Finally we would get the go or no-go. I almost did not care anymore what the outcome would be, I just wanted an end to this dragging situation.

We did not receive a reaction on the 14th of February, and the 15th went by without any news either. In the end I called Jaap myself: 'And?' I asked. 'What do you mean?' Jaap replied wearily. 'The board meeting! What have you decided?' I said impatiently. 'Oh that,' said Jaap. 'We haven't had time to discuss that yet, we had too many other important issues to deal with.' It was immensely frustrating. The meeting had been held, the moment had gone, and we just had to wait again until the next opportunity.

Two fruitless meetings and two proposals later, we received an arrogant letter in which EuroCollecte, acting as the watchdog of the charity industry, demanded 'consent in writing of all charities registered with Coins for Care'. They also gave us a list of conditions to which 'charitable actions as the Coins for Care scheme should adhere to before realizing a cooperation'. One by one all objections we'd heard over the past months appeared again and they added some new ones as well. The first objection was that before the start of a collection it should be agreed on how the money was going to be divided. Next to that our contract with Coin Co's should be annulled (they called it a 'monopoly', meant to 'force' other charities into unconditional corporation'). And last: we were not allowed to even mention our very low costs, whilst forbidding us to talk to the press.

Anita and I were completely overwhelmed. We weren't even sure anymore whether the EuroCollecte board had even seen our proposals, because they were now highlighting completely new issues. Now, for the first time they detailed, in writing, their reluctance to working together, and were apparently so convinced of their case, that they had cc-ed the letter to everybody involved: all charities, the government, Erica Terpstra ( a Dutch ex-sports star who was now into politics and had agreedto be an ambassador for the collection), they even sent the letter to Coin Co.

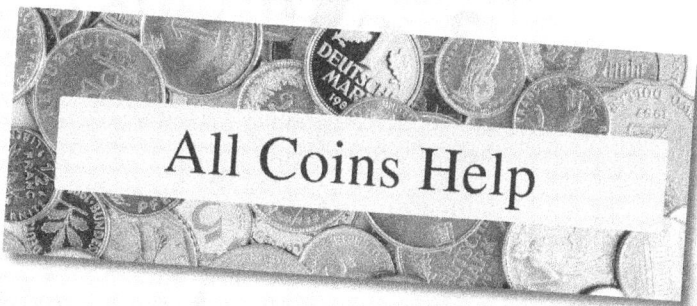

All Coins Help

'I've had enough! I'll tell them exactly what I think of them, those arrogant jerks!' I shouted, but Anita helped me to realize this was an official letter, which was going to be read by many people who did not know our history. 'You should see this as an opportunity to explain the situation to a wider and sympathetic audience. With a bit of luck people will realize what's going on and they will clearly see that EuroCollecte is making a fool out of themselves,' she added.

We put together a friendly and professional reply, in which we concisely dealt with every point made by EuroCollecte, invalidating all of their arguments. We added a lot of data and facts, and avoided the temptation to react angrily. 'They were probably hoping for an emotional reaction, so they could show how immature and unwilling we are,' Anita said.

## Victory March

**Obsolete Coins? Join Coins for Care!**

Who doesn't have a few Franks, Marks or Liras lying about at home? These coins will be obsolete once the Euro has been introduced. Coins for Collects there coins for charity. The total amount raised...

**Ernst and Young joins Coins for Care trial.**

In Eytem van december 2000 be we over het Coins for Care-proj inzamelingsactie van buitenland
...g van
...it proj
...n van
...dviezen
...st & Yo

Donate a 'worthless souvenir' to a worthy cause

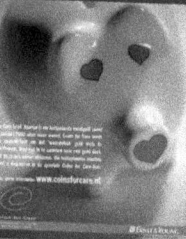

In contrast to our never ending negotiations with EuroCollecte, our campaign was taking shape rapidly. Even in other European countries initiatives for a coin collection were developing, and we were contacted by Coin Co who wanted to know how much capacity they needed to reserve for Coins for Care.

We did not have a clue, there were still so many unanswered questions: 'How many coins are we expecting to collect? How many coins fit in a collection box? How heavy is a full box? Will the box be strong enough? How often should the boxes be emptied? What is the average value of a kilo of coins?

The corporate campaign had been up and running for a while, and we decided to do a test run to see if we had everything in place before the start of the public action. We asked the companies to hand in the coins collected so far, and fortunately this answered many of the questions we had. We were even able to do an estimation of how much we would eventually raise. Another pleasant surprise was to find out we had received enough to cover the costs we had not been able to find sponsorship for.

**KLM dedicates fundraising total to Coins for Care**

De opbrengst van de inzamelactie voor Coins for Care van KLM Nederland werd vrijdag door de directeur van dit bedrijfsonderdeel. project. Esther Jacobs. KLM Nederland hield de inzamelactie van 14 tot en met 18 mei tijdens haar medewerkers vrijwilligers-

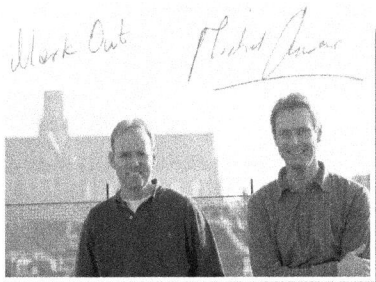

*Mark Out*    *Michel ...*

*"We never met anybody who so completely dedicates herself to a worthy cause like Esther."*

**WHERE'S FRANK?**

Kijk op pagina ... van deze krant!

Northsea FM and a few other radio stations offered to broadcast radio commercials for free, and I was introduced to *Double O Radio*, who could help us with the production of a radio advert. Mark and Michel were two young, enthusiastic, ex-advertising guys, who ran a radio station in their spare time, and who were experts in creating amazing radio commercials, jingles and other audio material.

During our first chat they had to stop every three minutes so they could put another record on... 'The show must go on!'. Mark and Michel offered to take care of all our radio adverts.

Mark and Michel organized the recording, and a few Dj's, amongst which Sylvana from Northsea FM, offered to record the voice over. We even got an address list of their contacts at other radio stations. These radio spots were very successful and generated a lot publicity.

**HAVE YOU SEEN MARK?**

Kijk op pagina ... van deze krant!

'Elsevier' and several other Dutch magazines, offered to place a free advert. Ted, our advertising agent came up with a great slogan: 'Mark, Frank and Penny: are you ready for the Euro?' I found a number of Dutch celebrities who agreed lend their image to support the campaign. It was a lot easier to get people interested as most people were by now familiar with our campaign and were happy to offer their services for a good cause.

We had earned the reputation of a trustworthy partner, and larger retailers like C&A and Videoland had now also agreed to place collection boxes in their shops. Due to all publicity it had become very attractive to join the campaign.

**DO YOU KNOW WHAT HAPPENED TO PENNY?**

Kijk op pagina ... van deze krant!

Disappointingly, Albert Heijn, the biggest supermarket chain, was still not showing any interest. I tried not to give it too much thought, and instead focused on all the parties who were taking Coins for Care seriously. You need to stay aware otherwise you might be drawn into negativity.

## Working together?

Not long after our reply, EuroCollecte invited Anita and myself to come to the Dutch Cancer Foundation's grand headoffices. 'We're ready to sign a cooperation agreement,' they announced to our surprise. The situation felt absurd; we were led into the directors' room, where Jaap, Raymond and Klaas van de Poll were already waiting for us, clearly nervous. Chairs were pulled out, drinks were offered; no effort was spared to make us feel comfortable.

Klaas van de Poll's haughty arrogance had disappeared, instead he was uncharacteristically reverting to small talk and trying to be funny. Jaap was all over us, his face fixed in his biggest smile. Only Raymond was keeping his distance, not saying much. Obviously, this had not been his idea.

The mood was so fake that Anita and I whispered: 'Where are the hidden camera's?' We couldn't resist asking what had brought on this sudden enthusiasm. 'After your presentation at the Fundraisers Association we have realized that Coins for Care is a trustworthy and professional organization, and it is no more than logical that we should work together,' was the diplomatic reply.

Anita and I smiled; had it not been EuroCollecte who had sent such an arrogant letter after the presentation? They hadn't been 'impressed' with us at all, far from it! Despite not knowing what had caused them to change their attitude so dramatically, we were happy something was happening at last.

We emphasized that Coins for Care was not happy with contributing to Euro-Collectes budget, which was estimated at 4.5 million euro. Jaap and Klaas were quick to agree: 'Yes of course, we should all take care of our own expenses.'

Because it was impossible to predict which of the two campaigns was going to be more successful, we suggested that each exchange a revenue share of twenty-five percent at the end of the project, which ensured both parties would profit from the success of the other. We also suggested to fix a maximum and minimum amount as we were much smaller than EuroCollecte: 'It will prevent any problems at a later stage and we think it's extremely fair,' we explained. The limitations on the amount to be exchanged was waived straight away by the three men: 'That's not important, it will all end up with the charities. Just sign here, everything will be fine.'

It was obvious that these gentlemen were not going to let us go before an agreement had been signed: they were all too willing to accept any demand we put on the table.

Anita and I felt like proposing all kinds of ridiculous things to see how far we could push things. We felt like anything was possible, but we kept ourselves in control and tried to keep a business view. 'What if they suddenly change their mind...?' we said to each other. Quickly we checked the most important points. EuroCollecte agreed with all the terms and again emphasized they really wanted to work together.

When we finally stepped outside, we felt a mix of relief and distrust. Had we forgotten something? How had it been possible that after this long, never ending battle, they were suddenly giving in to everything? We could not get our heads around it.

Afterwards I heard that the charities united in CollectePlan, all of whom had been present at the fundraisers conference, had written a letter demanding that EuroCollecte partner with Coins for Care as quickly as possible. I have never seen that letter myself. But how I would have loved to see the look on the faces of Klaas, Jaap and Raymond as they read it!

That one presentation had been a true turning point for us. Coins for Care had been taken seriously by the charity world, which meant EuroCollecte had no longer been able to ignore us. What had seemed impossible after a year and a half of negotiations, had now been achieved within one afternoon.

*'Be who you are and say what you feel because those who mind don't matter and those who matter don't mind.'*
*- Dr. Seuss -*

# Excuse 9:
## 'I've had a difficult childhood.'

*Dream what you want to dream,*
*be who you want to be,*
*you have only one life,*
*and one chance to do it all.*

*I wish you enough happiness to keep your spirit bright,*
*I wish you enough trials to make you strong,*
*I wish you enough sorrow to keep you human,*
*and I wish you enough hope to make you happy.*

'Happy Family' (1987)

*The happiest people,*
*don't have the best of everything,*
*they just make the best of everything*
*they have.*

*The brightest future is always based*
*on a forgotten past.*
*You can't go forward in life,*
*until you let go of your past failures.*

*When you were born you cried,*
*and the world rejoiced.*
*Live your life so that when you die,*
*the world cries,*
*and you rejoice...*

## Don't look back

'It's important to start with a clean slate,' Anita said. 'Forget all that's happened between you and EuroCollecte, and try to make the best of it,' she advised me on her last day. Anita was now heavily pregnant with her second child, and while looking after her first child, she had also taken on another project which was much larger than she had anticipated. 'There are still so many things to do before the birth, and I don't think I will have time left for Coins for Care,' she said with regret in her voice.

I wished Anita all the best with her pregnancy and project, and couldn't thank her enough for her help and efforts over the past year. 'I'll be fine,' I assured her. I completely understood her decision to stop, but I felt very sad that I had to carry on alone again, but over the past years people had come and had gone, and I had learnt that the most important thing was to trust myself.

## Strange bird

At school, I was always a bit of an outsider. I used to get good grades without having to study for it, and the clothes I wore were never very trendy; I guess I was a bit of a nerd. The other children picked up on this and, although I was

never bullied, I didn't have many friends. The girl next door was my favorite play mate, but other than that I preferred to be on my own.

It didn't bother me that I was never part of the group, intuitively I didn't want to 'belong', and I was happiest being left alone, living in my own fantasy world, drawing or reading, and spending time with my pets.

It was only when I attended high school, that I realized the importance of being with others but, being twelve years behind in understanding the social norms and values, I was not sure how to get about it... Struggling to find my own identity, I experimented being a 'punk' for a while, adapted the cute college girl image a few weeks later, and after that I became the joker in class. At the end of my teenage years, I had found myself. I had a few good friends, and had learnt to enjoy being amongst other people. Deep down, however, I would always be the loner, the observant, who feels most comfortable on her own.

After all these years, I still feel uncomfortable at large social gatherings. I will stick it out, but I'll never get used to the pretense on display. How is it possible that someone asks you how you are, while not even waiting for an answer, and already looking around for someone more important to talk to? How can you tell someone: 'let's have lunch soon,' while you don't actually mean it? I learnt to deal with it, and while marketing the Interglobe phone card, I even discovered I was quite good at networking, as long as I had a clear goal.

For a short while I was involved in all kinds of network marketing organizations, and I am ashamed to say I was always trying to sell, everywhere I went, until I discovered it was really not done, trying to sell something to your friends and acquaintances at parties. I vowed to never involve them in my business proposals again, and give up the networking altogether.

I made an exception for Coins for Care. At every drink, dinner, and party, I told everyone about this unique initiative and the problems we were facing. Step by step I found the right tone: 'Do you know anyone who could help me with...?' I would ask, instead of 'Can you help me?' which would put people on the spot, and was much harder to refuse. Strengthened by my new found strategy I did not felt so lost anymore, and started enjoying going to drinks and receptions!

My slow development at social interaction had its advantages: First, I had spent a long time studying how people communicate with each other, instead of picking it up subconsciously. Secondly, I am not afraid to cross the existing norms and values, which is why I sometimes dare to take that extra step, compared to someone who is more sensitive to how they are being perceived and, finally, I know it takes time for some people to get used to me, which means I have had to learn to be patient. Usually they come to appreciate me being different at a later stage.

Despite, or maybe thanks to, my social unawareness I experienced a carefree childhood. I always loved going to school and had a huge appetite for learning.

My parents had been very young when they got married, and when I arrived my mum was only twenty-two years old. While my dad was setting up his career across the other side of the country, my mum was at home looking after us. We did not see much of our dad, but financially we didn't lack for anything.

When I was seventeen, my mum announced she wanted a divorce. 'I have taken care of you for long enough,' she said, 'I need to think of myself now.' My fourteen year old sister, who had a very close knit relationship with our mum, burst out in tears and asked her if she did not love us anymore. 'Of course I love you, but you've reached a difficult age, I've always been there for you, but now it's your dad's turn.'

I think she'd always had a kind of part-time parenthood in mind but being left by her hit us hard. We had suddenly been abandoned.

It was a stressful time for all of us, even the dog suffered with epileptic fits caused by the tension in the house. My parents were constantly arguing about the divorce, often having heated arguments in our presence. 'If you continue like this, we're gone!' I warned my parents one day, but not much later they started at each other again, so I made sure my sister would be able to stay with the neighbors, and I moved in with my boyfriend.

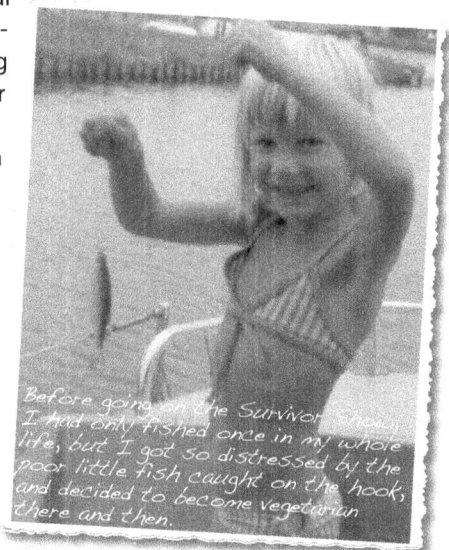

*Before going on the Survivor show, I had only fished once in my whole life, but I got so distressed by the poor little fish caught on the hook, and decided to become vegetarian there and then.*

149

Sadly, my parents were not able to sort out their difficulties, and both started court cases: against each other, against each others lawyers, and even against several members of the family. Being the oldest I tried to mediate. I was convinced that in the midst of all this emotional chaos, we could come to a rational solution. Unfortunately, my intervention was interpreted, by both my mum and dad, as choosing sides. I tried my best to protect my younger brother and sister, but it was all too much to handle, and in the end I had to choose for myself. I simply left them to it, and for the next year, I kept contact with my parents to a minimum.

My sister had been badly affected by the divorce and was having a very rough time. Luckily, our lovely neighbors had taken her in, and she was in good hands, being pampered and taken good care of. For me, it was quite a different situation. I had moved to the student campus at Nyenrode Business University, where everyone had a story to tell. About half of the students had experienced some tough times, there were people who'd lost one or both parents, while others had never settled anywhere for any longer than a few months.
The difference between the two groups was astonishing, students who had been through the mangle of life appeared to be a lot more streetwise and independent than those who'd enjoyed a reasonably carefree youth.

Once I used the *'but my parents are in a divorce'* excuse, but some people in my project group looked at me, indifferently, and said: 'So what? My parents have divorced too.'

FAM. JACOBS

My grandfather's family before the war.

My mother and her sisters behind the counter of the family grocery shop.

Soon enough I understood that at Nyenrode you had to distinguish yourself by your deeds, not by your background. The reigning mentality was to take control of your own life, regardless of where you'd come from or what you'd gone through.

The bond with my parents, especially the one with my mum, was put to the test regularly but I still kept the door ajar. Despite their endless arguing, the countless court cases, the disappointments, and promises that were not fulfilled, despite the house moves, and the many, many reproaches, I kept giving my parents another chance. On the other hand, however, I put up a wall around me, and swore never, ever, to be dependent on anyone again.

My father came from a Jewish family, who'd gone into hiding during World War II. They'd lost all his extended family and my father tried to escape from this traumatic family history by working hard and building a new existence with

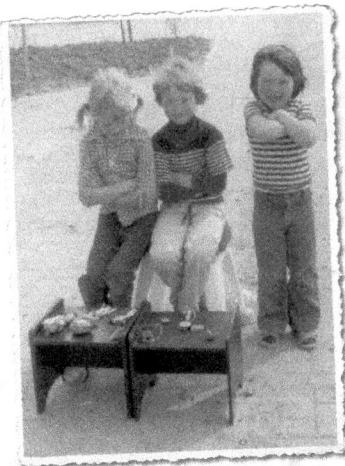

my mum. Money offered him the opportunities his family had never had.

My mum was from a simple grocer's family, and was one of seven children. By marrying my dad she'd been hoping to move away, to be able to build a life of her own, and being appreciated for that. She was used to having very little money, and worked wonders with whatever they had in those first years of their marriage. True to her grocer's mentality, she was always counting her pennies, even when my dad was earning decent money. I sometimes wonder if she ever really enjoyed the times when they were

Street vending with neighbor (centre) and sister (right).

151

well off. Like many other housewives she struggled with the lack of appreci-ation for all the 'invisible' things she did, which eventually led to their divorce, and all misery that came with it. 'Stubbornness seldom leads to appreciation' is what I learnt.

I was raised with both a Jewish as well as a grocer's mentality towards money and subconsciously I felt that money meant 'survival'. As a young child I became somewhat obsessed with it, and saved every penny I had, and would even sell my toys if I had a chance! During the divorce, however, I saw how emotions and frustration were translated in terms of money, and I vowed never, ever, to argue about money; it was just not worth it. If I could do it all over again, I would not change anything. It might sound weird, coming from someone whose childhood wasn't easy, but these experi-ences turned me into an individual with unique personal characteristics, which I can use for better or worse. For instance, a lot of people see me as a pushover, but once I used my determination during my charity action, all of a sudden it was called 'perseverance'!

'The strongest oak of the forest is not the one that is protected from
the storm and hidden from the sun. It's the one that stands in the open
where it is compelled to struggle for its existence against the winds
and rains and the scorching sun.'
- Napoleon Hill -

In a sense the whole EuroCollecte affair shows similarities with what I went through as a teenager, but I have vowed not to make the mistake of looking back reproachfully; this will never allow you to make a new start, instead I decided to leave all negative experiences behind and make a fresh start.

'I am a peacemaker,' I told Anita, 'and I think that has helped me in the nego-tiations with EuroCollecte. It's been a slow start, but at least it's taught me, that it takes time to establish a course of action, and you should be careful to burn your bridges behind you.' 'Indeed, she who perseveres wins,' smiled Anita, 'but don't count your winnings too soon, Esther, and never give up. Good luck!'

## Two worlds.

I was so happy and proud that we had finally come to an agreement. During the past few months, many people had said I was crazy to keep trying, but I had known all along that the possibility existed that it could work out. Coins for Care had been a new, unknown party, with no track record and it had needed some time before EuroCollecte had been convinced that it was indeed best to combine forces with the hundred and forty-three participating charities.

March April 2001

EuroCollecte was a valuable contributor to the campaign; they had experience and an extensive network, and I was glad we didn't have to struggle with the logistics all by ourselves.

Press conference with Jaap and Raymond.

I still found it hard to digest that EuroCollecte was paying for everything. From recent experience, I knew that it was possible to organize sponsorship in most cases, and I must have driven Jaap and Raymond to despair at times: 'How much is that going to cost?' 'Can't we do that cheaper?' 'With Coins for Care we used to organize that for free.' My attitude wasn't always constructive, and even caused irritation and tension; I knew I had to relax, and stop asking so many questions. In fact, EuroCollecte had a decent budget, and I realized it was quite acceptable to pay for certain things.

Overview of the free radio and TV adds.

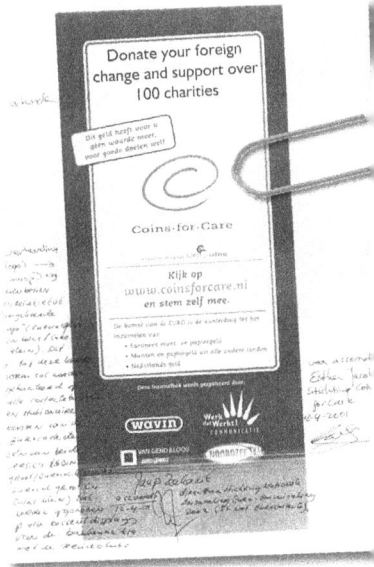

With six months to go before the official start of the campaign, we agreed on the details of our cooperation, and prepared a joint press conference. We still had to decide on a name. I thought it would be logical to continue with Coins for Care, as we had received so much publicity recently and were now quite well known nation wide. EuroCollecte, however, disagreed: 'It's important to have a clear, Dutch name, including the word *collection*. That's what the public and our charitable partners want.'

After an exhaustive discussion we agreed on publishing the logo's alongside each other, just a little smaller in size. It would be 'Coins for Care in partnership with EuroCollecte' and vice versa.

Donate your foreign change and support over 100 charities

Coins-for-Care

The final 'contract' with our agreements on the name, logos, stickers and distribution of coast. Officially signed by Jaap and me.

To be on the safe side, I had it recorded that we would contribute inkind to the campaign: 'Coins for Care will generate publicity worth millions of euros with their free radio adverts and other promotions, and will offer use of the Coin Co contract.'
It was clear we would not share the costs of the publicity, or any other plans of EuroCollecte, for which they had 4.5 million euros budget at their disposal.

At the end of March, Jaap and I signed the final contract, which had turned into a scrappy piece of paper, following all the adjustments and amendments. 'I didn't think it necessary to convert the draft into an official copy, it's all been finalized and the operation is running smoothly,' was Jaap's apology.

## A slow start

After the long tug-of-war over the Coin Co contract, I was surprised to find that EuroCollecte didn't join the exclusive contract straight away. 'We would like to explore other options first,' Jaap and Raymond said. I was astounded: with no more than three months to go before the start of the campaign, Euro Collection still did not have their money processing organized!
Coin Co's patience was about to run out. 'Are they joining yes or no?' asked John. 'I need to know, so I can make the necessary preparations. I need to ensure I've got enough people, cars and storage capacity.' I mediated between the two parties and we decided on a deadline before which EuroCollecte should finally make up their mind.

We needed a national network of depots and delivery locations, where our own people and volunteers from the Service Clubs could hand in the collected money. It seemed more than logical to organize this mutually, but Jaap and Raymond were in no hurry: 'We will notify the Service Clubs of

your ideas,' Jaap promised when I asked him about it. But a few days later they would tell me my idea hadn't made it onto the agenda, or the Service Clubs had to consult their supporters first, which meant weeks of delay. Nevertheless, I remained optimistic, and was convinced it would work out fine eventually. Didn't EuroCollecte have a wealth of experience in this kind of business?

An immediate advantage of working together was that our respective databases could be merged. All shops, banks, volunteers and depots needed to be registered, as well as the proceeds of the participating clubs. Jaap and I visited a data processing company. Noticing Jaap being treated with the highest respect, I couldn't help wondering how much money had been involved with creating and maintaining this database. Despite asking a few times, my question remained unanswered. 'Don't worry, we will fully cover the costs; Coins for Care only needs to pay any surplus costs, if applicable,' he said.

We spent weeks discussing how this database should be organized. Jaap and Raymond wanted to add things like relationship management and other extra's which, in my view, were completely unnecessary for this one-off campaign. I just didn't understand how they could spend so much time and money on something that was not going to be fully used anyway. Even the database company suggested a smaller package, which was refused by Jaap and Raymond, and I had to remind myself of my 'clean-slate' attitude, and withstood the temptation to get involved.

## Biting my tongue

One day I arrived a few minutes early for a meeting at the EuroCollecte offices. The management team was just finishing another meeting, and I noticed their guest had laid out a collection of sealable plastic bags on the table. I understood that EuroCollecte was about to order money bags for the collection. When their visitor had left I stepped into the office and said with a straight face: 'You know Coin Co distributes these bags for free?'
'We're still not sure whether to work with Coin Co, so we have decided to order some ourselves,' answered Jaap. Raymond looked away, clearly annoyed. 'Well, in that case you might want to consider using different colored bags, so we can distinguish between EuroCollecte, Coins for Care, and the Banks.' I suggested.
'We've just placed our order, it's done and cannot be changed,' Raymond snapped. 'We're not giving in to her!' he warned Jaap.

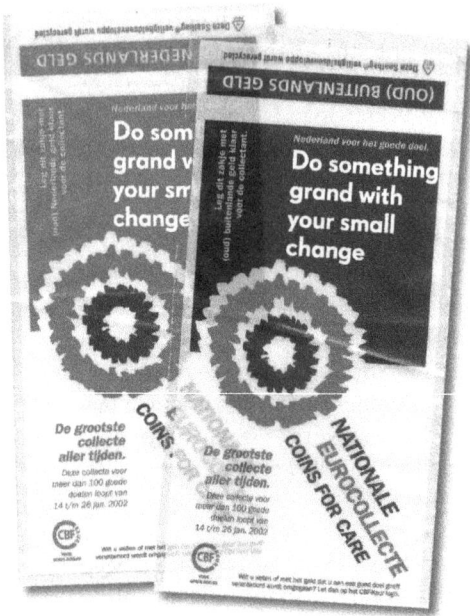

'But it does sound like a good idea, we could easily change the color,' Jaap said, and turned round to me. 'Leave it to me, I'll make sure the bags will have another color,' he whispered. I thought of the games played by Amal and his CEO in Geneva, and recognized the pattern but wasn't sure what to make of it. I could just feel the tension rise, every time I opened my mouth.

Why is Raymond so annoyed with me?' I asked Jaap some time later. 'Do you think he feels threatened by me?' 'No, no, it's nothing like that,' said Jaap, realizing he needed to give some kind of explanation for Raymond's strange behavior. 'You know, uhm, it's your voice...you got quite a shrill voice, just like my daughter, and some people simply can't stand it...'

I kept running into problems with our so-called cooperation. For example we desperately needed an overview of participating stores. I suspected the development of the shared database was going to take forever, so I started looking for an alternative. After dealing with the European Bank and Publicis, I knew it was better to take action instead of waiting until it was too late.

I met Rob Decker, an IT guru, who managed to design a tailor-made, smooth running database which was up and running within two weeks. Rob even lent a helping hand, putting in the retail addresses which we had delivered in Excel format. Of course, I offered EuroCollecte to make use of this database, but wasn't even surprised when they rejected the offer: 'We'd rather stick with our own suppliers, thank you,' they said.

*'What you need to know about the past is that no matter what happened, it has all worked together to bring you this very moment. And this is the moment you can choose to make everything new. Right now.'*

*Esther gets reactions from all over the country. In this picture she meets two pupils and their teachers from a High school in Apeldoorn who are involved in several projects regarding the introduction of the euro and support Coins for Care.* ©photo: Jaap Wals.

# Excuse 10:
## 'I don't have the time for this.'

*'Time is flexible.*
*Fifteen minutes seems short when you're in love,*
*but lasts an eternity when you're stuck in an elevator'*

© www.hermanwouters.nl

## Busy, busy, busy

Thinking back to the summer of 2001 makes me dizzy; setting up this campaign was not your average nine-to-five job, and I don't know how I managed; my to-do list seemed never-ending.

My first priority was to act as an account manager for more than a hundred and twenty charities and about four thousand shops, making sure they were prepared for the start of the campaign. I also had to keep our existing sponsors happy, and look out for new sponsorship deals.

At the same time, the collection boxes were being produced, and solutions were required for the storage and transport, as well as a thousand volunteers, who needed careful instruction on how and when to empty these boxes.

The increased media attention created a lot of additional work in terms of TV and radio appearances, and to top it all off we were dealing with hundreds of phone-calls and e-mails per day.

I was so busy and didn't have time for any income providing jobs, let alone for a private life. 'How do you do it?' people would ask me. 'I don't really know,' I'd answer, 'I don't have a strategy... All I know is that time is relative: when you're really passionate about something, or trying to achieve a goal which is close to your heart, you'll always manage to make time for it.' This is exactly why I had been able to continue these frustrating negotiations with EuroCollecte. I'd put this high on my priority list as I saw a lot of advantages in working together, and now it was important to invest the time in shaping our tender cooperation.

I only just managed to keep all the balls in the air, but it was a precarious juggling act, and I constantly had to reset my priorities and think of how to use my time more efficiently.

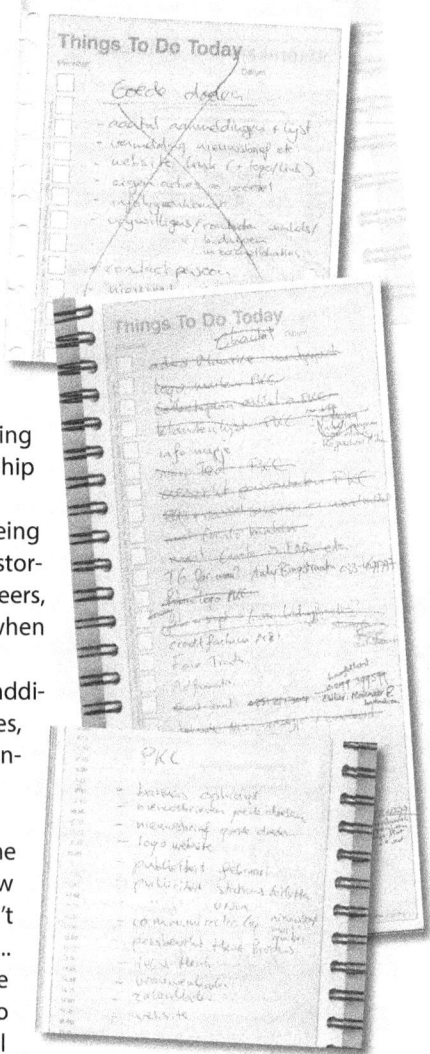

*The official launch of the campaign by the Dutch Minister of Finance, who could not keep his eyes of the model dressed in a 25kg dress made entirely of coins.*

## It's about time to prioritize!'

After the announcement that Coins for Care and EuroCollecte had become partners, my cell phone and two landlines didn't stop ringing. During every telephone conversation I would receive seven voicemail messages, and before I'd even listened to these, another phone call would come in. On top of that we received hundreds of e-mails on a daily basis. This situation lasted for weeks, I became a specialist in multi-tasking. Driving the car would be most efficient: I could return calls, drive to meetings, and eat at the same time!

worked long hours, starting at five in the morning, continuing through the evening and well into the night, trying to work my way through the backlog of e-mails. Every morning at eight o'clock the phone started ringing again, its compelling ringing making me sick, literally. I was desperate for a break, however, I still managed to force myself to answer with a friendly: 'Coins for Care, how can we help you?'

The weekends gave me a chance to catch up, not being disturbed by the phone. I worked hard to clear the list of e-mails before the start of a new week. I received all sorts of requests: coin collectors looking for certain coins, but also charities and retailers asking to join our scheme. I tried to answer every mail within a few days, and taught myself to scan-read, filtering out what was important. It worked well, but there wasn't any room for error, if the internet connection would not work for a day, it would take me a week to catch up. I had to keep going, and it was impossible to take a day or even an hour off. And this was just the beginning, the campaign was not even under way yet!

Few people knew how I operated, I had succeeded in creating the impression that Coins for Care was a huge organization. The 'office' was situated on the first floor of my house in Amstelveen, with me as its sole employee!

Charities reacted surprised when they got me on the phone directly, expecting a receptionist instead: 'Hey, Esther, how nice of you to answer the phone your-self...' I also received many positive reactions to the fact that I was responding to the e-mails personally. 'We don't usually get such a quick reaction!' I was complimented.

## Key support

'You're incredibly busy, aren't you,' my friends said after I had declined a dinner party invitation for the third time in a row. 'Can't you just hire some-one, or look for a company who can help you out?' They had a point, but I was swamped with work, and simply didn't have time to even think about this.

Unexpectedly, our publicity campaign had started to pay off, and Coins for Care was becoming a household name. Just when I thought I couldn't be any busier, I was contacted by KeyNet, a customer contact center, who spontaneously offered to deal with my calls and e-mails for free!

My prayers had been answered!

I was over the moon with this offer but, not having much experience with del-egating, I was surprised at how much time it took to fully explain the campaign to KeyNet. 'If you provide us with a FAQ-list, including the answers, we'll be able to handle about forty e-mails a day,' was KeyNet's promise. I did have an idea of the most common questions, but I'd never kept any records, and I real-ized that if I wanted to outsource some of my tasks, I'd have to put a few things on paper, in a structured way.

With KeyNet's support, I arranged a sponsored freephone number at World-Com, using an automated phone answering system which would handle most standard phone calls.

Of course, there were still calls that had to be dealt with personally, but the pressure was off, at least for now...

## Van Gend & Loos Distribution

VAN GEND & LOOS
*EURO EXPRESS*

Since my negotiations with the Body Shop, I had asked the retailers if they could arrange the distribution of the collection boxes themselves. It saved us a lot of work; all we had to do was to deliver enough collection boxes to the distribution centers, and I'd found a well known national logistics company, Van Gend & Loos, who were prepared to assist us with this.

I was greeted with a warm welcome from the whole management team: 'Esther, how nice to meet you, we've heard a lot about Coins for Care in the media and we think it's an amazing initiative! Please tell us what we can do to help.' Wow! I'd wish it would always be this easy!

I told them I needed the collection boxes transported to the retailers.

'No problem, consider it done,' was the reply. I was impressed with their efficiency, but then they said: 'And, because we think this is such a fantastic campaign, we've decided to give you a discount of a whopping fifty percent!' Everybody around the table looked at me in excitement, but my face darkened. Apparently it had not been clear how Coins for Care operated. I hesitated: 'We don't have a budget at all...'

The men around the table stared at me in disbelief. 'But surely you're running a complex operation, you're making revenue, aren't you? What about your salary?' When I explained I was the organization, and that I didn't get paid for my work at all, they were perplexed. They briefly looked at each other, a few men nodded their heads, and then the director said: 'Okay, we're also doing it for free! Just give us a list of how many boxes we need to take where, and leave the rest to us.' In my euphoria, I completely forgot I'd have to structure all this information before handing it over.

As the meeting came to an end, one of the men asked me: 'Where are you going to store all these boxes before they go to the shops?' It was something I hadn't thought of yet. Of course, these boxes couldn't stay on site at Fotolight... Noticing my bewilderment, the guy who'd asked said generously: 'Don't worry, we'll take care of that too; just give us a buzz when we can pick them up, and we'll hold on to them until the time of transport.'

I couldn't have hoped for a better partnership agreement, and utterly relieved I went home.

## Everything at the same time

Every so often, I would be contracted by CapGemini to lead one of their work-shops, which would earn me the necessary money to pay for my living. As Coins for Care grew, it became increasingly difficult to leave for a few days; the back log of phone calls and e-mails would grow to monstrous proportions.

Once I got myself into trouble, during such a workshop, trying to deal with a few phone calls and e-mails, instead of focussing completely on the job. 'Esther, we know how occupied you are with Coins for Care, and we understand

IDENTITY

USE

VISION

BUILD

INTENT

ENGINEER

INSIGHT

*Cap Gemini's Creative process-model.*

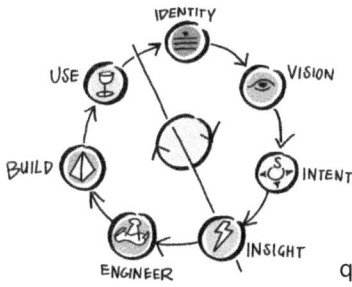

you've got a huge responsibility, but we have hired you to concentrate on our clients,' I was reminded by CapGemini.

One of the last workshops I ran was in the spring of 2001, when preparations for the campaign were in full swing. In order not to waste any time, and to not disturb the participants of the workshop, I quickly checked my voicemail messages in the ladies' room. Just when I switched on the phone it started to ring and, foolishly, I pressed the answer button. 'Good afternoon Miss Jacobs, this is the editor's desk of De Telegraaf, the biggest Dutch newspaper. Would you mind answering a few questions on Coins for Care? Tell me...' I quickly assessed the situation: I was in the ladies' room with a journalist on the phone; I couldn't flush and continue the conversation outside, as it was strictly forbidden to make a phone call on the work floor; I wouldn't have an opportunity to call back later, nor would I be available for the rest of the week. I realized I'd no other option but to talk to the man from my little cubicle. Speaking as quietly as I could, I prayed to God there wasn't too much of an echo. After I'd finally hung up, I got out of the cubicle and bumped straight into a colleague who looked at me, suspiciously. 'I thought I heard someone talk,' she said. My heart sank, this was it, I'd been caught in the act, it would be the end for me at CapGemini!

Fortunately, my colleague had the complete wrong end of the stick: 'It was as if you were in there with someone else!' she laughed.

## Eat that frog!

After completing the CapGemini workshop, there was a lot of catching up to do; I was submerged in my Coins for Care work, and I didn't give myself

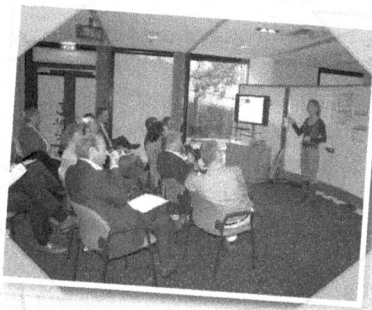

*Workshop at Cap Gemini.*

# burn-out?

**burn out**

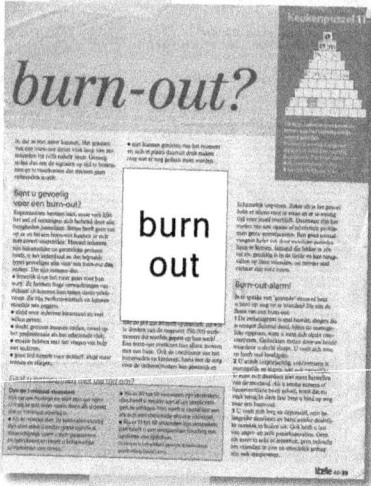

*Pitfall:* 'Once I've finished this job,
I'll be OK'. Small changes or longer
breaks don't help when you're close to a
burnout. © Libelle

a moment's rest. I knew I couldn't go on like this forever, I was completely stressed and even had trouble sleeping, but taking a break was not an option; the amount of work would spiral out of control. I thought working a little harder would get the backlog out of the way, and for a while it seemed to work, but there were still only twenty-four hours in a day. My only alternative was to optimize the way I worked.

I remembered a lecture on time management, with a famous professor conducting an experiment using a glass bowl, a bag of stones, a bag of sand, and a jug of water. 'This glass bowl represents your day,' he said. 'Now, imagine the stones, sand, and water are your activities for this particular day. How are you going to manage to complete all of them?' he asked. Then he piled up the stones in the tray and explained: 'These big stones symbolize your main activities and will take most of your time. It's important to plan these first.' Then, throwing in the sand, he added: 'The smaller activities fill up the spaces nicely.' The tray was now filled to the brim and, without hesitation, the professor poured in the whole jug of water, which was immediately absorbed by the sand between the stones. Triumphantly, he looked around the auditorium: 'If you organize your day well, you can always fit in something extra,' he said.

## During the last minute you're always more productive.

According to one of my friends, people usually confuse what is urgent with what is important, and deal with the urgent things first, while the important issues are being left for last. I didn't think it applied to me; I'd always been able to prioritize what was most important in my work for Coins for Care, and right now, I was focussing on the media. Free publicity had made this campaign possible; it was our lifeline. I could not afford to postpone calling back a journalist: it might ruin my chance of free advertising.

I tried to fix everything immediately, so I would not have to worry about it anymore; a short email was usually enough to set certain things in motion.

I also found that other parties would act quicker, if I answered their mail promptly.

In the meantime the workload remained high, and to make matters worse, problems kept occurring. At some stage we didn't have enough volunteers in a certain part of the country, or there would be a problem with the collection boxes. I was also busy organizing a mailing to the charities, communicating the latest details of the campaign.

Occasionally I'd be overcome by despair, thinking of everything that still needed to be done. 'It's never going to work,' I'd think, but it would be during those darkest moments that, somehow, an idea would pop into my head.
Over the years I've developed a method of cutting any problem that seemed too big into bite size chunks. If I'm facing a seemingly insurmountable problem, I look at how to cut it into pieces and solve them one by one. The trick is not to be overwhelmed by the magnitude of what needs to be done, you just need to start somewhere.

Years later, long after the Coins for Care campaign, I was given a fascinating book on time management which, surprisingly, described what I had been doing all along! It's called *Eat that Frog*, and it advises to focus on a difficult task first. 'If you do need to swallow that frog you might as well straight away, instead of staring it in the face all day.' The book also described how to set priorities: 'If you can do something in five minutes, don't bother putting it on a list, just do it.' I smiled, I'd already come to that conclusion myself, without the help of any book!

## Power cut

On average, I received about one hundred and thirty-five e-mails a day, including the weekends and holidays. Archiving or filing my e-mails was not my strongest point, I was only using my inbox and a sent box, as I didn't have time to familiarize myself with the system.
The sheer volume of e-mail messages caused many problems caused by pop accounts, spam and viruses; my humble computer couldn't handle it, and crashed frequently.
In a panic, I phoned Jaap, who had a friend working in IT, and was willing to take a look at what was going wrong. Shocked at the size of my e-mail data, the first thing he did was compress all my computer files. This was, however, only a temporary solution, and I'd have to change the way I was organizing my

e-mails, but at that moment I was only thinking about the short term; I had to get back to business as soon as I could.

The frequent computer mishaps taught me a valuable lesson: once my PC was up and running again, some of the 'urgent' messages had been solved already, without me having reacted at all! I realized that a quick response was not always necessary.

I also learnt a lot about myself. I became aware that I felt personally responsible for any problem or, worse, for being deliberately obstructed, like during the EuroCollecte negotiations. Being so passionately and deeply involved meant that I found it hard to separate myself from the project, and it was difficult to keep a healthy distance.

On the other hand, I drew a lot of energy from it. The positive reactions, all those enthusiastic people helping me out, that's what kept me going. A new sponsor, a new shop, or a newly registered charity gave me such a boost, and I realized I should take a moment to look back on what I had achieved so far, instead of worrying about what wasn't going so well, or still needed to be done. Frustration eats up your energy, while success gives you the drive to continue.

*'Life is not measured by the number of breaths you take, but by the moments that take your breath away.'*

## Reinforcements

I'd hoped that working with EuroCollecte was going to save me time but, on the contrary, it created a huge amount of extra work, and I had no choice but to outsource some tasks. Luckily, due to all the publicity, we received many spontaneous offers from people who were keen to help. I was struggling to find the time to meet all of them personally, but I did manage to assign some projects to a couple of these volunteers, however, only halfway into the job, these people decided to pull out; I was annoyed, having wasted much of my valuable time, first introducing them to the task, and still having to complete the jobs myself.

I asked some other people, who'd offered their assistance, to write a proposal requesting extra sponsorship or government subsidies; we were in urgent need of money. Unfortunately, Coins for Care did not seem to tick any of the regular boxes, and writing a proposal was a difficult and time consuming task; these volunteers dropped out one by one as well...

Fortunately, not all offers were futile; my friend's brother took care of all our communication with retailers, and a young airline purser who had considerable experience with charities and volunteering, became our main contact for the charities. Michel would maintain the address database and register any new participants. He would also supervise the charities' own campaigns and keep contact with the CBF. He had one small request: 'The main problem...' he said reluctantly, 'is that I will have to give up one day's work, which makes it hard to provide for my family.' I was so desperate for a pair of extra hands that I, for once, abandoned my principles, and decided to compensate him for his work. He'd get a thousand euro per month, and I'd pay it out of my own pocket, if necessary. Michel was the only one at Coins for Care to receive a salary.

## The Abcoude Jackpot

Receiving a mail from Karel de Snoo from Abcoude, meant the start of a new era for Coins for Care. Karel had seen me on television and, having toyed with similar ideas, he'd been impressed with my initiative.

He wrote: 'I am nearly sixty-five, and I'll be retiring from my job in a couple of weeks. Maybe I could make myself useful by helping you out?' Karel was a quiet, amiable man, with a consulting background in logistics. 'That's wonderful, I'm absolutely clueless!' I laughed, and explained we were at the stage of setting up a network of depots and delivery points for the volunteers, and immediately Karel offered to outline a solution. I was thrilled!

*Karel and his friends processing buckets of coins.'*

I had another appointment after meeting Karel, and when he heard I was going to deliver some collection boxes for the corporate campaign,

he looked at me in surprise, and said: 'Are you still doing that yourself?' Now it was my turn to look surprised: 'Yes, of course, who else?' 'Well, that's going to be the first thing I will do for you. From now on you're not going to waste your time delivering collection boxes. I'll organize some people who can do that for you,' was Karel's decisive reply.

He then mobilized all of his friends, most of them retired, and these dedicated people took care of everything I didn't have the time for, or hadn't even thought about yet. They'd drive thousands of kilometers during the course of the campaign, covering the country from north to south in a car and trailer, picking up bags of money. All I had to do was to send an e-mail, and the Abcoude volunteers would swing into action. They even took care of the Coins for Care mailings, folding letters, putting them into envelops, and sticking on the addresses.

Karel's experience, his rationalism, calmness, and clear business view, made him an ideal sparring partner. We became a close knit team, and before he knew it he was working harder than before his retirement!

Karel's help was invaluable, and his sense of humor put the enormity of the work into perspective. He once showed me a picture of his grandchildren, sticking addresses onto envelopes: 'Would you believe it, Coins for Care is promoting child labour!' he roared with laughter.

After my interview was featured in Quote magazine, I was approached by Leonie, who was looking for a new challenge after the sale of her events organizing agency. 'I have granted myself a sabbatical to think about what I would like to do next, and I think I've found my project!' she told me during our first conversation.

Leonie was an independent woman, used to organizing things, and we agreed that she would have a kind of 'sweeping up' role within Coins for Care, being responsible for all the action points which had not yet been taken care of.

She drove all over the country to visit the depots, picking up money when we didn't have any volunteers available, and helped out with a lot of other tasks. It was such a relief to be able to call either Karel or Leonie when I needed a hand.

I had learnt to think in solutions rather than problems; By intelligently prioritizing my day, outsourcing many tasks, and working very hard, everything was now running smoothly; the campaign was ready to take off!

Shortly EuroCollecte would start their part of the campaign as well, and I was looking forward to start focussing on generating even more publicity. The worst was now behind us. Or so I thought...

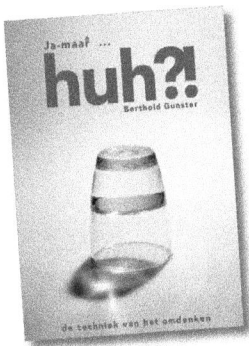

*'For some the glass is half full,
For others the glass is half empty.
You could philosophize about it for
hours, but it's better to ask:
"Where is the tab?"'
- Berthold Gunster -*

## Excuse 11:

## 'What I want is not possible.'

'I know God won't give me anything I can't handle;
I just wish He didn't trust me so much....'
- Moeder Theresa -

# MISSION:
# IMPOSSIBLE

## Fight with Free Record Shop

The idea to collect foreign coins was not new. In 1993 Free Record Shop had held a similar campaign, accepting any foreign coin as payment, as well as reward points collected at gas stations. This radical campaign had caused much controversy and the gas stations had been extremely unhappy with their reward points being used somewhere else. They were making a huge loss and eventually paid Free Record Shop an enormous sum of money to have the scheme stopped. 'Operation kitchen draw' had been a great success, financially as well as publicity wise.

I'd come in contact with Free Record Shop while looking for retailers who'd be interested in joining us. Being somewhat in awe of their bold, rebellious business approach I was very excited to meet Hans Breukhoven, its notorious CEO.

The Free Record Shop head offices were modern, decorated with big extravagant artworks in bright happy colors. I'd never seen such a huge, luxurious boardroom. One wall was completely made out of glass, offering a full view of the surrounding fields. Hans looked exactly like the pictures I'd seen of him: smart suited, tanned face, a big smile, and clear sparkling blue eyes. Hans had started his career as a market trader, with a charming boyish attitude. He was sharp, quick, and straight forward; a cunning business man not taking any nonsense from anybody.

I told him about Coins for Care. Hans was very impressed with the sponsoring schemes we had realized, and he asked if I'd heard of their 'kitchen draw' campaign, telling me how he had played the trick on the oil companies. 'So, collecting foreign coins is nothing new,' he said, half jokingly. 'You're absolutely right, but the timing is perfect, as well as the fact that all profits go to charity,' I replied, asking him how he felt about joining us. Hans thought about it for a minute, and said: 'Listen Esther, I think it's fantastic what you have achieved so far, but I'll be honest with you: I'm a business man, and I'd only join if I could make a profit myself; that's all I am interested in. I don't have any intention of getting involved in any collection campaign, at least for now,' he added.

It wasn't what I'd been hoping to hear, but at least he was being honest. Somewhat disappointed, but very impressed by Hans' candor, I drove home, Free Records Shop had been worth the try, but I'd need to move on and find other parties who'd be interested. How was I to know then that this wasn't the last I would hear from Hans...?

A few weeks later I received a phone call from a young man, who asked if I were Esther Jacobs from Coins for Care. He sounded very insecure, but when

171

Competing euro exchange campaign
Charity furious about Free Record Shop
door Michiel Hoogers
AMSTERDAM, vrijdag
Free Record Shop spoils charity collection
MARC LAAN
AMSTERDAM – Hans Breukhoven, eigenaar van de platenketen Free Record Shop, is erin geslaagd
Woordvoerder Rob Hermans van de Free Record Shop vindt alle boosheid van de collecteorganisaties onzin. "Wij bieden onze klanten een keuze: of ze brengen hun naar het goede doel, of

Free Record Shop: 'Coins for Care is too late.'
Free Record Shop wil consumenten die thuis nog het
NOG 20 WEKEN DE GULDEN
Bickering about Coins
bij Free Record Shop
waard!
sen, onder bepaalde voorwaarden, cd's kunnen kopen met buitenlands geld. Het is de bedoeling dat buitenlands geld uit de deelnemende euro-landen in een speciale envelop wordt gestopt. Bij inlevering in de winkel kunnen hier cd's voor worden teruggekocht.
De actie heeft kwaad bloed gezet bij Coins for Care, de organisatie die in september in winkels collectebussen wil neerzetten om buitenlands geld in te zamelen voor het goede doel.
Rob Hermans, marketing manager bij Free Record Shop, moet Coins for Care meer naar
'Zij kunnen niet
met een campagne moeten komen om bekendheid aan hun actie te geven.'
Coins for Care verwijt Free Record Shop ook het idee voor de actie te hebben gestolen.
'Onzin', weerlegt Hermans. 'Wij hebben in 1993 al een soortgelijke actie gevoerd.'
De actie van Free Record Shop loopt door tot 6 januari 2002.
De muziekwinkelketen verwacht hiervan een extra omzet van vijf miljoen gulden.
Halo-ef
Het halo-effect waarnaar VN onderzoek heeft gedaan [zie week 23, p. 7, red.], zou de uit geld kunnen kosten. Adverte willen in de meeste gevallen bepaalde doelgroep bereiken als daarbij te veel ruis optree de 'kleuring' van een bepaald

I'd confirmed it was indeed me, he hesitantly told me the reason for his call: 'I work as a shop manager in one of the Free Record Shops. I've read a lot about Coins for Care in the papers, I think your campaign is great.' I urged him to tell me more. 'I've just returned from a secret meeting with all our shop managers, and our marketing director has announced we are going to set up a foreign coins campaign, starting in June 2001.' I was dumbfounded, Hans had told me he wasn't interested in a collection program! 'That's not all,' the guy continued, 'when I asked why our campaign would start before the Coins for Care scheme, I was told that it has been arranged to play a 'good trick' on the charities.' According to the shop manager, the Free Records campaign had been hastily put together, following the increased publicity for Coins for Care. They'd been preparing their plans in the deepest secrecy, and the shops would receive the advertising posters only one day before the launch of the campaign, so nothing would be leaked prematurely.

Free Records Shop was looking to create a controversy similar to 1993, hoping it would bring them a whole lot of free publicity. 'I think it's disgusting, that's why I have decided to give you a call, even if it means I will lose my job,' said the courageous shop manager.

I was appalled that Hans Breukhoven hadn't been able to withstand the temptation to create a competition. I thought his plans were completely misplaced, this time round it wasn't some powerful global oil company he was taking on, but a nonprofit charitable organization!

What could I do? I had no chance of standing up against such a large and wealthy corporation as the Free Record Shop. They were going to get much publicity from this controversial action, and alerting the press would only add to that. It was best to stay put, and I waited frustratingly until the press would find out and come looking for me.

On the first day of the store's campaign my phone didn't stop ringing. The press reveled in the details of this new development and, dramatically, public opinion turned mostly against the Free Record Shop, who argued that their customers were free to choose how to get rid of their coins, however, they had correctly anticipated their youngest customers would spend their leftover coins on a CD or DVD, rather than donating to a charity campaign.

The marketing director of Free Record Shop even had the audacity to call me up, requesting we'd process their foreign coins for them. I made it very clear that we didn't support any commercial schemes, and we'd only consider helping out if Free Record Shop was willing to share their profit with the charities.

'Who does your coin processing?' he then asked, and I replied it wasn't a secret that our partner was Coin Co International.

Shortly after, I received a phone call from John at Coin Co, who told me he'd spoken to Free Record Shop, asking if he could process 20.000 kilo of foreign coins. According to our contract, John had referred them to Coins for Care.

The next day John phoned again. Roaring with laughter this time, he told me how he'd been contacted by an obscure company from Belgium, who had

Spending of foreign coins - in % basis:
has foreign coins at home (n=167)

| | |
|---|---|
| donate to charity/ coins for care etc. | 43 |
| exchange at bank | 27 |
| spend in applicable country | 21 |
| Nothing, just keep | 13 |
| Spend at Free Record Shop | 10 |

exactly 20.000 kilo of foreign coins which needed to be processed. 'When I asked them if it had anything to do with Free Record Shop, they hung up on me!' John laughed.

Free Record Shop's plan was seriously backfiring, and their actions became increasingly reckless; I was called by the editors of a popular consumers' television show who had been tipped off by Free Record Shop that it would cost Coins for Care thirty percent of the total value of the coins to have them processed, instead of the 2 to 8 percent we had communicated. Disgusted by the fact that Free Record Shop had turned to these kind of unprofessional practices and even indisputable lies, I decided not to hold back and inform the TV show in detail of all the contact I'd had with the chain.

'So their 'tip off' is a straight attempt at putting Coins for Care into discredit!' was the editors' conclusion, sensing a good story. There was no stopping them: the show exposed all the dirty tricks played by Free Record Shop. No stone was left unturned: the aim to play the charities a 'good' trick, the 20.000 kilo of coins they hadn't been able to dispose of, and the pathetic attempt to discredit Coins for Care.

*Satiric television show focusses on Free Record Shop stunt*

I was so relieved, there'd been justice! I'd survived a seemingly impossible battle, appearing dignified and unscathed, while my mighty opponent had shot himself in the foot.

## Logistical challenge

FREE RECORD SHOP CANCELS COIN EXCHANGE

Our biggest challenge would be setting up a national network of locations for the storage of collected coins. I was hoping to organize this together with EuroCollecte, but they informed me they didn't have resource available yet. I couldn't believe they were going to leave something that important to the last minute, the start of the bank campaign was planned for the October 15! I didn't want to wait any longer and decided to go ahead without them.

Karel drew up a system based on a hundred and fifty regional depots covering the whole country. It was a big challenge to create these locations, and we approached all kinds of organizations, from churches to women's institutes, who might be willing to allow their premises to be used as a depot for our coins.

Eventually it was Dorcas, one of the participating charities, who came to our rescue, offering the use of their existing collection points which they used for clothes donations. When we received the list of addresses from Dorcas, we couldn't help but smile: our coins would be stored at all sorts of locations: in bible kiosks, homes for the elderly, second hand clothes stores, at peoples' houses, in churches, and even in a lighthouse!
With Cordaid helping us out in the South, we'd nearly covered the whole country. Karel quickly called some of his old friends and acquaintances, who lived near or in these areas, and persuaded them to let us borrow their garages or sheds. Despite its unique character, our network would prove to work perfectly, still, at this stage, no one had the faintest idea of how many coins we would receive...

## Third time lucky

Albert Heijn, the country's largest supermarket chain, kept rejecting our request to join. Their biggest objection was the timing: 'It's estimated that most people will exchange their guilders in our supermarkets, which will create a huge amount of extra work, we'll need to organize additional security also,' explained a spokesperson. 'Until the government officially announces what is expected from us, we will not be considering any charitable collection campaigns.'

A few months later I approached Albert Heijn again. Although it was now clear what their role would be during the introduction of the new coin, they gave me a completely different excuse: 'The scheme doesn't fit our consumer policy.'

I refused to give up that easily and would keep trying to persuade them. Purely by chance I met one of the companies' spokespeople and got connected to the board of directors. 'As the largest supermarket in the country, and brand-leader, you simply can't lag behind,' was my argument. The Coins for Care campaign was now widely known, and the board of directors agreed they should become involved too. It was a decision which wasn't appreciated by those who had previously rejected my request, however, they had no choice but to cooperate.

'There's a difference between interest and commitment. When you're interested in doing something, you do it only when circumstance permit. When you're committed to something, you accept no excuses, only results.'

- Art Turock -

A few months later, I received a message from my contact person at Albert Heijn. 'I know we've given the go ahead, but there are still a few people who have concerns about the risks involved,' he said, and asked us to come to their offices and discuss the issues they still had. We were prepared for a tough meeting.

When we entered the meeting room, Karel and I were welcomed by a group of about ten men, who introduced themselves as Head of Sales, Head of Security, Head of Operations, Head of Logistics, et cetera...; It seemed that all the 'Heads' were present! They had also hired an external consultant, who was assisting with the euro-introduction. 'The reason for inviting you is that we still have some serious doubts about the campaign,' the Head of Security commenced, and all the other Heads nodded. 'One of our main concerns is the security, we're talking about a significant amount of money here,' added the Head of Security. My usual argument that foreign coins had little or no value as they were not exchangeable within the Netherlands, was immediately dismissed. 'You've already said that, and it sounds plausible,...' said the Head of Sales, 'but others may have a different opinion. I'm going on holiday next week, to France, I could probably use a few French Francs!' he said defiantly.

Karel stood up: 'Sir, you're absolutely right,' he said, 'foreign change certainly has a value, and that is exactly why I've brought this bag of coins.' With these words he tipped up a big bag over the table, and within moments everyone was rummaging through the pile of coins. 'Just see if you can find anything useful for your holidays,' Karel continued with a straight face. The Head of Sales found a few coins of ten or twenty centimes, but had to admit it wasn't going to make him a rich man, and began to realize his security concerns seemed unfounded.

'It might still be a risk for our employees to have these boxes located next to the tills,' said another Head. We'd expected this question and I reacted straight away: 'I suggest putting the boxes right in the centre of the stores, next to the bottle return counter, so the collection boxes will be associated with recycling, rather than money exchange.' For a moment it was quiet, I looked around to see if anyone objected to this, but it was all smiles, except for the Head Security who said: 'Well, it's still possible for someone to pick up the box and just walk out of the store.' Karel scooped up the pile of coins from the table into a collection box, which he'd brought along, and he added another ten kilo's of coins. 'Gentlemen,' he said, 'I invite you to have a go at lifting this box which isn't even half full, but already too heavy to be carried around easily.' A skinny man volunteered; with much straining he managed to lift the box a few centimeters into the air, but almost immediately the weight forced him to drop it back down. Most of the men were now convinced, except for the strongly built Head of Security, who obviously wasn't impressed by the smaller man's attempt.

At the close of the meeting, we politely asked the Head of Security to help us carry the collection box to the car. All too willing to demonstrate to his colleagues that it wasn't that difficult, he lifted the box onto his shoulder, however, when we walked down the corridor towards the elevator he said: 'Sorry, but this box is much heavier than I thought, could you mind giving me a hand?'

The Albert Heijn meeting is one of our favorite memories. Karel and I had so much fun during this meeting and, being prepared thoroughly, we showed our hosts that we had become experts in this field and succeeded in removing all their worries and concerns.

## Wasteful spending

One of our main objectives had been to raise as much money as possible, while keeping costs at an absolute minimum, however, I had my doubts as to where the loyalties of EuroCollecte lay. Why else would they keep working with their trusted, but incredibly expensive suppliers, instead of accepting the sponsored help I'd organized?

We needed to develop a shared website, and the EuroCollecte management insisted on having this created by a renowned web design agency, instead of customizing our existing sites, or even using the web designers at Ernst & Young who had created the Coins for Care website. They also rejected my offer to use our sponsorship deal with KeyNet, but rather stayed with the company who currently maintained their database, and

answered all their phone calls and e-mails, for the rather costly price of two and a half euro an item!

When I heard they had special collection boxes designed for their bank campaign at a cost of ninety euro each, I stepped in, protesting that it could be

done much cheaper using simple sewage pipes, nevertheless EuroCollecte decided not to contact Fotolight.

I'd also managed to secure a sponsorship deal with Boomerang, a direct marketing company who distributed free postcards in bars and restaurants nation wide, and they'd agreed to create a card in honor of our mutual campaign. EuroCollecte's reaction was disappointing; instead of being happy, they were upset! 'I'd just arranged a meeting with Boomerang myself,' Raymond grumbled. 'We could have gotten a twenty-five percent discount!' complained Jaap, and the men acted as if defeated. I was shattered and just couldn't figure out what was going on; was it something personal?

Ted was still doing all our advertising, he had already done plenty of good work for us, and had also designed our communication strategy. Now he was even offering to do our publicity campaign for free. EuroCollecte, however, insisted on staying with their advertising agency, who had three people working for them at a whopping rate of a hundred and fifty euro per hour, spending their time in endless meetings, discussing every single minute detail. By the time that Ted had delivered a complete publicity campaign, they were still at the early stages of drawing up a communication plan.

Fans Bruijs **Communicatie**
Tesselschadestraat 11
1054 ET Amsterdam
Telefoon 020 6167779
Fax 020 6633230
E-mail: fbruijs@euronet.nl
ABN AMRO 44.58.84.296
KvK 33321599

**12. Budgettering scenario 1 en 2**

|  | Scenario 1 | Scenario 2 |
|---|---|---|
| Internet | 150.000 | 250.000 |
| TV shows | 1.000.000 | 1.000.000 |
| Dagbladen (netto) | nvt | 100.000 |
| Radio (netto) | 350.000 | 475.000 |
| Sub-Totaal | 1.500.000 | 1.825.000 |
| Bureaukosten | 200.000 | 200.000 |
| Productiekosten | 100.000 | 115.000 |
| Reserve/extra: | 25.000 | 25.000 |
| Drukwerk muntsticker | 90.000 | 125.000 |
| Werving sponsors | 1.000.000 | 1.500.000 |
| H-a-h- mailing | 250.000 | 500.000 |
| Landelijke SNE promotie | | |
| Totaal | 3.165.000 | 4.290.000 |
| Te financieren via sponsorbijdrage | 1.465.000 | 2.590.000 |
| Budget | 1.700.000 | 1.700.000 |

Alle genoemde bedragen zijn in guldens en incl. 19% BTW

This total inefficiency and unnecessary waste of time frustrated me immensely, but what I found most upsetting were the tons and tons of money being squandered. A mere two weeks before the start of the campaign this 'essential', overpriced communication plan was ready, the conclusion being: 'It needs to be a nation wide action plan.'

Even Karel got fed up: 'Why can't they just set their pride aside and use the advantages of the sponsorships we already have in place,' he sighed one day. We talked this over in great detail. We suspected Jaap and Raymond's budget to be based on successfully setting up a collection for the banks. They would probably be compensated accordingly. If they would give up control of that campaign, they wouldn't be able to justify their exorbitant spendings. 'And don't forget their huge egos, too,' said Karel. 'We've entered their world, their kingdom, and they don't want us there.'

## Race against time

With only a few months to go until the start of the campaign, I realized we were running out of time. The participating retailers needed at least two months to place a collection box in each of their stores, which meant the boxes had to be ready by mid July. It would take Fotolight at least six weeks to produce four thousand boxes, so Wavin should deliver the cut-to-fit sewage pipes at the beginning of June. It was nearing the end of May when I came to this conclusion; time was running out.

I received an alarming call from Wavin: 'We've got a problem. We're approaching the summer holidays, and the production schedules, which were established a while ago, don't include any pipes which would be suitable for you.'
'Well, if that's the case, I can forget about the whole campaign,' I said defeatedly. Wavin promised to look for a solution. A few days later they phoned back: 'We've got permission to adjust our production scheme!' an enthusiastic voice on the other side of the line said. They would be able to free one of their machines in a couple of weeks.
'Let's start printing the stickers,' decided Fotolight. The sticker design we had used for the corporate campaign needed some adjustment: we'd now reached a total of a hundred and twenty charities, and our sponsor NorthSea FM had to be added, as well as EuroCollecte's logo. We showed Jaap a proof of the print and he gave his approval.
Then Wavin delivered the collection boxes, and we could finally start putting the stickers on. It was a nasty job; the stickers were static and difficult to handle, and it was awkward to stick them neatly on the rounded pipes.
We'd been working at it for a couple of days, when there was another hitch.

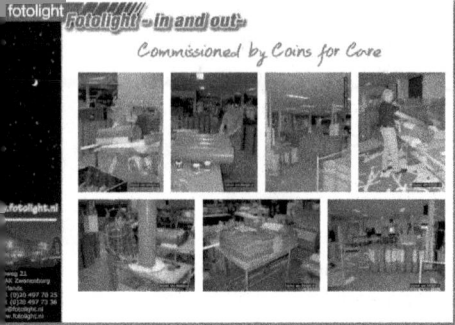

Commissioned by Coins for Care

'Our board has decided they would like a common logo after all, they think this is very important to emphasize our partnership,' Jaap announced out of the blue. That had been exactly my argument which Jaap and Raymond had so bluntly rejected during our negotiations! I gathered they'd not even discussed this with their board, and had taken the decision to use separate logo's all by themselves.

Do something grand with your small change

This put us in an impossible position. I panicked, I didn't think we'd have time to organize new stickers, but EuroCollecte didn't share my anxiety: 'What do you mean, we've got plenty of time left,' they said. 'The collection doesn't start until January and the bank campaign doesn't start until Oct 15.' They weren't even aware of the start of our campaign on Sept 1st...
We didn't have a choice. The Coins for Care stickers were peeled off the collection boxes, new stickers were printed, and those hard working people at Fotolight, started putting them on all over again.

Donate your foreign coins and support

Coins-for-Care

## An unpleasant surprise

In the meantime Albert Heijn agreed to handle the delivery of the collection boxes to all of their six hundred supermarkets themselves. 'As long as we receive the boxes well in advance,' warned my contact person. I hesitated: 'We are a little delayed because of a problem with the stickers, so it might be slightly later,' I said cautiously. Immediately, I sensed panic at the other end of the line. 'Listen, you've got no idea what I've had to do to get this organized,' my contact person

BEUMER PACKAGING BV

snapped, 'please make sure the plans stay as they are, otherwise we have a prob-lem.' It was a clear warning, there should be no delay. 'And another thing,' he continued, 'did I already tell you that we need the collection boxes delivered in cardboard boxes? Our system can only handle square shapes.' I couldn't believe this, now we had to get six hundred special boxes for the Albert Heijn stores. Not wanting to frustrate the situation even more, I asked for the specific details and measurements and promised I would look into it. How was I going to solve this?

Then I remembered an e-mail I had received months ago from Beumer packaging; this was the perfect moment to take up their offer to support Coins for Care! I called them and asked if they could design a box which would meet Albert Heijn standards. 'Of course!' was their reply. 'You name it, we package it!'' Could you do that within a week, on a no-cost basis?' I asked. It wasn't a problem for them, and I am eternally grateful to Beumer for donating six hundred, perfectly fitting boxes, which could be handled by the Albert Heijn logistics system. Phew, another problem solved!

*'Opportunities never come to those who wait...they are captured by those who dare to attack.'*
*- Paul J. Meyer -*

## July Crisis

On July 4, 2001, less than two months before the start of Coins for Care, EuroCollecte was having a board meeting. I'd never met any of the board members and, after that miscommuni-cation about the logo, I thought it couldn't hurt to raise a few points, and I asked Jaap if I could accompany him. Jaap, however, insisted that it wasn't a good time: 'Maybe another day, right now we're too busy with internal matters.' The night before the board meeting I quickly checked my e-mail and found an official message from Jaap in my inbox, stating that 'EuroCollecte's board is not happy with the existing clauses regarding the financing of the mutual activities, which (might) endanger the current cooperation.' Jaap contin-ued that 'the 2% cost percentage has been mentioned in an article about Coins for Care, whereas we'd agreed this would not be communicated to the press'. I didn't understand where this was suddenly coming from.

The financing had been included in our - signed - contract, and we'd accepted to each be responsible for our own costs, while Coins for Care would organize free publicity and sponsorship. It was true that I'd been asked not to boast about the 2% costs, but at the same time this information was freely available on our website, and it was frankly bizarre that it had raised questions with EuroCollecte's board. My heart was in my throat.

I got straight onto the phone with Jaap: Are you seriously considering canceling the whole cooperation?' I asked. 'It depends on what decisions are being taken in our board meeting tomorrow,' he said, and he added that, obviously, it wouldn't make any sense for me to come over for our weekly work meeting the next day.
I tried everything, begging him for an answer: 'Tell me at least what to do with the collection boxes, do you want me to get on with that or not?' 'Just wait for the letter from the board,' said Jaap, and hung up. I was outraged, I knew that Jaap and Raymond were up to something, and felt completely excluded and help-less. Would this be the end of us working together, something I had previously looked forward to?

The next day Karel and I wrote an urgent letter to EuroCollecte, explaining our precarious situation, and requesting clarity as soon as possible.
'Let's see what options we have,' said Karel. 'If we continue with putting the stickers on the boxes, at least we'll be ready in time, even if the logo is incor-rect, waiting for an answer from EuroCollecte will put us in a vulnerable posi-tion as it will definitely delay the process.'
'There's another alternative,' I said, 'we could start printing the Coins for Care stickers, and take the others off the boxes, then we'd still be ready time. We decided to go for it; if EuroCollecte would change their mind we could still add their logo, and damage would be limited to the printing costs.

A week went by, and we still hadn't heard anything. 'It does not bode well,' Karel sighed when our e-mails, calls, faxes, and a second urgent letter remained unanswered. Time was ticking on and Fotolight urged us to make a start with the collection boxes, with pain in our hearts we decided to replace the mutual logo with the freshly printed Coins for Care stickers. Karel and I both felt very unhappy with how things had turned out, but despite the unpleasantness of the situation, it felt good to make a decision; we were no longer dependent on EuroCollecte and had taken control; at least the bins would end up in the shops on time. Our problems weren't completely over yet. 'Sorry, but I simply can't ask my people to take off these stickers again, they've only just put them on!' Tim from Fotolight reacted when I told him about our change of plan.

It was a disaster, where were we going to find enough people in time? I imme-diately started contacting everybody I knew, asking for help, while Karel was on the phone with his Abcoude friends.
We managed to pull quite a few people together, and worked solidly for three days. To be honest, despite the blisters on our fingers, we had a great time; the weather was good, some people had organized a bit of music, and there was plenty of food and drink.

Volunteers peeling of the stickers for the third (!) sticker change due to EuroCollect politics.

It was heartbreaking, however, to see so much money being wasted, we had containers full of unwanted, peeled off stickers. Finally, all collection boxes were clear, and Fotolight started applying new stickers for a third time.

A few days later EuroCollecte came back to us: The board had decided in favor of continuing the cooperation, but the exchange percentage of twenty-five percent needed to be reviewed. Karel and I were appalled, the campaign hadn't even started yet, and already they were going back on our agreements. What was the reason for these contradicting signals and arguments? Right away, we replied that we were shocked, explaining the decision would have far reaching consequences for the campaign if this wasn't resolved fairly soon.

Fourteen very long days after Jaap's first e-mail, Karel and I were finally invited to meet with two members of the EuroCollecte board; it would be an interesting conversation, to say the least.

## Board Meeting

EuroCollecte had arranged a private room in Motel Breukelen where we were going to meet their two new board members: Paul Nouwen, former CEO of the Dutch Automobile Association, who had been recently installed as chairman of the board, and Erik van de Merwe, who had been appointed by private bank Mees Pierson to watch over the 4.5 million euro loan.

We were prepared for the worst; Karel had warned me to stay calm and not let my emotions take the lead. 'Paul and Erik are two reasonable people,' he said. 'They both have a background in business, and they joined EuroCollecte only recently; they may not be aware of everything that has been going on.'

We were greeted by Paul, a quietly dignified gentleman, who told us he was happy to finally meet us, and came to the point straight away: 'I understand you've been somewhat reserved in your communications with the board,' he said, looking me directly in the eye.

I couldn't believe what I was hearing; I hadn't been 'reserved' at all! I'd done everything to arrange a meeting, but Jaap and Raymond had made it impossible! 'I'm also sad to hear that you want to cancel our cooperation, I deeply regret that,' Nouwen continued. Karel, noticing my outrage, gave me a warning look, but I couldn't stop myself: 'That is absolutely not true! Time and time again we've been trying to convince you of the benefits of a partnership and, even after we've signed a contract, you're still being difficult when it comes to working together. Whether it's the organization of the logistics, organizing the volunteers, or the money processing, you just refuse to partner up with us. I find it incredibly difficult to agree anything with EuroCollecte; I'm not allowed to attend your board meetings, and every week you seem to have another objection to working with us. Let me tell you one thing: time is running out; we've got to get these collection boxes distributed, we only have six weeks left to get them into the stores, why haven't you replied to any of our letters?'

Shaking with anger, I immediately regretted my outburst. Karel had been right, I should have controlled my emotions and dealt with the issues one by one. There was a long silence, I looked up and saw Paul and Erik staring at me in complete astonishment. Paul was the first to speak and, casting a brief glance at Jaap and Raymond, he said: 'If this is all true, I am afraid we've been misinformed.' Erik nodded: 'Could you please tell us again exactly what's been going on?' he asked. Karel had been right, Paul and Erik were not aware of the situation at all!

Calm as ever, Karel explained that the campaign was being seriously delayed by EuroCollecte's inability to come to a decision. He described our current situation, how it had been two weeks since we had last heard from EuroCollecte, and how time and money were being wasted. Karel concluded this was intolerable and we had to find a solution, so we could be assured it wouldn't happen again.

Now all eyes were on Jaap and Raymond. 'We've asked you a couple of times to arrange a meeting with Coins for Care, why did you tell us they weren't interested?' Paul and Erik asked. 'What about the logistics, the volunteers, it would make sense if we would organize this together with Coins for Care; why didn't you ever mention this?' Jaap and Raymond stared at their shoes, not knowing what to say. 'We'll deal with you later,' said a visibly angry Erik.

It was refreshing to talk to Paul and Erik, we were on completely the same wavelength, and they told us they thought it was very important to display both our logo's on the collection boxes, to emphasize our partnership with this campaign.

I informed them that most of the boxes had already been distributed to the stores, it would be terribly costly to get them all back and have new stickers fitted on. 'Don't worry about that, it's our mistake, we'll take full responsibility and cover all costs,' Paul and Erik proposed, and added EuroCollecte would also take care of organizing the volunteers, so we could focus on labeling the boxes. Karel and I were thrilled, we'd never expected such a positive outcome!

## Aftershock

Karel and I were delighted with EuroCollecte's renewed support, and despite being very angry at Jaap and Raymond's sabotaging actions, we didn't linger on it for too long; there was too much work to be done.

I contacted Fotolight and informed them of the latest developments: stop the current production and start taking the stickers off. All volunteers were contacted once again - some of them still had blisters on their hands from the previous week! - and all collection boxes were correctly labelled. Thanks to Albert Heijn and Van Gend & Loos, we still managed to get them in the stores on time.

My problems were not over yet, in all the delays and confusion I had made a huge error. With all boxes safe and sound in four thousand stores across the country, I received a phone call from NorthSea FM, asking me what had happened to their logo, I had completely forgotten to add them to the most recent version of the stickers...!

It was an unforgivable mistake; our trusted sponsor was hugely disappointed. I thought of all kinds of ways to create some publicity for NorthSea FM to compensate them, but damage had been done. 'We have to review our

**NOORDZEE FM**

marketing plan completely, we were counting on those four thousand boxes. Our board of directors is not impressed, and I am afraid we have decided to step down.'

Fortunately they kept playing our free radio commercials, and they completed the current activities, but there was not going to be any further advertising campaign.

I had succeeded in getting everything back on track, but it had come at a cost.

## One last chance

If it hadn't been for Paul and Erik, I'm sure we would have failed in our attempts to work with EuroCollecte. We had tried everything we could to make it a successful partnership, but Jaap and Raymond's stubbornness and silly politics had made it impossible. Erik and Paul's involvement, however, offered a multitude of new opportunities, which encouraged us to invest more time. Erik had suggested to hold a meeting at his house every two weeks, so he could keep an eye on Jaap and Raymond, and make sure they would stick to their agreements.

So with renewed enthusiasm we continued to work towards the launch of our campaign.

'Anyone can give up,
it's the easiest thing in the world to do,
but to hold it together when everyone else would
understand if you fell apart,
that is true strength.'

# Excuse 12:
# 'What if it doesn't work out?'

"Success is not final,
failure is not fatal: it is the courage to
continue that counts."
- Winston Churchill -

# By the Skin of one's teeth

'Stop feeling sorry for yourself,' I told myself. 'Just get it done!' I was updating our contacts database, thousands of addresses needed to be added manually. I was concerned we did not yet have enough volunteers to cover all four thousand stores, we had to make a start with sending out the instructions on how, when, and where to empty the collection boxes.

My house had become the administrative hub of this operation, there were piles of paper everywhere. The kitchen became the storage room for the welcoming letters to the volunteers, my office was stashed with the letters of instruction, and the rest of the house was covered with address stickers and other piles of paper. My garden shed was cluttered with the special screwdrivers for opening the collection boxes, the result of a generous sponsorship deal with DIY giant Gamma. Even my garden was being used as a depot for the plastic money bags.

It was a real challenge to match the address stickers with the correct instructions, location, and number of plastic money bags. I was constantly running up and down, between my office where the simple printer was doing overtime, and the rest of the house, desperately trying to bring some order into this mass of paper. All the while both my two landlines and mobile phone were ringing non-stop.

Despite their promises, EuroCollecte had failed to deliver the necessary volunteers, and at the last moment we had to turn to Dorkas, who - once again - came to our rescue with their network of enthusiastic supporters.

A couple of weeks before, I had been contacted by my cousin from Canada, she was traveling to Europe with a friend and had asked if they could stay with me for a few days. I had said it wouldn't be problem, expecting to be finished around that time, suggesting I would take the time to show them around the Netherlands…

In the midst of the Coins for Care chaos I had simply forgotten all about them, and was shocked when they suddenly appeared at my doorstep. My house was one huge mess, I hastily tidied up one room, so they had at least a place to sleep. Realizing I wasn't going on any outing, they politely asked me if they could help with anything, and instead of sightseeing trips to the Dutch country side, they spent the next two days and nights helping me putting letters into envelopes...

## Peeping Minister

We'd asked Gerrit Zalm, Minister of Finance, and Erica Terpstra, chairperson of the Dutch Olympic Committee, to officially announce the start of the Coins for Care campaign. At the Ministry of Finance they were the first to publically depose some coins into our special collection box.

As a festive touch to the official start I had contacted the young designer who had created the famous dress out of foreign coins. Maurice Spapens helped his model into the extraordinary outfit, which weighed at least twenty-five kilograms. Very carefully the model tottered around the room in the revealing, low cut coin dress, drawing much attention. Just before the official photo shoot with Minister Zalm, the designer had to adjust the dress, as the model's nipples peeped right in between the coins! Eventually the daily newspaper *De Telegraaf* did not publish the official photograph, but one in which Mister Zalm admires the results of the low cut back of the model's dress...

The grand opening was a huge success, we received a lot of publicity and the whole country was now aware of our campaign, and the cooperation between Coins for Care and EuroCollecte.

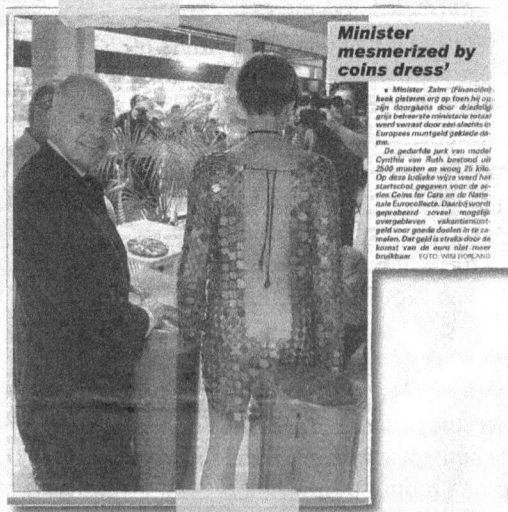

'Minister mesmerized by coins dress'

© De Telegraaf, Sep 2001

Sept/
Oct
2001

# Tempted by money and status

Some time previously I had gratefully accepted Michel's
offer to help out. One of his tasks was to coordinate the registration of the
various charities, but he seemed to cause
a lot of confusion, for example, communicating different deadlines which resulted
in awkward situations for several organizations who were not sure whether they
had been accepted or not. I also received
an email from a charity referring to the
pleasant chat they had with 'the director of
Coins for Care.' Naively, I took it for a simple
misunderstanding.

Another of Michel's tasks was to coordinate
the private campaigns. There were certain
charities who held their own collections
amongst their own supporters, and we had
agreed they would keep half of the funds themselves, and donate the other
half to the larger Coins for Care pot. We would take care of the money processing and divide the total amount over all the participating charities. We received
many questions about this, some charities had been running their own
campaigns for years, and wanted to be sure they weren't going to lose out. I
thought it was important to communicate a consistent story, so I had detailed
everything on paper, and instructed Michel accordingly. Strangely enough I
kept receiving reactions from the charities which suggested we offered a variety of options. Michel however, assured me he had been communicating our
policy clearly to the charities involved.

According to me, Michel should be given the responsibility to sort things out
himself, but Karel thought he needed more guidance: 'Otherwise these kind of
miscommunications will keep occurring. Leave it with me, I'll sort it out with
Michel,' he suggested.

We had our hands well and truly full with putting the new stickers on, when
I received a weird phone call from one of the charities. The caller felt clearly
uneasy about what he had to tell me: Michel had suggested that they should
not donate their money to Coins for Care, but have it exchanged by Michel
himself. The charity would then receive eighty percent of the value instead
of the agreed fifty percent. I was in shock, this could not be happening, had
Michel started his own little business?

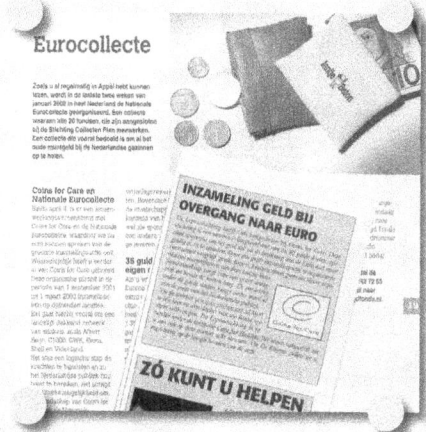

'Of course we haven't accepted Michel's proposal,' said the caller, 'but we're concerned that others may have, that the balance between the charities has been disrupted, and with that the confidence in Coins for Care.' I swallowed hard, this could have serious implications for our campaign. I promised to look into it, however, my whistleblower didn't want me to use his name, nor the name of his organization, so I would not have any proof. What could I do? Should I call Michel, and ask him what he had done? He would probably deny it, which wouldn't leave me any wiser. Should I call all hundred and twenty charities? First of all, I didn't have the time for that; secondly, they would also deny any involvement, and thirdly, I probably should let sleeping dogs lie, and not stir things up any further. The situation was bad enough as it was.

Deep down I knew this story was true, and I decided to get some advice from a private detective whom I knew. 'You won't be able to do anything without evidence,' he said. 'If your informant wants his identity to remain anonymous, you will need to gain proof yourself.' We agreed he would call Michel, pretending to be running a charity, while recording the conversation. Hopefully, we would find out if Michel was sticking to the Coins for Care agreement, or whether he was indeed promoting his own little private business.

'Not good at all,' the detective said when he got back to me. Listening to his tape brought a chill to my back. Michel had been recorded saying things like: 'If you want to exchange money you've come to the right person' and 'Such a good choice'. It really hurt to find out to what extent he'd abused my trust. His actions did not only disadvantage the charities, he was also endangering the whole campaign; Michel had to be stopped immediately.

That night Leonie and I paid Michel an unannounced visit. I had a million questions for him, and Leonie was armed with pen and paper, ready to take notes. At first Michel denied all of it, but when he realized we knew all about his dealings, he started listing the charities he'd approached with his proposals. Leonie quickly scribbled everything down, aghast at the vast number of organizations. It was an incredibly long list, I found it particularly hard to take that Michel had cheated on all of us. He looked very uncomfortable himself, and didn't dare to look us in the eye. We didn't have another choice than to fire him instantly, asking him to sign a statement in which he agreed not to act in our name ever again.

Michel's house was also being used as one of the money-depots, however, no longer trusting him, we decided to take all the bags of coins with us. Despite Coin Co having called the day before to collect money, there were still hundreds of money bags left in Michel's shed, some even had their seals broken and were opened! We couldn't take all bags in one go and would have to come back the next day. On the way home, we had to drive extremely carefully, the car was dangerously low to the road, heavily loaded with the coin bags. Both Leonie and I were quiet, overwhelmed by the situation. Apparently Michel had been so desperate for some acknowledgement and respect, that he had abused his position, and despite the stolen money, we actually felt very sorry for him.

It didn't end there; the next day I received a phone call from a money exchange office: 'We thought we should inform you that we've been contacted by Michel, who wants to empty our money boxes. He's asked us to put an earlier date on the receipt, so it looks as if he was here a few days ago.' I was astonished, had he not learnt his lesson yet?

Beside myself with anger I called Michel: 'You really need to stop this!' I snarled at him. 'you aren't working for us anymore, you've signed a statement yesterday! Your stupid actions put the whole Coins for Care campaign in jeopardy!' Michel was in tears: 'I only wished help, I really wanted to collect the money for you and save you some work,' he said, and I was stupid enough to believe him...'Michel, you're only making things worse, don't you understand...,' and I explained again what the consequences would be. He promised it wouldn't happen again. 'If you ever contact another charity, I will contact the police,' I warned him.

A few hours later, Michel turned up at my doorstep, his car filled with moneybags. He had tears in his eyes, and sniffed: 'I really want to come clean with you,' and confessed there had been a lot more charities he had done a deal with. I was very relieved that Michel had decided to come clean, but hugely disappointed by the number of charities having accepted his offer.

# 'Dirty laundry'-dilemma

It was sad to discover that the idea of widespread partnership was not being shared by all charities. Some had accepted Michel's offer, and their excuse was they had simply thought it was legitimate. I struggled to believe this; they must have had their suspicions; Michel's arrangement went against everything Coins for Care stood for, and our policies had been clearly communicated in the contracts, e-mails, and on our website.

Karel and I knew that excluding these charities from our scheme, would only cause further bad publicity and damage to the campaign. Instead we contacted the charities which had been approached by Michel, and most of them apologized, admitting they had suspected something wasn't quite right, but had been persuaded by the thought of the extra money. One organization, however, insisted that business was business and refused to make any adjustments.

It took a lot of effort to renegotiate, but in most cases, we came to an arrangement which was in accordance with our original policies.

The whole episode had not only absorbed a lot of valuable time, but we also found ourselves in a very precarious position, and were not sure how to handle it. Should we solve this behind closed doors and let Michel go quietly, or should we be open and transparent, explaining we'd been having some internal problems which had been dealt with, risking bad publicity?

We decided to spare Michel a public verdict; his main motive hadn't been so much financial gain, but was a cry for attention and respect. I still think, however, that openness and transparency are extremely important. You should be honest about mistakes being made, clear about the measures being taken to ensure it won't happen again; that shows respect for those who support you, and that's why I am telling this story. I haven't used Michel's real name, as I want him to have the chance to improve his life. Deep down he is a good guy, with his heart in the right place.

Fortunately this was the only incident of it's kind, which paled into insignificance compared to the positive example of the thousands of volunteers dealing with bags of money every single day, behaving impeccably, which is far more noteworthy than that of one person who wasn't able to withstand temptation.

## Injustice and difficult decisions

We had formulated five guidelines on the allocation of the collected money:

1) The Dutch public should decide how the money will be divided over the participating charities.
2) All charities, no matter how small, should be given an equal chance to participate in this unique scheme.
3) The allocation of the money should be completely transparent and understandable for everyone.
4) Donors need to be encouraged to take part in the allocation process.
5) Charities should be rewarded according to their active contribution to the campaign.

Unlike EuroCollecte, the press, the public, and the charities were unanimously positive; the donors would have more control over the money they were donating, and participating charities could exert an influence by calling up their supporters to vote.

The Christian charities, in particular, were very quick in mobilizing their loyal followers. It wasn't surprising they had made a head start, those religious groups are responsible for more than half of all the funds being raised for charity in the Netherlands, and the names of radical religious organizations, like 'Word and Deed' and 'Christians for Israel' were soon topping the list as the most popular charities.

When the Reformed Daily Newspaper started to ask questions about this, EuroCollecte was the first to jump onto the bandwagon, suggesting we had committed fraud.

Soon I was being chased by the press, asking for a reaction, and I told them that 'certain Christian charities have been very successful in encouraging their supporters to vote for them. There hasn't been any wrong doing.' Disappointingly some journalists ran their own story, and

© De Telegraaf

### Christian charities head race for 50 million in coins

door Nathan Vos

AMSTERDAM, vrijdag

#### Voting manipulated on Coins for Care site

Van onze binnenlandredactie

AMSTERDAM – Woord en Daad en de VBOK stonden ten onrechte in de top van de lijst van Coins for Care. Sympathisanten van deze organisaties hebben zich niet aan de regels gehouden bij het aangeven van hun voorkeur op internet.

Dat zegt Esther Jacobs van de stichting Coins for Care. Deze organisatie organiseert samen met de Nationale Eurocollecte een landelijke actie voor het inzamelen van buitenlands munt- en papiergeld ten behoeve van het goede doel nu de euro wordt ingevoerd. Bij de verdeling van de opbrengst wordt gekeken naar het aantal keren dat de naam van de deelnemende charitatieve instelling op de website www.coinsforcare.nl is aangeklikt.

De bezoekers van deze internetsite kunnen kiezen uit meer dan 100 namen van goededoelorganisaties. Tot voor kort werd de lijst aangevoerd door de reformatorische stichting Woord en Daad, die zo'n 1500 voorkeursstemmen had verzameld. Ook de VBOK scoorde hoog.

Internetgebruikers mogen maar één keer hun stem uitbrengen. Volgens Esther Jacobs van Coins for Care is er door stemmers gemanipuleerd. „We hebben vastgesteld dat het vooral ging om sympathisanten van Woord en Daad, VBOK en stichting Ontmoeting. Kennelijk wordt in die kringen doorverteld hoe je de beveiliging kunt omzeilen."

Woordvoerder H. de Pater van Woord en Daad zegt blij te zijn dat mensen zijn organisatie een goed hart toedragen, maar betreurt het dat zij zich niet aan de regels hebben gehouden. Woord en Daad is nu naar een 19e plaats geduikeld, Ontmoeting staat op 34 en de VBOK op 45.

Zie ook png. 3: "Stemfraude nog duister".

© Reformatorisch Dagblad

© Het Parool

in huge headlines it appeared in all newspapers: FRAUD BY CHRISTIAN CHARITIES AT COINS FOR CARE. A scandal was always more interesting than the truth.

## Coins for Care fears fraud

Internetstemmen te manipuleren

The tide had turned against me, instead of generating further positive publicity for Coins for Care, I found myself having to guarantee the security of our website: 'No website is a hundred percent safe, not even NASA's website!' I protested. 'Our aim is to generate as much public involvement as possible, not to build a hermetically sealed website!' Eventually I asked Ernst and Young to execute a specially designed test on our electronic security, which dramatically decreased the possibility of manipulation, and could recognize any duplicate votes. It was to no avail, *de Volkskrant* newspaper published an article of an IT student proudly announcing that he'd developed a program which could issue numerous votes in one go, and he'd managed to let two charities improve their position in the list.

I found out who this student was and gave him a call: 'What do you think you're doing?' I asked, and told him how his actions were damaging our reputation, putting us in a very difficult position. 'I guess I wanted to prove that it's possible to manipulate any result by hacking into a website,' was his answer. 'Well, that's no surprise, is it?' I snapped. 'Why didn't you contact us and help us with securing our voting system, instead of going to the papers and endangering our whole campaign?' and the poor guy stammered it was all being blown out of proportion by the press, and apologized a thousand times.

**Coins for Care**

Coins for Care enquiry into security measures of voting module.

ERNST&YOUNG
FROM THOUGHT TO FINANCE

A few weeks later, I was invited by Kassa, a consumer TV-show, to explain how our voting system worked. It would have been a perfect opportunity to put all misunderstandings right, once and for all, were it not for the IT student, who had been invited also. On live television, in front of millions of viewers he demonstrated how he could move charities up our list; there was nothing I could do, but watch in horror as he hacked our website, completely violating our voting system.

Kassa continued to pour oil on the flames by focussing on the top three charities. 'I don't want my money to go to an organization like Word and Deed' said a woman. 'That's exactly why we've got this voting system,' I replied, 'but there are also people who do support Word and Deed.' 'What about the *Society for the Protection of the Unborn Child?*' the same

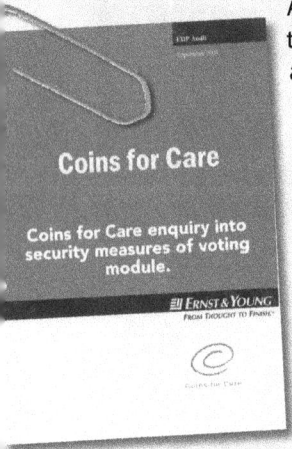

woman continued, 'I'd rather throw my money away than giving it to them!' I tried to explain that the money would be allocated according to the wishes of the public, 'The list will consist of a variety of charities. Some people have more sympathy for certain charities than others, and that's why we're asking everybody to vote!'

A few days after the show, EuroCollecte suggested to end the internet voting...

'I can't stand it,' I said to Karel. 'I keep having to justify our voting system, but nobody seems to be interested in the facts! I feel the public is ruled by emotions rather than logic, they've turned against us, and I'm fed up with having to defend myself...Let's cancel the internet voting,' I decided. 'That's probably the best thing you can do, a very courageous step,' said Karel, and admitted he'd been hoping I would reach that conclusion sooner rather than later.

I was still determined, however, to let the public have a say in how their donations should be divided among the charities, and now the internet voting had been called off, I had to think of something else. I came up with an idea for a public survey, and to my relief, the board of EuroCollecte accepted my proposal and even offered to pay half of the costs!

It put an end to the discussion about the security of our website, but the controversy about extreme charities, radical religious organizations and anti abortion movements had left its mark. Choosing a film at my local video store, towards the end of 2001, I noticed the Coins for Care collection box had disappeared. When I asked the manager about it he said, without knowing who I was: 'That Coins for Care supports all kinds of weird charities, and that's why we decided to remove the box.' I can't tell you how upset I was.

Echte 'gevecht' om verdeelsleutel buitenlandse munten moet nog beginnen

## Still no clarity on voting fraud

„Duizend adressen per persoon mogelijk"

## Internet voting difficult to secure

### Coins for Care in favor of pro-life movement?

De gedachte achter de Coins for Care-actie was nobel: geld inzamelen voor het goede doel. Tragisch echter dat de Vereniging ter Bescherming van het Ongeboren Kind (VBOK) de stemming op internet, die de sleutel is voor de verdeling van de miljoenen, misbruikt door haar leden massaal tot stemmen op te roepen. Ondanks haar minimale aanhang voert de anti-abortuslobby inmiddels de ranglijst aan in de miljoenenrace. Esther Jacobs, initiatiefneemster van Coins for Care, vindt het allemaal best. Ook als Osama Bin Laden en Stichting Jojo's voor Zuid-Nepal zich melden? "Als ze erkend worden door het Centraal Bureau Fondsenwerving, dan spreken de stemmen." Eén stem die alvast bezorgdheid uitspreekt, is die van Rebecca Gomperts, initiatiefneemster van de abortusboot. "De VBOK heeft al genoeg geld. Er moet zeker een tegenactie komen." (MR)

In de trendy strandtent serveerden ze zeer exclusive cola-tics.

*Nieuwe Revu Magazine was forced to rectify this article"*

## Dispute about funds raised by Coins for Care

© Trouw.

### Problems for Coins for Care

© Het Parool.

AMSTERDAM - De organisatie van Coins for Care maakt zich zorgen over de fraudegevoeligheid van de internetsite waarop mensen hun stem kunnen uitbrengen op een goed doel. Het bestuur komt deze week bijeen om te praten over eventuele sluiting van de site. De opbrengst van de collecte van overtollige buitenlandse munten valt tegen; in twee maanden is een miljoen gulden opgehaald. Pagina 3

*This photograph was taken when I heard that – besides the usual building and construction fraud– we also had a fraudulent voting module, hence the raised eyebrow. My compliments for daring to change the system whilst halfway.*

*Fortunately there were still volunteers who could see the humor of the nasty situation we had found ourselves in.*

## My savior

Of all the organizations who had accepted Michel's offer, only one had been reluctant to renegotiate the proposal. I wrote them a letter, explaining the complexity of the situation we had found ourselves in, hoping to find a solution. The next morning Karel came into the office announcing he'd got fed up with this charity and had written a letter to force a breakthrough. 'Would you mind reading it through before I post it?' he said. I laughed: 'Only if you read mine!' By complete coincidence we had both written letters, identical in tone and style, using similar arguments and suggesting the same solutions.

Working with Karel was such a joy. He was like a father to me, he was my rock during difficult times, supporting me in everything I did. We were a good team, striving for the same ideals. 'The grey dove and the young puppy,' Karel used to call us.

My theory was that most of our problems occurred because people didn't fully understand what we were doing. I was convinced raising more awareness and giving out information was the answer, but Karel taught me a wise lesson: 'Esther,' he said, 'there are always people who disagree with you, especially if they have a hidden agenda, no matter how right you may be. It's not a big deal, you just have to accept that they'll never admit they're wrong, and trying to convince them is of no use, it will only create more resistance.' I learnt to keep my mouth shut at times, and cut senseless discussions short. 'Choose your battles wisely' reads a famous saying, and I decided not to waste my time on every little bit of injustice, but to save my energy for those moments and topics which really mattered.

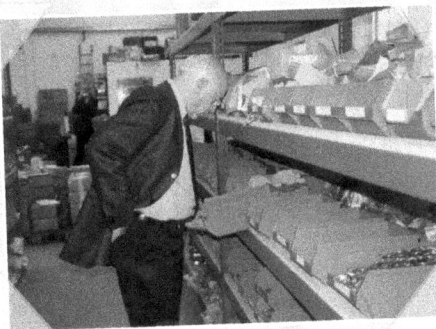

Karel on site at CoinCo.

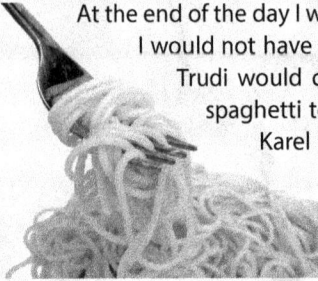

At the end of the day I would usually give Karel a call to catch up. Knowing I would not have time to prepare a proper meal for myself, his wife Trudi would call out in the background: 'Esther, we're serving spaghetti tonight. Dinner at six!' I loved those evenings with Karel and Trudi. We had an unspoken agreement that we didn't talk about Coins for Care during meals. Instead we chatted about family, the grandchildren, and what had been happening recently in the tiny village of Abcoude lately. I was intensely grateful for this loving 'oasis' in Abcoude; a place where people respected and helped each other. Such a stark contrast with what my daily life had become...

## A dead-end street

During the work meetings at Erik's home it became painfully clear that Jaap and Raymond had a complete disregard for any agreement we had made. Their promise to deliver five hundred volunteers for Coins for Care had not been met. Nor did they respect Erik's demand to obtain at least two quotes if they wanted to hire a third party. They obstinately persisted in doing things their way, not hindered by any one else, and they had gotten away with it.

Until Karel and I discovered they had changed the minutes of our weekly meetings... They were clearly in the process of covering up something and we were not willing to find out what that was.

This was the final straw for us. We had tried everything to turn this partnership into a success, but it still wasn't happening. Feeling disillusioned, demotivated and defeated, we decided to call off the cooperation with EuroCollecte.

> 'If at first you don't succeed, try, try again. Then quit. There's no point in being a damn fool about it.'
> - W.C. Fields -

In a letter to the board of directors at EuroCollecte we stated that, regretfully, we were not able to work any longer with their management team, having serious doubts whether these men had the campaign's interest at heart.

We suggested that, for the sake of the charities, we would continue to act as partners towards the outside world, but we didn't want any further dealings with either Jaap or Raymond.

Following our letter, the board ordered an audit into the finances of EuroCollecte, which found 'severe financial irregularities'.

Even though that did not surprise us one bit, this news shattered us. How can established charity people keep putting their own position and finances over the cause itself?

It was the end of December, and I needed a break. I took a three week holiday in South Africa, far away from it all. One night Karel contacted me with the latest news: 'Listen, EuroCollecte are in real trouble, their campaign is far from ready; Jaap and Raymond have been so busy with collecting 'evidence' against Coins for Care, that they haven't organized anything, no volunteers for the collection, no processing of the money, nothing!' said Karel, while I listened in astonishment. 'The board told me that if it hadn't been for our decision to withdraw, they wouldn't have discovered this in time. They've now appointed an interim manager to sort everything out.'
I was happy to hear that our radical decision had, at least, led to something positive.

Many more skeletons tumbled out of the closet. 'We suspect, albeit hard to prove, that the agreements with the advertising company and the other par-

# Collection management more focused on prestige than on charity

Door Achille Prick
**Den Haag**

Terwijl het Nederlandse publiek braaf zijn oude muntgeld verzamelt voor het goede doel, rollen de directeuren en be-

omdat deze stichting een wanprestatie leverde. Hij stelde onder meer dat de SIA niet berekend was op haar taak.
Nu is het de beurt aan de SIA, een stichting die onder leiding staat van de heren J. Zeekant en R. van

Coins for Care en de Nationale Eurocollecte. Daar heeft het bestuur niet goed opgetreden en toen was het conflict geboren."
Volgens Schravenmade zag het bestuur zijn fouten in en trad het begin december vorig jaar af

© *Amerfoortse Courant*, Jan 18th 2002.

ties were made beforehand,' Erik told me. It had become clear that certain people in the charity industry had been looking after each other.

Despite these revelations, the board of EuroCollecte refused to take action. It wasn't until Erik and Paul refused to take responsibility, threatening to step down, that the board dismissed Jaap and Raymond. 'They've obviously established some close ties,' sighed Erik, who stayed in touch with Karel and me.

Even though our partnership had ended, we kept communicating the same message to the public: 'It doesn't matter where you donate in your coins, it will all end up with the same charities.'

Then Erik brought some bad news: 'It seems that the majority of the board thinks Coins for Care is in some way responsible for this mess, I don't really understand why, but they want to skip the 25% revenue share exchange,' he said. 'That's not possible! It's in the contract!' I called out. 'I know,' said Erik, 'I defended you strongly, and although it's extremely unfair, I strongly advise you to agree with a reduction from twenty-five to seventeen and a half percent, otherwise, I fear you will be left with nothing.'

# Only half of EuroCollecte ends up with charities

Van onze verslaggevers
AMSTERDAM

Slechts de helft van de opbrengst van de Eurocollecte komt terecht bij goede doelen. De andere helft is opgegaan aan kosten voor de organisatie. Dit heeft bestuursvoorzitter Paul Nouwen donderdag gezegd. Eurocollecte hoopt over enkele weken de definitieve rekening te publiceren met de goedkeuring van de accountant.

Eurocollecte werd in 2001 opgericht om Europese munten en briefjes in te zamelen die door de invoering van de euro waardeloos zouden worden. De organisatie zou het geld sorteren en naar de centrale banken van de EU-leden brengen. De collecte – via duizenden collectanten en bussen in bankfilialen – bracht 13 miljoen euro op. Nu blijkt dat iets meer

dan de helft daarvan bij de goede doelen terecht komt. Het verwerken van de munten kostte drie miljoen euro. Daarnaast was Eurocollecte 3,3 miljoen euro kwijt aan kantoorkosten.

Nouwen vindt de kosten niet buitensporig hoog. 'Het sorteren van het geld en het transport naar de buitenlandse banken kost nu eenmaal veel geld.' Ook de kantoorkosten zijn volgens de ex-voorzitter van de ANWB niet hoger dan normaal. 'Deze kosten maak je altijd voor personeel, advertenties en collectebussen.'

Esther Jacobs, die ook buitenlands geld heeft ingezameld met Coins for Care, is dat niet met hem eens. 'Wij waren slechts 4 procent kwijt aan kosten. De rest van het geld ging naar het goede doel.' Coins for Care had in Groot-Brittanië een bedrijf gevonden dat de munten goedkoop kon sorte-

ren. Eurocollecte kon hier volgens Jacobs ook terecht, maar weigerde, Nouwen ontkent dat.

Eurocollecte kwam begin 2002 in opspraak vanwege financieel wanbeleid. De directie werd aan de kant gezet. 'Zij brachten niet wat noodzakelijk was', zegt Nouwen nu. Op geruchten dat de tweekoppige directie gezamenlijk een jaarsalaris van 700 duizend kreeg, gaat Nouwen niet in. 'Wij hebben dat contract niet afgesloten. Je moet bij Collecteplan zijn.' Collecteplan, die Eurocollecte oprichtte, is niet bereikbaar voor commentaar. Een van de opgestapte directeuren, Jaap Zeekant, doet de geruchten af als de 'grootst mogelijke onzin'. 'We kregen een normaal salaris.' Nadat de directie was ontslagen, stelde het bestuur een interim-manager aan. Ook die zou een riant salaris hebben gekregen.

Unwilling to put up a fight once more, we reluctantly accepted receiving only a fraction of the money we'd initially agreed upon, and bitterly concluded that the only good thing to come out of this latest mess was that we wouldn't have to deal with Jaap and Raymond ever again.

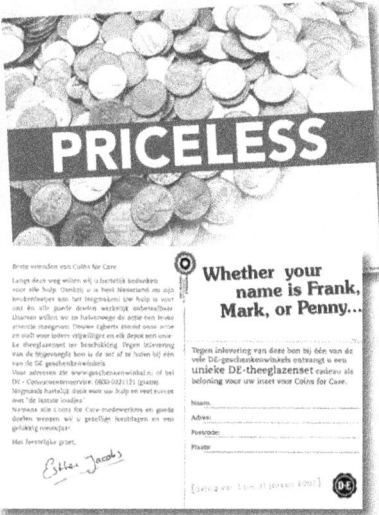

## Big thank you to all volunteers

Behind the scenes thousands of volunteers were working day and night, ensuring the smooth running of the campaign. We could not have succeeded without their help, and to express our gratitude for their valuable work, we asked Boomerang to design a card with a special thank you message on the back, which was sent to every volunteer.

I kept looking for some other small gift, something to remind them, a little keepsake, but whatever I found was either too expensive or not practical. Good old Carola came up with a great solution, she was now working as a marketing manager at Douwe Egberts, a Dutch coffee producer, and she donated two tea glasses to every volunteer. They could be picked up at any Douwe Egberts shop, in exchange for the voucher on the 'priceless' postcard we sent to all of them. It turned out to be a great success and nearly all the glasses were collected.

Before we had parted company, I had also offered the tea glasses to EuroCollecte, but they had their own plans for thanking their volunteers. 'We're having special badges made,' Jaap had been very pleased with himself. But when the board became aware of the costs involved, he was summoned to cancel the

*Thank you so much!*
National EuroCollecte Association

## One guilder badge creates problems for EuroCollecte

Van een onzer verslaggevers    collecte. Het publiek kon via    bouwd en hebben een prima
ROTTERDAM - De voormalige    het web aangeven welke goede    reputatie in de sector. Als de

© Algemeen Dagblad

order immediately. After Jaap and Raymond had long gone, however, a box of badges arrived; the order hadn't been cancelled. EuroCollecte sent the badges to their volunteers after all, and while writing this book, January 2009, I still see a few being advertised on Ebay...

EuroCollecte strains under weight of coins

## NOVA

Since our holiday in India, where I thought of the idea for Coins for Care, I hadn't seen much of my boyfriend. Our relationship had hit rock bottom as I'd been so busy with Coins for Care, and it had been difficult to find time for each other. A few weeks after the final incident with Euro-Collecte we managed to meet up, and in an attempt to breathe new life into our relationship we decided to spend the evening watching television together, snuggled up on the sofa. 'It's time you took it easy,' my boyfriend said while putting his arm around me. I tried to empty my head and give in to an evening without Coins for Care.

Just when I started to relax, I saw the preview for Nova, a current affairs program which was scheduled for later that night. 'Fraud and Failure at Coins for Care.' The words appeared in big letters on the screen. I jumped up as if stung by a bee: 'That's not fair!' I shouted at my boyfriend who wasn't sure what was going on. 'This should be all about EuroCollecte but now everybody will think WE got ourselves into a big mess!' I was now walking up and down the room, thinking about what options were available to me. 'Why don't you call and ask them to correct it?' suggested my boyfriend.

Trying to contact the news desk of a current affairs show one hour before they are due to go on air is not easy, but I did it. I sank my teeth into it like a pit bull and didn't let go until I was finally speaking to someone. 'You've made a huge mistake!' I shouted through the telephone. 'This story refers to EuroCollecte!' I quickly explained their mistake and was reassured they would change the name on the internet and discuss what to do during the show.

What should have been a relaxing evening on the sofa, turned into a nightmare; I was nervously waiting for the phone to ring and checking the internet. After half an hour the text on the Nova website was adjusted to 'Fraud and Failure at EuroCollecte.' I breathed a sigh of relief and settled down again in front of the television. 'You're shaking all over,' my boyfriend said, sounding concerned.

Then the program was announced for a second time that evening: 'In half an hour we update you on the fraud and failure at Coins for Care,' the presenter said. I nearly cried in frustration 'It is not COINS FOR CARE!' Quickly, I called the news desk again, but they did not wish to come to the phone. 'If you do not immediately solve this, I'll get my lawyer onto you!' I threatened in despair.

Eventually I spoke to someone who explained it was impossible to change anything this close before broadcasting. 'You did manage to change it on your website,' I said suspiciously. 'That's another news desk,' was the reply. 'But what you're broadcasting is not correct!' I insisted, and I was put through to the chief editor. 'Please, just explain to me what the problem is,' he said wearily, and I told him that EuroCollecte and Coins for Care were two different organizations, and the names were being mixed up.

'So why does everybody confuse EuroCollecte with Coins for Care?' asked the editor. 'Because Coins for Care is best known out of the two,' I explained 'Well, there you go, at least everybody knows who we're talking about,' concluded the editor. 'Look, I really have to go, if you have any questions or further suggestions you can put them to us in writing. Good evening,' he said before I could reply. There was nothing I could do but watch and witness the damage being done.

NOVA showed pictures of Jaap and Raymond, detailing their negligence, and focussing on the fact that by the end of December they still had not finalized any collectors for the mega collection starting in January.

Every time they used the name Coins for Care in relation with any malpractices, it was as if I was stabbed with a knife. I had worked so hard, for so long, not earning a single cent, and it made me furious to see my brainchild being named and shamed on national television. However, there was nothing I could do.

Nova had neatly listed all the blunders made by Jaap and Raymond and on screen appeared, in full view:

*Only a few hundred volunteers
instead of 10.000*

AT LEAST 40.000 GUILDERS WERE MADE AVAILABLE TO COINS FOR CARE FOR THE COR-
RECTION OF AN ERROR MADE BY ESTHER JACOBS IN RELATION TO THE STICKERS ON THE
COLLECTION BINS.

'What?' I called out in astonishment. My boyfriend, who'd been following from
a safe distance, decided it was best to stay out of my way for a while. 'That
error, that mistake was made by Jaap and Raymond! They were the ones who
couldn't make up their minds whether to have a mutual logo or not; they failed
to inform us in time, which meant we had to change the stickers THREE TIMES!
And it was their board who decided to compensate us for the extra costs,
because they understood that THEIR management had been in the wrong!'

I rattled on and on, while tears were running down my face. It was so unfair.
Immediately after the show I wrote an angry letter to NOVA, cc-ing all sponsors and retailers. I knew it would be hard to reverse the bad reputation we
now had. Most people and organizations who knew me personally were
equally shocked by the program but, unfortunately, there were also those who
thought that 'where's smoke there's fire'.

Of course, if I'd known beforehand that our cooperation would end in such a
dramatic outcome, I would never have pursued a partnership with EuroCollecte so stubbornly. But at least I had tried, and I had learnt that working with
a well established organization is never a guarantee for success. I decided to
look forward, focus on what had gone well, and have confidence in our ability
to manage this campaign ourselves.

'It is not the critic who counts,
Or how the strong man stumbled and fell,
Or where the doer of deeds could have done better.
The credit belongs to the man who is actually in the arena,
Who knows the great enthusiasms, the great devotion
And spends himself in a worthy cause.
If he fails, at least he fails while daring greatly.
So that he will never be one of those cold and timid souls
Who knew neither victory nor defeat.'
- Theodore Roosevelt -

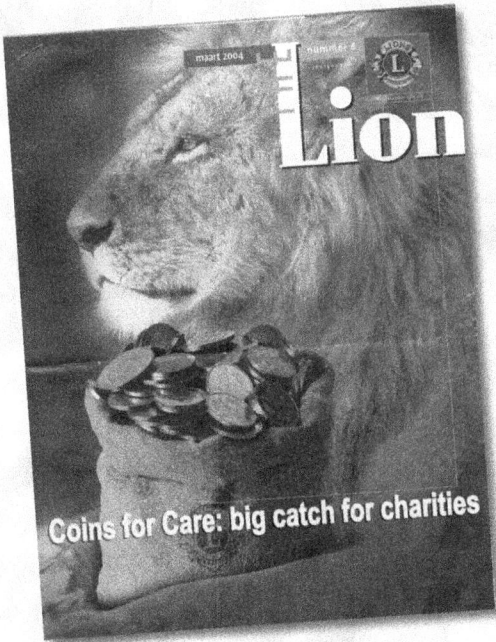

Coins for Care and EuroCollecte were mixed up on a number on occasions. Fortunately this also led to some amusing confusion. The Lions Club featured 'Coins for Care a huge success' on the front cover of their club magazine. However, they actually participated in EuroCollecte.

# Excuse 13:
# 'What if I do succeed?'

*Our deepest fear is not that we are inadequate. Our deepest fear is that we are powerful beyond measure. It is our light, not our darkness, that most frightens us. We ask ourselves, who am I to be brilliant, gorgeous, talented and fabulous? Actually, who are you not to be? You are a child of God. Your playing small does not serve the world. There's nothing enlightened about shrinking so that other people won't feel insecure around you. We are all meant to shine, as children do. We are born to make manifest the glory of God that is within us. It's not just in some of us, it's in everyone. And as we let our own light shine, we unconsciously give other people permission to do the same. As we are liberated from our own fear, our presence automatically liberates others.'*

*- - Nelson Mandela's inaugural speech - \* Marianne Williamson -*

## A flying start

© photo: ANP

Queueing up at the GWK Travelex.

Shortly before the start of our campaign, GWK Travelex announced that they would stop the intake of foreign coins per September. This led to chaotic scenes in their branches, with long queues of people who, true to their Dutch nature, emptied their kitchen drawers, jam jars, and piggy banks, and hurried to the nearest GWK office to get some return for their soon to be obsolete coins.

We received a call from a panic stricken GWK employee: 'We're soon to join the EuroCollecte campaign, but it is not due for another six weeks, and it's such a madhouse here, can we still join Coins for Care?' I couldn't resist a smile, and quickly organized a collection box for all the GWK Travelex branches.

As GWK Travelex only accepted four major currencies, most people donated the coins that were not exchangeable to Coins for Care. Some people just couldn't accept they weren't getting anything in return for their foreign coins, and sulkily took the coins back home.

'What are you going to do with these coins? They're useless, why not put them in the collection box? It's for charity, you know' a journalist asked a woman who tried to sneak away. You could see the embarrassment and shame on her face; she'd obviously hoped for a nice return on her foreign change, and not only had that not worked out, now she was being portrayed as a greedy money grabber too.'

There were also people who couldn't be bothered to queue for that long, and simply donated all their coins to Coins for Care. It was proving to be a very successful start to our campaign.

'Success is a journey,
Not a destination.'
- Ben Sweetland -

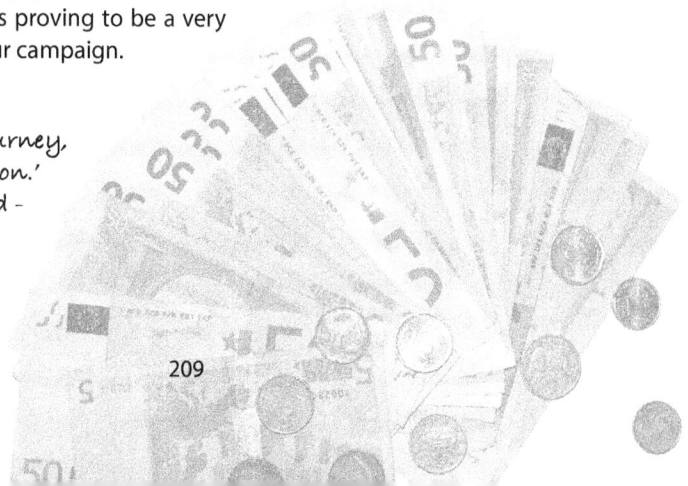

The collection bins were about a meter high, and we had expected it would take weeks for them to fill up. But to my surprise, on the very first day of the official launch of the campaign, we already started receiving the first reports of full bins. I still hadn't quite completed the allocation of all volunteers. This meant that we had to manually look up who lived nearest to the stores, and call each one of them with the request to empty the bins as soon as possible. I explained that Coins for Care had - unexpectedly - made a very successful start. 'We're a little overwhelmed, we have not been able to sent you the plastic moneybags and the special screwdriver yet; could you please bring your own? The coins will need to be delivered to a depot in your area, I'll send you the address details shortly.'

Later we heard there had been some hilarious scenes. Many elderly ladies had volunteered to help us and, not driving a car, these brave women set off on their bikes for the GWK offices. Only to find collection boxes weighing over a hundred kilo's which was of course impossible to transport on their trusty two wheelers. Fortunately, in all cases, the women managed to find someone with a car, and safely deposited the coins. I was moved to see such determination and enthusiasm.

© *Huib Jans/Mec Studio.*

## The volunteers brigade

The campaign was finally well under way, and it gave me such a buzz, I felt such pride when I saw a Coins for Care bin in a store.

Our thorough preparations were beginning to pay off. Volunteers from all over the country were emptying bins, and the depots were steadily filling up with bags of coins.

We realized we were demanding a lot from our volunteers; they were working so hard. Whilst it was physically challenging to move the bags of coins, it was also dirty work, because the collection bins were sometimes used as thrash can, and we had to sift through chewing gum and other rubbish. Even so, moral was high.
In the center of Amsterdam one of our volunteers was cleverly avoiding the steep parking meter rates by borrowing a car with a disabled parking permit. Another volunteer had mistakenly been allocated to a depot which was a long distance from where he lived. He had a great sense of humor, which he dis-

played in the letter he sent us: 'As a geographer I am, indeed, very interested in the landscape. I'm grateful to be responsible for this far away depot; It was a long drive, which allowed me to see the whole of the area. I really enjoyed myself.'

> 'To laugh often and much; to win the respect of
> intelligent people and the affection of children...
> To leave the world a better place...To know even one life has breathed
> easier because you have lived. This is to have succeeded.'
> - Ralph Waldo Emerson -

A few weeks into the campaign we received an urgent call from an older lady in Hilversum, she lived in a residential care home and had kindly offered to have her room used for storage of the money bags. 'Do you think you can come and collect the bags fairly shortly?' she asked timidly. I told her a pick up was not due for another week, at which the lady replied quietly that she had difficulty getting into her room! I immediately notified Karel, who alerted the Abcoude volunteers' network and they called in the next day and relieved the woman of the coins.

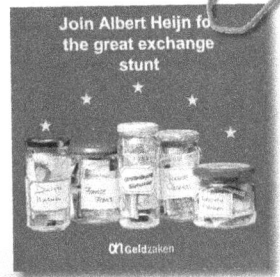

Join Albert Heijn for the great exchange stunt

Two garages in Abcoude became our emergency depots, and soon enough these were filled to the roof as well, the concrete floors cracking under the enormous weight of the bags.

## Money stinks!

It was unbelievable what was thrown into the collection boxes. We found gold teeth, wedding rings (what kind of story could be behind that?), a love letter, and a bracelet with old silver coins attached to it. One generous inhabitant of Scheveningen obviously thought the collection wasn't going quick enough and spontaneously threw a note of fifty guilders in the collection box.

A big-hearted truck driver, who'd been collecting all kinds of foreign currencies for the last thirty years, presented a shopping bag full of coins to one of our volunteers.

# Love letter and wedding ring found in coin box

e inzamelactie van Coins for
Care heeft tot nu toe munten
pgeleverd uit 189 landen. Over
e totale opbrengst kan de organisatie nog niets zeggen omdat

Coins for Care.
Vanaf het begin van de actie
rijden vrachtwagens met buitenlandse valuta naar het geldinza-

trouwring in de kokers.
Tot begin deze maand stonden
inzamelbakken in diverse winkels. Mensen konden in de bak-

van de opbrengst verdelen. In
eerste instantie was het de bedoeling dat er kon worden ge-
stemd via internet op het favorie-
te goede doel. Omdat dit erg frau-

*Annie Bakkertje die de muntenactie startte met de bloemen en Jan Keizer van de SSNV met de cheque van 'Coins for Care' t.w.v. €52.090,-*

## Coins for Care collects €52.090 for burn victims

In addition to the 36.000 euro which was collected by Annie Bakkertje

**Samen met de actie "Coins for Care"** September vorig jaar ging de muntenactie vorder samen met "Coins for Care". Hiervan was de grote organisator Father Jacobs, waarover Annie Bakkertje prima heeft samengewerkt. Na heentle min niet meer het muntgeld te sorteren en kon het in emmers afgeleverd worden. De muntactie van munten in Havendtat en Willem Egger ging gewoon voort. Vijftig procent van de eigen actie was in Volendam voor de SSNV en dit werd ook weer even €14.676,-!! De totale opbrengst van de actie "Coins for Care" was € 3.762.789,- over 118 goede doelen verdeeld.

stemming op internet kon men het goede doel aanwijzen. De SSNV kwam in de hoogste categorie en kreeg een bedrag van €37.416,-, met de 50% van de eigen actie (+ € 14.676,-) werd het totaal voor de Stichting Nederlandse Nieuwgeboorenid Volendam het mooie bedrag van € 52.090,-. De cheque werd maandag in Het Anker overhandigd. Eigenlijk leverde de buitenlandse muntenactie van Annie Bakkertje met de 36.000 euro circa dus € 10.000,-. op. Dit bedrag kan nog verder oplopen, want de verwachte bijdragen van de buitenlandse euro's tegenwoord kan zien over de waren.

There were some funny requests, like the Saab Car Dealership in Amsterdam, who wanted to know if they could buy some old guilders. Normally we would refer collectors to Coin Co, but this was such a special case: 'We've only just found out that our coffee machines do not accept the new euro coins, they only work with guilders! Please help us out, or we can't have our morning cup of coffee!' they said, adding they would double the price, as it was for charity.

The charities' privately organized collections would also add to our grand total. One day we received a call from the Association of Burn Victims in the fishing village of Volendam, were recently a big fire in a local bar had taken many victims and left several young people with horrible burns. 'We've held a collection and now have an enormous load of coins waiting for you. When can you pick it up?' I asked one of the Abcoude volunteers to go to the fishing village to collect the donations. Later that day he called me, laughing:

*"Try not to become a man of success, but rather to become a man of value."*
*- Albert Einstein -*

'Esther, don't they say 'money doesn't smell'? Well, let me tell you, money from Volendam does smell! They've put the coins in fishing buckets! My entire car reeks!'

I also pitched in, collecting moneybags from different locations. My car nearly went through it's axels, with the boot full of coins. This made the headlights shine upwards instead of straight forward; the car almost failed its annual safety test!

## Coins from Japan

The Coins for Care campaign had encouraged many enthusiastic creative people to start their own collection. I was approached by the Japanese Women's Club in Amstelveen, who'd been keen to collect coins in Japan. They were such kind, willing people. However, I found that the communication required some effort, as the Japanese are keen on formality and hierarchy.

To be honest, I had completely underestimated the significance of the Japanese collection, it just wasn't on my list of priorities. When the first load of coins arrived in the Netherlands, I was invited to come along to Karel's depot in Abcoude and meet the Japanese organizers.
I was just getting into my car, wearing my jeans and a T-shirt, when Karel called: 'Esther, please make sure you wear something formal, I've got a whole delegation of official looking Japanese people on my doorstep!' The Japanese Women's Club had done an excellent job; to our amazement they had even succeeded having Japanese Airlines take care of free transport from Japan to the Netherlands!
I had hastily changed into something more appropriate, and made my way to Abcoude where I met the CEO of Japan Airlines, the Japanese ambassador, and the proud representatives of the Japanese Women's Club.
In a neat line we walked from the Japanese limousine to the depot with boxes full of money. 'Please don't tell them the depot is actually just my shed,' whispered Karel who felt awkward with such important guests walking through his garden. I'm sure our welcome was somewhat disappointing, but the Japanese never showed it. The official pictures of the handover were taken and, with many bows and formality, I was presented with a beautiful drawing. I felt terribly embarrassed for not organizing anything for them. I had not even thought of a thank-you-present. I should have made a bigger effort.

The Japanese Women's Club had collected six hundred kilo's of coins, and a box full of European paper money, with a total value of twenty-thousand euro! What an amazing achievement!

*The Japanese Women's Club in Karel's shed! :-)*

FROM PERSBOOM-ISHIKAWA
fax: 31 20 4841835   1.17.02 12:56  P. 3

# Persbericht
## プレス リリース

Amsterdam, 17 Jan. 200

オランダ語（オリジナル）版の

### 日本大使、ご自分の旧貨を
### "COINS FOR CARE" の募金箱へ

**2002年1月18日（金）、ホテル・オークラで開催の新年会にて**

2002年1月18日(金)、ホテル・オークラで開催される合同新年会に招かれている600名のゲストた...、コインズ・フォー・ケア協会 Stichting Coins for ...ale Eurocollecte 共催による" あなたの小銭を大...d " のキャッチフレーズでお馴染みの有名な募金...の旧貨を投じる。...キャンペーン活動が実施されていると知り、この日...ティーに紹介し募金を開始することにした。

...ルテンス Leonie Martens が出席する。パーティ...ションはスピーチのあとに行なわれる。

日本十四時以上日本商工会議所 (JCC) 主催

...キャンペーン

JNS 宛に、話送することも...
郵送・問合せ宛については...
収されたコインは、2月の...

**お問合せ先 infor...**

オークラでの新年会。
日本橋「日蘭協会」での...

[ Coins for Care コイン回収...

### 日本発信 ≫≫≫ COINS for CARE

---

2月19日（水曜日）　　　12版 ◇　　18

### ユーロ導入で旧通貨となる各国のコイン

### 眠っているコインが役に立つ

自宅に眠っているコインをユーロ（欧...材料一週間...に替えて役立...て来ませんか...。来年から...ヨーロッパで...ユーロが導入...、硬貨が導入...れるのに合わ...せ、オランダ...ダリト...

...ロに替え福祉...

---

### 日本から空を飛んで届けられたチャリティー・コイン」プロジェクト

　北海道から沖縄まで・・・。1000通以上の郵便に託された日本中の皆さまのあたたかいお気持ちが、『 チャリティー・コイン 』にすがたを変えて日蘭協会まで届けられ、オランダまで飛び Coins for Care のお手元に渡されました。コインに添えられていたお便りの一部を、日蘭協会のご好意によりここにご紹介させて頂きます。　　　　　　　　（JWC編集部）

● 先日はコインズフォケアのポスターご送付有難うございました。娘の幼稚園と友人からの募金を先日逗子へドライブがてら持っていきました。多くの人の協力と善意により欧州各国の通貨が集まりました。[大磯町在住 女性]

● 大雪の候、平成不況という暗い雲が日本全体を覆いつくし、連日心を痛める事件が後をたたない毎日です。当地の「秋田新聞で魁新報」にて欧州旧コイン募集を知り、多少しかございませんが提供しようと思いました。少しでもお役に立てるのであれば本望です。昔より、「衣食住足りて礼節を知る」と申します。まずは氏の生きていく糧を与え満たしてあげて下さい。私どもも半世紀前までは、大変ひもじい思いをしたやに聞き及んでおります。戦争を知らない世代がどんどん増えていくことは大変よろこばしいことですが、いま一度ご先祖達の苦渋の日々を思い起し暴飲「礼節を知る」の城にて日々を過ごせる繊細うもの...

## Estimation upon estimation

We were thrilled with the extensive media coverage. Our commercials were broadcast widely on radio and television; newspapers and magazines were publishing articles detailing the progress of the campaign, and journalists wanted to know how much money had been raised so far. I tried to avoid having to answer this question as I really didn't have a clue, but at some point we owed it to the public to come up with an estimate. Besides, we were very curious ourselves to find out how the campain was doing so far.

During the corporate campaign, we had estimated that one kilo of mixed foreign coins had an approximate value of twenty-four euros, and this enabled us to inform the public of a mid-collection result: 'Although not officially confirmed yet, we think we've raised about a million guilders so far!' I announced to the press. The news spread rapidly. 'The first million is in!' It was an enormous boost for the volunteers, the sponsors, and everybody who'd worked so hard to turn this campaign into a success.

> 'In order to succeed your desire for success should be greater
> than your fear of failure.'
> - Bill Cosby -

## Head above the parapet

I was overwhelmed with all the positive and heart warming reactions I received. Every day my inbox was bulging with e-mails from people expressing their support for the campaign, which gave me the energy to get through the difficult stages.

However, I was surprised by the number of people who didn't seem to have anything better to do than moan about everything. The Advertising Code Commission contacted me twice during the course of the campaign, informing me there'd been complaints regarding our radio commercials.

One man objected to our slogan 'Whether your name is Mark, Frank or Penny...'. He thought it was misleading, suggesting the British Pound to become obsolete as well. Someone else criticized us for creating the impression that European Coins would become completely worthless. We had to follow the official procedures to reply to each and every one of these complaints.

In the end we were able to counteract all these and other complaints, but it didn't feel good having to focus on these kind of insignificant and negative aspects.

## Creative with publicity

My relationship with the press had changed drastically. When I had started Coins for Care they were positive and sympathetic, showing a lot of goodwill

*Official letter from advertising code commission containing the complaint against our commercial.*

RECLAME CODE COMMISSIE

**STICHTING RECLAME CODE**

Dossier 01.0455

RECLAME CODE COMMISSIE
COLLEGE VAN BEROEP

Postbus 12252
1100 AJ AMSTERDAM

Stichting Coins for Care
T.a.v. de Directie
P. Lastmanweg 12
1181 XG AMSTELVEE

De Commissie acht voldoende duidelijk dat de namen Mark, Frank en Penny als persoonsnamen zijn gebruikt en beschouwt de associatie die deze oproepen met de valuta van bepaalde landen van ondergeschikt belang. Bovendien is niet gebleken dat de naam Penny een verwijzing moet zijn naar de Britse pennies die na invoering van de Euro blijven bestaan. Ierland, dat wel overstapt op de Euro, kent ook pennies, die dus wel verdwijnen. De Commissie acht de uiting niet misleidend.

dossier 01.0557

16 oktober 2001
Amsterdam

Geachte heer, mevrouw,

Wij ontvingen een klacht, gericht tegen een van u afkomstige recle de e-mail van A. de B    d.d. 21 september 2001 treft u hierbij aan

Klager/klaagster gaat ervan uit dat deze wijze van adverteren in s Nederlandse Reclame Code. Hierbij zenden wij u de tekst van de Reclame Code, alsmede info werkwijze van de Reclame Code Commissie en het College van

De Commissie ziet gaarne binnen veertien dagen na dagtekenin schriftelijke opmerkingen ten aanzien van de klacht tegemoet, of de tekst van de commercial. Wij verzoeken u eventuele bijlagen bij uw brief in 8-voud bij te v

De Reclame Code Commissie zal bovengemelde zaak behande vergadering van **dinsdag 13 november a.s.** Indien u de zaak ter vergadering wenst toe te lichten, verzoek binnen 14 dagen na heden aan het secretariaat te laten weten, toepassing onder opgave van de personalia van degene(n) di zal (zullen) zijn.

Opgave van het tijdstip van behandeling ontvangt u indien u laat weten dat u ter vergadering zult verschijnen

Hoogachtend, namens de Reclame Code Commissie

Mr P.E.C. Ancion - Kors

6. **De beslissing**

De Commissie wijst de klacht af.

Partijen hebben, voorzover zij in het ongelijk zijn gesteld, de mogelijkheid tegen deze uitspraak beroep aan te tekenen bij het College van Beroep, onder gelijktijdige storting van het voor de behandeling van het appel verschuldigde bedrag. Het beroepschrift dient binnen 14 dagen na dagtekening dezes in het bezit te zijn van het College van Beroep, waarvan het secretariaat gevestigd is te Amsterdam. Het postbusnummer van het secretariaat is postbus 12352, 1100 AJ Amsterdam.

De Voorzitter

mr J.A.J. Peeters

De Secretaris

mr S.L. van Eijk-Brons

Gewezen door mr J.A.J. Peeters, voorzitter, drs. R.C. Leijns, W. van der Palm, R. Schippers en mr M.M. Wolff, leden.

Amsterdam, 31 oktober 2001

and generating loads of free publicity. This had created the image of *the girl next door with a good idea.*

Together with communication guru Lucas Stassen, I constantly thought of new ways to put Coins for Care in the picture. We eventually resorted to a more targeted perspective. In magazines and articles aimed at women, we emphasized that the campaign had been started by a woman. While for the men's magazines (who were more interested in the hard figures) we detailed the number of coins and currencies. With some clever profiling strategies we managed to get coverage in every newspaper, magazine, and radio or television program. Sometimes even more than once in the same magazine or program!

However, at one point, everything changed. After the commotion surrounding the EuroCollecte debacle, the Free Record Shop row and the disastrous voting module, the press attitude changed from friendly and supportive to hostile. Journalists were now actively digging for dirt.

I launched a major counter offensive, promoting the campaign through the consistent release of positive news, and funny anecdotes, refusing to comment on any problems we had with EuroCollecte. The campaign was well under way, running smoothly and I felt all attention should go to the deserving volunteers. When I watch myself on videos from that time, pretending that we were all one happy family, I don't look very convincing. Of course, the journalists picked up on that.

Whilst I was the face of the campaign, all focus was on me, but I wanted to shift the spotlight to the volunteers and sponsors. It became a personal challenge to pay tribute to my dedicated helpers whenever I could. I had to be very creative to use any given situation to fit a 'thank you' in. It became like a game .

One very early morning I was being interviewed for the breakfast show 'the Bus-stop', in which I had to pretend I was waiting for a bus. 'Good morning, Esther,' the interviewer said, 'where are you going?' 'I'm on my way to our depot in Abcoude,' I replied, creating an opening to talk about the Abcoude network. I was also interviewed by RTL Z, a business news channel. At the end of the interview the presenter asked me to name my favorite stock. I was at a loss, I didn't know anything about the stock markets. From the corner of my eye I saw a screen displaying a current market overview and, fortunately, I was able to make out a few familiar names: 'Well,' I said, 'I don't have any specific advice, but I would most likely pay attention to those companies supporting the Coins for Care scheme,' and I reminded the audience that they could donate their old coins at Albert Heijn (Ahold) and other retailers listed on the stock market.

RTL Z

Despite the publicity not everybody was aware of who I was, or my role in the organization. The manager of the local *Rabobank* once asked me what I did for a living, and when I told him about Coins for Care, he said admiringly: 'Oh I know that name. Isn't that the national collection of foreign coins? I definitely have heard of that! How nice, so you are taking care of the local collection here in Amstelveen?'

## Sharing lessons

I learnt many valuable lessons during the Coins for Care campaign. I thought I should use my experiences for advising other charities, and published a 'Tips and Tricks' sheet on fundraising. I was overwhelmed by the reactions. I had never imagined there would be so much interest in my ideas. Our low cost policy proved especially popular. I was even asked to give a workshop on the topic, and Leonie (the event manager volunteering for Coins for Care) and I organized a few meetings in which charities could exchange experiences and be inspired by each other.

## A very special day

We had set a date to announce how much money had been raised and the exact amount each charity was going to receive. On February 27, 2003, we organized a festive event at the Cobra Museum in Amstelveen.

'I'm absolutely exhausted,' I said to Karel, after working all through the night to get all the numbers and percentages right. At the very last minute I had pulled it off, and everything was ready for that afternoon. I could hardly wait to get it over with...

All charities, volunteers, and the press were invited, and I had prepared a cheerful presentation focussing on our achievement, and the fun we had. I avoided spending too much time on our darkest moments, and would only briefly mention EuroCollecte, the Free Record

*Burst into tears this afternoon after talk with Karel about how to wind up CFC. It will be such a relief. No energy to get anything organized, it's affected me more than I thought*

Shop, and the problems surrounding the voting module.

My mum was attending too, however, my dad was back home in the US after visiting me the week before. 'It's such a shame he can't be here, he would have enjoyed it,' I said to Karel. 'I'm sure he would love to be here, he is very proud of what you have achieved,' Karel reassured me.

The museum was only a short walk from my house. On my way out, I looked over my shoulder and saw a big mess. I hadn't tidied up in days, there were dirty dishes everywhere, and paper and clothes all over the place. It was as if a bomb had gone of. 'I'll clear that up later,' I thought, 'nobody will visit anyway.'

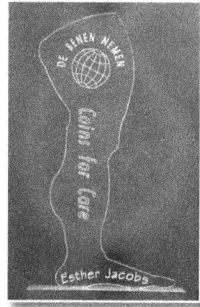

*Eefphotography.com*

*I was given this trophy by an organization specializing in protheses for people who had lost a leg.*

When I arrived at the museum I was welcomed by hundreds of people, queueing to shake my hand and say a few kind words; I was overwhelmed by so much attention. Karel's wife and her friends from Abcoude were welcoming all the invitees.

'You enjoy yourself girl,' they smiled, 'this is your moment!' Just before starting my presentation to the audience of more than three hundred people, I thought I saw my brother in the crowd. But I must have been mistaken, he was at home in America. I didn't give it much more thought as I needed to focus on my presentation.

I introduced Coins for Care, using a powerpoint slideshow with lots of pictures and headlines, presenting our entire history from beginning to end. 'I had no idea what I was getting myself into,' I admitted, 'and at times I was close to giving up, but thanks to so many great people and organizations, we pulled through and were able to turn the campaign into a success.'

The audience, consisting of charity representatives and volunteers were listening intensely. I made sure to make eye contact, and smiled: 'This is your story as well!' I noticed my mum was crying, and I had to look away quickly not wishing to let my emotions get the better of me, yet...

The national news had wanted to know when I was going to reveal the final amount of money raised. 'No idea,' I'd answered, 'just take a seat and all will be revealed. During my presentation the camera man lay before me on

219

the ground, trying to get a good angle. It was a little distracting and, at the moment of truth, I confused the euros with guilders! The whole audience burst out laughing, but not the camera man: 'Can you repeat that please, this time correctly?' he asked, irritated. I tried a second time:

'And the grand total raised is…', but again I mixed up the two currencies. The audience was roaring with laughter by now, and the camera man got increasingly annoyed. 'One more time!' he shouted. 'We've raised the unbelievable total of 16 million euros!' I said. This time I nailed it although all spontaneity had evaporated.

The camera crew left immediately, their work complete. It took me a few moments to regain my composure and resume my presentation, the encouraging smiles and cheers from the audience helping me to get back on track. 'In total we've collected 160 million coins, from a 189 countries, weighing 529.688 kilo's' I shared with the audience. 'If you would pile up all these coins, you'd have a tower of more than 28 kilometers high. If you would lay them side by side, you would be able to cover a tenth of the earth's circumference.' Karel had calculated this, just for fun, and it helped to visualize the enormity of the amount of money.

'We've made the impossible possible! With a cost percentage of only 4 percent we are happy to tell you that Coins for Care will divide five million euros over the 118 participating charities!' I concluded.

*'Success is to be measured not so much by the position that one has reached in life as by the obstacles which he has overcome.'*
*- Booker T. Washington -*

Then Karel strolled up to the microphone. 'We have got a little surprise for you, Esther,' he said, smiling at me. At that moment the mayor of Amstelveen walked into the room, wearing his official regalia and mayoral chain. Making eye contact with me, he walked up to the microphone.

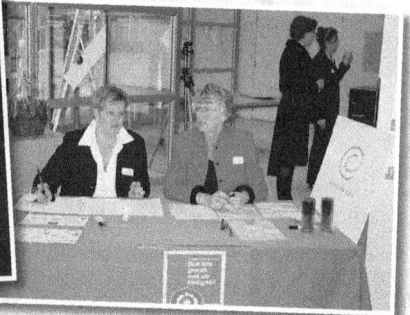

In his short speech he highlighted the importance of volunteering work, and spoke about setting an example for society, all while looking in my direction. I initially thought I was going to be made an honorary citizen of Amstelveen. Most of his words were lost on me anyway. My thoughts turned to my tearful mother, my brother in the audience, and I frantically tried to piece it all together:...

'Is my dad here?' I asked Karel, who just laughed and said: 'You just wait and see.'

At one point he mayor asked me to step forward and presented me with an official looking medal.

'This is the first time I need to pin an honorary medal onto a leather jacket,' the mayor smiled. 'An honorary medal?' I said in astonishment. 'Yes, Esther, you are now a Knight in the Order of Orange-Nassau,' the mayor said, and guided me in the direction of the microphone for a reaction.

I was speechless, overcome with emotions, and initially couldn't say a word. Eventually I managed to compose myself and thanked everyone.

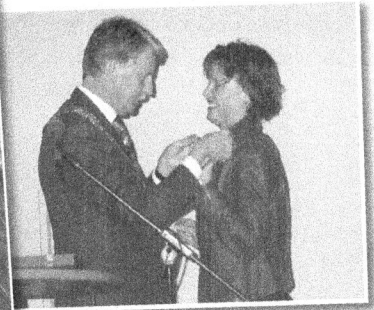

My first thought when I was knighted was "Jaap and Raymond, I am a knight, and you are not, haha!..." Quite immature, isn't it? I can only say my sense of justice is still playing up every so often.

Good old Karel gave me a big hug. I felt a lump in my throat. Karel's love and support meant so much to me. We'd gone through so much together, and I knew I couldn't have managed without him.

Karel then confirmed that my father and brother had come all the way from the US, to be with me on this very special day.

The rest of the afternoon I was in a daze. Everybody was queuing up to speak to me. I finally got to meet many of our trusted volunteers, dedicated people who have played an essential part in turning the campaign into a success.

I met so many lovely people who all tell me how they are inspired by me and by Coins for Care. I does me the world of good! One lady took my hand and didn't I let go anymore, that's how affected she was.
Someone tells me that Holland's one and only Professor of Philanthropy, Mr. Schuyt started referring to me as 'Robin Hood'.

At 7pm we finished. Finally time to talk to my dad...

## Surprise

I was exhausted. 'I don't want to do anything, just sit down,' I told my dad as we were walking home. 'Yes, you should put your feet up and relax,' he replied with a twinkle in his eyes.

My father, brother and sister hiding while the major arrives at the Cobra museum.

When I opened the door into the living room, ready to flop down onto the sofa, I was welcomed by a house full of friends and family who were all cheering and applauding me. So many, lovely people! It was a complete surprise.

I wanted to say something, but was overcome by emotions. There was no holding back; I burst into tears. It was too much; Coins for Care succesful despite all the setbacks, the late nights, the hard work, the Knighthood, and now all these people who had come especially for me...

My sister had been responsible for organizing this secret Coins for Care 'after party', and she had magically turned my house into a true party venue, complete with candles and plenty of food and drink.

I found her in the kitchen: 'Goodness, I can't believe it, what a difference,' I said, 'when I left this morning, it was such a mess!' 'You can say that again,' my sister laughed, and gently pushed me back into the living room to mingle with my guests.

At about eleven o' clock at night all guests had left, and I literally couldn't stand on my feet anymore. I crawled up the stairs to get to my bed, when the doorbell rang; it was Carola. 'I've been at a meeting all day so I couldn't be with you this afternoon, is it too late to celebrate?' she said. 'You're never too late,' I smiled, and turned the lights back on. Over a cup of tea we reminisced about our Coins for Care adventures, laughing at our blunders: 'Do you remember how we managed to persuade Shell?' I laughed. 'And what about that visit to the Quote office, when Jort Kelder invited you to sit on his lap?' Carola giggled. When I finally lay down in my bed, I thought about all the wonderful things that had happened that day, and with a big smile on my face I fell asleep.

For the next three days I was in a daze, it had been such an honor being Knighted. I had always thought it was priviledge being awared to old, wise and important people. 'You've showed the world that nothing is impossible,' Karel and Leonie said proudly. 'Despite all the problems, you have achieved what you set out to do; raising an enormous amount of money for charity, while keeping costs to a minimum.'

I knew Karel and Leonie had moved heaven and earth to get me nominated. Except for a few Olympic, gold medal winning athletes, I was one of the youngest Dutch people ever to be Knighted. It was such a great token of appreciation; to me it meant that my efforts had not gone unnoticed. I decided to dedicate my medal to all the people, especially the volunteers, who'd helped me realizing my dream, hoping it would be an inspiration for others to follow their dreams also.

'A successful man is one who can lay a firm foundation with the bricks others have thrown at him.'
- David Brinkley -

My brother made this drawing of Karel, Leonie and me, all wearing the medal!

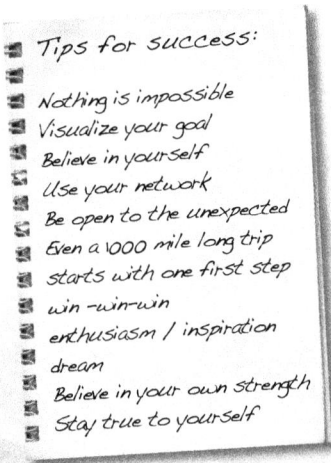

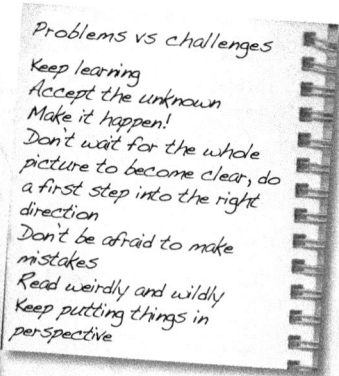

Tips for success:

Nothing is impossible
Visualize your goal
Believe in yourself
Use your network
Be open to the unexpected
Even a 1000 mile long trip
starts with one first step
win -win-win
enthusiasm / inspiration
dream
Believe in your own strength
Stay true to yourself

Problems vs challenges

Keep learning
Accept the unknown
Make it happen!
Don't wait for the whole
picture to become clear, do
a first step into the right
direction
Don't be afraid to make
mistakes
Read weirdly and wildly
Keep putting things in
perspective

Abcoude, 6 april 2002

Dear Esther,

I'd never thought my mail from March 2001 would lead to what has been a fantastic year! What seemed like a bit of simple volunteers work, has grown into a full-time job. I have very much enjoyed working with you. Esther, you put your heart and soul into this project, completely selflessly, and all for charity. Don't ever tell me that young people lack ideals. I have a deep respect for you.

Your golden idea was not immediately accepted by the charity world. You found out about the nonsense, politics, status and plain self interest that exist, unfortunately, even in this industry. You were not deterred by this, but kept going, thinking up creative solutions for difficult problems. You won people over, convincing them by your performances at events and on television. You found sponsors, retailers and CoinCo. Remember the fun we had during the meeting with Albert Heijn?

You were sabotaged many times, and I witnessed how hurt you were by the scheming against you, but time again you got up and try to make the best of it, always working hard for charity. You've had to endure some horrible things, indeed, but you've also seen that there will always be people who are willing to help. All those hundreds of volunteers have held out under your enthusiastic management.

You've been very careful with the spending of the collected money. An acquaintance here, a friend there, you always seemed to be able to find a cheap and simple solution. You've done everything in your power to keep costs to an incredible low. The campaign has become a huge success: a great result!

Trudi and I both enjoyed having you around. It was lovely when you would come round for dinner. The Abcoude troops will miss you! It's going to be quiet without your mails and phone calls.

Dear Esther, we wish you - after a beautiful trip - all the best and fortune, also in your personal life. You are a special -and vulnerable- young woman. We hope you will visit us two oldies in Abcoude every now and then!

Take care of yourself.

Karel de Snoo

# Excuus 14:
# 'Why change? Things are fine the way they are.'

'When winds of change blow, some build walls, others build windmills.'
- Chinese proverb -

## From resistance to action

Now the Coins for Care campaign was over I fell into a rut; I was exhausted, disillusioned, and had no physical or financial reserves left. 'I don't ever want to get involved in any charity project again,' I said, but deep down I knew I should put my experiences of the past years to use.

In the summer of 2003, I flew to New Zealand, hired a motor home, and toured through this amazing country, discovering the beautiful landscapes and fabulous scenery. I enjoyed the solitude and the peace and the setting was perfect for gathering my thoughts and putting the experiences of the past years to paper. It brought back some long forgotten memories, and I started wondering again if I had made the right decision to partner up with EuroCollecte.

By the end of the summer I had written a book. I thought my story had all the ingredients for a good soap opera, and I had given it the working title *Good causes, Bad causes,* referring to the popular Dutch soap-series *Good times, bad times.* I had written extensively about the dirty politics being played within the charity industry, and had reconstructed all my conflicts with the establishment in the minutest details. Retelling it again was nearly as frustrating as it had been in real life.

After rereading my story I understood it would probably cause a scandal in the charity world, and that wasn't my goal. All I had wanted was to be constructive rather than destructive, so I decided to leave the book as it was and find another way of revealing what I had seen.

Despite my wish to retreat from the charity world, I was still being approached from all sides by people sending large amounts of coins and, on average, I received about two hundred e-mails per day. 'How do I know whether a charity is legitimate?' was one of the most common questions, other people even reported cases of corruption, and asked me if I could do something about it. 'I

*My thought of tonight:*

*You can't make darkness disappear by fighting it. The only thing you can do is to bring in light.*

have played my part,' I replied. 'I've raised a lot of money for charity and I know there are things happening which are not right, but I really can't do very much about that.'

*'To sin by silence when they should*
*protest makes cowards of men.'*
*- Abraham Lincoln -*

The queries and messages kept coming in, however, and much of my time was spent on telling people I wasn't the right person to turn to. Slowly it dawned on me that I did have a choice, and I could start using this energy a lot more efficiently. 'If I push myself one more time, maybe I can go that little bit further and make a real change this time,' I thought. I knew I wouldn't be on my own, I now had the support of all those anonymous donors who were discontented about how the charity sector was operating.

*'It's easier to do a job right, than to explain why you didn't.'*
*- Martin Van Buren -*

## Frustrated by the charity world

© NRC, February 23rd 2003.

'Frustrated by the charity world'
*Initiatiefneemster Esther Jacobs over 'Coins for Care'*

Egbert Kalse was the first journalist who I confided in. This young, enthusiastic, reporter worked at the economy desk of the NRC newspaper, and wanted to look deeper into the charity world. He was honest and straightforward, well informed, asking intelligent questions; I immediately felt at ease with him. 'I would like to openly talk about my frustrations with the charity world, but I don't want to cause any scandals,' I explained the dilemma I was in.

After Egbert had promised me he wasn't going to write anything I didn't agree with, I told him everything I had learned and seen, while

Friday lots of mail. telephone calls and radio interviews. Lots of reactions to the harsh NRC article. Frustrated by the charity world. I call the journalist to tell him about the positive reactions, and he tells me he's even received a text from Wouter Bos (chairman of the ruling parliamentary party)! What on earth is happening?

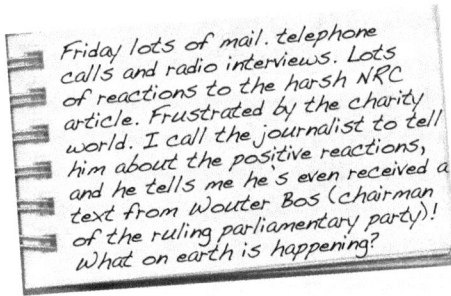

arguing for more transparency in the charity industry. 'If all charities publish their figures on their websites, then the donors can decide for themselves whether they think that organization is operating well or not,' Egbert transferred my thoughts to print perfectly. It was a well written article, however, I wasn't entirely comfortable with it being so straightforward; until then I'd always made sure I was noncommittal in my communication with the press, but Egbert assured me: 'These are your personal statements, your feelings, your experiences, a very well argued, criticism of the charity industry. You illustrate your case with plenty of examples and explanations and offer solutions for the existing situation, believe me, it's a perfectly balanced, coherent story.'

I couldn't have known the article titled "Frustrated by the Charity World" would cause so much upheaval.

## The donor association

**donateurs**vereniging
nederland

The NRC article did stir things up. A year after its publication I was still receiving e-mails from individuals and companies offering their help, as during the Coins for Care campaign. There were a lot more people out there, who were trying to make the charity world more accountable. 'I recognize these issues only too well' or 'I have tried for years to promote more transparency, why don't we join forces?'

One of the people who wrote to me was Diane, an old university friend from Nyenrode. I hadn't seen her for a long time, and we decided to meet for a coffee. During Coins for Care she'd been working for War Child and we had clicked immediately. It was so nice to chat with a like-minded soul, who just wanted to do good without having a hidden agenda. We shared the same ideas about how to fundamentally change the charity industry, and there and then we had the idea for the Donor Association, a consumer organization for donors, with the objective of initiating a dialogue with the charities. We wanted the donating public to become more critical of the charities they were donating money to.

sponsored business cards
for the Donor Association

The current affairs show NOVA was broadcasting an item about charities from the Millionaire's Fair. They wanted to interview me and discuss my experiences. 'You see, we're looking for someone with an independent view, who can objectively comment on the charity sector,' they said.

'Diane, it's a perfect opportunity for introducing the Donor Association on national television!' I said enthusiastically. 'We should have a website we can refer to, which contains all the information we have collected so far,' added Diane. 'Oh my god, the recording of the show is in only two days time!' she looked at the invite, but then her eyes lit up: 'It'll be tight, but I think I know how to officially establish the association and have a website up and running in time,' she said. 'You wait and see!'

# Donors United

Donors demand transparency

How good is a good cause?
Donors want to know their money is spent.
Now there is a website.

Don't ask me how we did it, but it worked. A lawyer we knew helped us register the association, and Diane and I spent a whole night finalizing the content of our website. 'I'll ask Jordan van Bergen whether he can put it online,' said Diane, and explained that this super volunteer offered internet solutions through his *GIVE for Free* foundation, which was available to all small charities. Jordan spent on average twenty hours a week of his free time on this foundation and had been doing so for the last eight years. He could work wonders and within a few hours a he had the website up and running.

Forty-eight hours later we arrived at the Millionaire's Fair, exhausted but thrilled with what we had achieved in such a short time. I was asked to tell my story on camera, while strolling through the fair, interviewing a few Dutch celebrities about their experiences with charities. That same evening, the Donor Association was officially launched.

## Critical mass

One of our first initiatives was organizing some brainstorm sessions, bringing together all those people who had offered their help. We thought this might lead to some innovative ideas. Many people had been actively trying to change the charity world for years, but had never met or cooperated with each other.

These sessions were incredibly informative, even for someone like me, who was quite familiar with the sector. We were able to figure out which tasks would be realistic for the Donor Association, but I also noticed that change within the charity industry was not always appreciated by everyone.

We needed to find out how many charities had been registered in the Netherlands, estimations varied from a few hundred according to the CBF, to 250.000 charitable foundations and associations as registered by the Chamber of Commerce. Registration was not obligatory anywhere, except at the tax office, but they did not publish their figures. Putting all the available information together, we estimated there were about 30.000 active charities in the Netherlands. 'They have an approximate revenue of between four and twenty-billion euros,' I was told.

During one of the brainstorm sessions we discussed the possibility of creating some sort of overview of the legitimate charities. 'Can't we have some kind of check mark or stamp, so it's immediately clear which charities are considered a high quality and which are not?' Unfortunately, although it was a feasible option, the information was just not available and in addition Dutch charities aren't even obliged to publish their annual reports. 'The only thing we can get is an overview of all active charities and publish their details on our website so the donors are able to contact them if they have any questions on what happens to their donations,' we decided. We had already created an original name for the project: 'DonorInformer'

After assessing what information should be included in the DonorInformer, we found a sponsor who would build the internet system at no cost. We informed the government of our new database.

Then something strange happened. Instead of working together with us, the CBF and VFI started a counter offensive, building their own system, which obviously required a significant amount of funding. Another entrepreneur who had attended our brainstorm sessions, also came up with his own scheme. The tax office designed a new registration process, only available to them, and the Ministry of Justice launched a terrorism alert system for charities. In the space of a few months, about five, more or less similar systems were developed, and charities were being approached by all these different parties asking for their data. Again, money, time, and energy were being wasted, because people stubbornly refused to hand over control over their own projects, choosing not to benefit from a shared system.

Despite the five different DonorInformer copies, a first step towards transparency had been made, and determined to stay positive, we organized another brainstorm session. I suggested we should grant an award to the organization with the most transparent annual report. To my surprise I was approached by PricewaterhouseCoopers, a well known accountancy firm with similar plans. 'Why haven't you done anything yet?' I asked surprised. 'We had not found the right partner yet. But now we do: would you be interested in joining us?' they replied.

Together with PricewaterhouseCoopers, we outlined the conditions which should be met by the charities' balance sheets, as well as a tough procedure to come to an objective judgment. Morris Tabaksblatt, a well known Dutch captain of industry, agreed to be the chair of the jury panel. I was asked to take seat in the jury.

A few months later the first prize was awarded to the Dutch Cancer Foundation.

*de **transparant** prijs*
voor de beste charitatieve verslaggeving

'Once we have all the figures from the charities, we can just put them next to each other and do a simple comparison' I had thought when we started. Unfortunately, it was not as easy as that. One of the charity experts explained that you can't just assume that the charity with the lowest expense rate is also the best charity. 'Some charities only raise funds in the Netherlands, but their mother organization is situated in another country, like SOS Children Villages International, so the money is transferred abroad. Other charities, like Medeçins sans Frontières have medical personnel on their books and execute their own help aid relief missions. This will entail completely different costs structures. You just can't compare the two.'

'Surely it's possible to compare two organizations which are doing essentially the same thing?' I tried. 'There will always be a difference between charities, even if they are not so obvious at first sight. You just can't standardize, it would be like comparing apples with pears. Take, for instance, two organizations in South Africa, both dispensing condoms to fight the Aids epidemic, one working in the cities, the other in the rural areas. The charity in the city has an advantage when it comes to logistics, the city is where most people live and they are able to hand out many condoms against relatively low costs, whereas the costs per condom are much higher for the other organization. The importance of their work, however, is no less. I was very impressed with these vivid explanations and decided to use them on our websites and in our interviews.

# The critical donor

*87 percent of all Dutch donaors want to know how their donations are being spent*

Nederlanders geven jaarlijks zo'n 1,7 miljard euro aan goede doelen – een redelijk stabiel bedrag. De laatste jaren wordt de roep om transparantie wel steeds groter. ,,Waar komt mijn geld terecht? En heeft dat effect? Dat zijn hele legitieme vragen."

Wilma van Hoeflaken

tell me, want ze wilden uitleg over de goe- de doelen. En inmiddels zeggen ze *show me*, want ze willen het zelf zien."
Die ontwikkeling is al een paar jaar gaande. Daarom verstrekt het Central Bureau Fondsenwerving (CBF) sinds 1996 keurmerken aan goede doelen. Het CBF, in de jaren 20 van de vorige eeuw op- gericht om de armenzorg te coördineren en tegenwoordig nauw betr... spreiding v...

dt kosten die de goede doelenorganisatie maakt om geld te werven, bijvoorbeeld de kosten van een reclamecampagne of een mailing of de salariskosten van de medewerkers die zich met fondsenwer- ving bezighouden. De gewone bureau- kosten zitten er bijvoorbeeld niet bij." De drempel...

233

## Overhead costs

Another huge point of discussion were the overhead costs, which the CBF describes as: 'Costs which are not directly related to the goals of an organization.' This is not very objective or specific, so I decided to investigate.

I proposed the following scenario to many 'experts', asking for their opinion: what is a charities objective is to provide wells in Africa. There is no doubt the 'man with the spade' who is actually digging the wells, is definitely part of their objective. However, transport is needed to take him to the waterhole; a permit is required to start digging, and most likely, a bribe in order to obtain this permit. You might also need to set up a local office to administrate. Which or all of these costs should be included in the 'costs directly related to the objective' and which were to be considered overhead cost? There didn't seem to be a simple answer to this question.

Charities were very reluctant to talk about which part of their funds was being spent directly on their objective and what was spent on their overhead. Every organization suggested a definition which was as favorable to them as possible. The charity trade organizations like VFI didn't dare to come up with a calculation, because they knew they would always disadvantage a few groups they were representing, and still until this day donors have to guess.

## A History lesson

The brainstorming sessions had been incredibly valuable, it had provided me with many new insights on how the charity industry works. I now had some good ideas to prepare the sector for the changes which were needed to create more transparency. The smaller charities were very enthusiastic: 'We've been trying to bring change for a number of years, but it's hard; we're up against the big guys,' they said, it appeared the inner-circle of established charities dominated the sector with their cooperation schemes. Their influence was enormous, something I had encountered personally during the Coins for Care campaign. It was only when I learnt about their history that I started to understand why that was, and why they were so opposed to change.

**"An annual report is a confidential document"**
Transparency is not common at charities

Ruim de helft

In the early days health organizations like the
Cancer Foundation, The Heart Foundation, and the
Foundation for Arthritis raised money by door-to-
door collections. These long established charities
united themselves with CollectePlan, and until this
day they decide who participates in the annual collection weeks. 'It's impossible to get in between,' the
other charities complained.

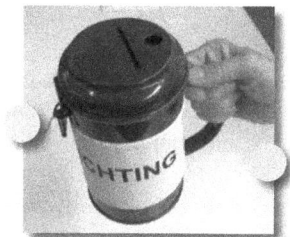

In 1925 CollectePlan launched a national monitoring agency, the CBF, in order
to distinguish themselves and protect their position. Although the CBF is said
to be an independent and objective body, its board is formed by members
of CollectePlan, and a few mayors representing the councils, with a view to
organizing the necessary permits. The VFI, the charities' branch organization,
was also created by CollectePlan; they supply three of the five members of the
board. This was why the VFI had been so uncooperative with informing their
eighty non-collecting members of a possible participation in the Coins for Care
scheme.

The VFI also runs the secretariat of the NGF (Dutch Society for Fundraisers) at
whose annual congress I experienced such an unexpected success with my
Coins for Care presentation. It showed how much influence the established
charities had; how the shared power was divided amongst an old boys network
of friends and acquaintances, and how members of boards simply swapped
positions between the different organizations.

It wouldn't benefit the interests of the establishment if the exact number of
registered charities were published, the CBF had given out approximately
three hundred quality labels. If the total number of charities would turn out to
be much higher, it would dramatically diminish the CBF's authority, and the VFI
would also lose its significance with the limited number of one hundred and
twenty members. It was obvious that these organizations wanted to leave the
infrastructure unchanged, especially since they were seen by the government
as the main advisors on regulation and registration, with which huge govern-
mental subsidies were linked.

*'You can fool some of the people all of the time, and all of the*
*people some of the time, but you can not fool all of the people*
*all of the time.'*
*- Abraham Lincoln -*

235

## Moldova

Dorcas, the charity that had helped Coins for Care tremendously by providing most depots and volunteers for Coins for Care, invited me to visit a few of their charity projects. Armed with a box full of pencils for the local children, I got onto the plane towards Moldova. It was a perfect opportunity to see a real-life aid effort in action.

Moldova is one of Europe's poorest countries, bordered by Romania and Ukraine. Unemployment is high with nine percent of the population out of work. The local Dorcas representative explained that alcohol, violence, and incest are amongst the countries problems. Young girls often become the victim of international human trafficking. Hoping for a better life they are lured abroad, but then sold into prostitution or, in extreme cases, the organ trade.

I traveled with a number of entrepreneurs who were looking to adopt a project. We visited two refuge centers for young girls, a cantina (soup kitchen), an activity centre for young children, and the homes of a few local families. The poverty was heart breaking.

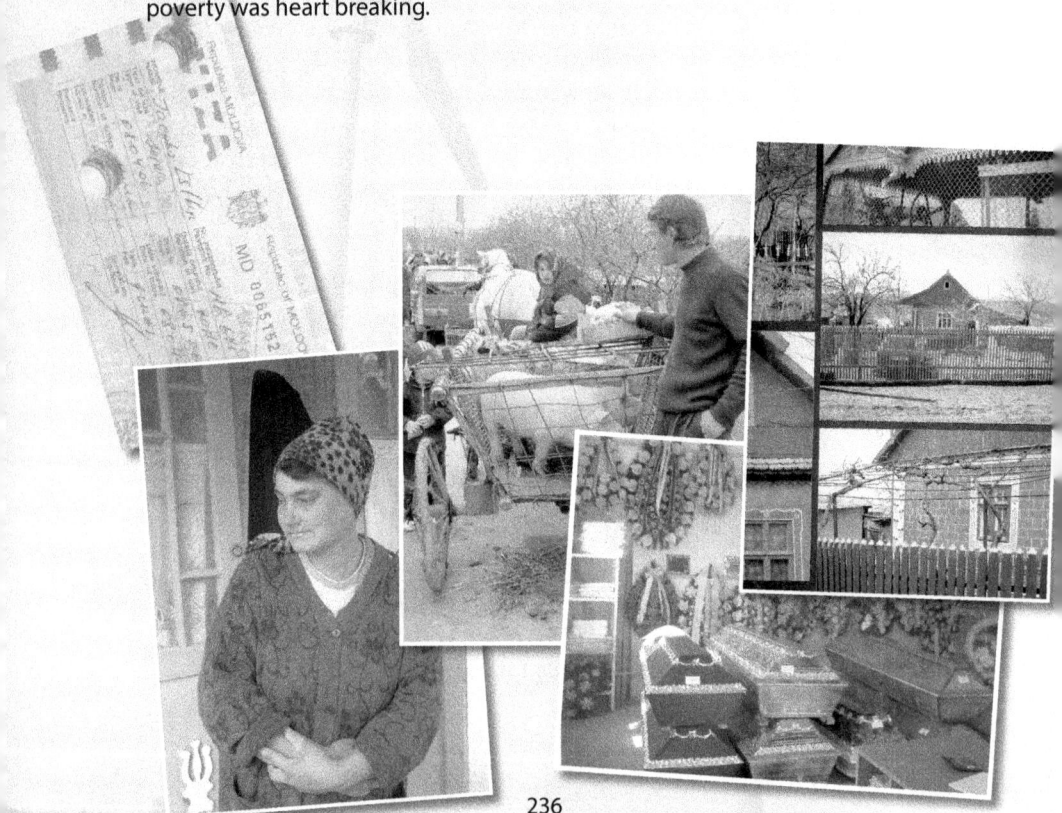

We couldn't help everyone. How on earth were we going to decide on who needed help most urgently? 'The Moldovans are a proud people, which can be deceiving,' explained our guide. 'They'll try to portray themselves better than they are. They rather paint their house before buying food. They sometimes even lie about their dire situation.'

I indeed met a family who were impeccably clothed, but it was clear they had not eaten any decent food in days. Another family were the proud owners of a cow, but their house was in shambles. It was impossible to decide who was worst off.

We had no doubts in the case of a terminally ill woman, who was in hospital with cancer, not even forty years old and slowly dying. She had no other option than to leave her four children, the youngest still a baby, with her alcoholic husband in their tiny, cold house, that had only two rooms. I felt numb and powerless, she deserved so much better, and we decided to help her and her family.

After a day of 'disaster tourism', exhausted by seeing so much hardship, we went back to the luxury of our hotel, but for the poor woman and for so many others there was no such escape…

In Moldova I was confronted with the dilemmas faced by so many aid programs: how to determine who needs help and also, who doesn't? Should you help people according to your own standards, or to the local standards?

Another important issue was the role of religion or evangelization, as the local orthodox institutions sometimes objected to help from foreign churches. We also spoke about the situation after a charity pulls out of an aid program; will the local people be able to continue the project, or does it collapse? There are no simple answers to these questions: good or bad, black or white, giving aid isn't as straightforward as sometimes thought.

After this experience I was even more motivated to find a method to judge the work and efficiency of the active charities, it all depended on the readiness of charities to be registered and the publication of their figures. We needed transparency, which would provide us with the information and details needed to set up a standard of comparison.

## Share, explain, repeat

The brainstorm sessions, the numerous chats with people from the charity sector, and my own experiences, had given me a clear picture of the dilemmas facing the charity industry, and through this I was able to better profile the Donor Association and its aims.

Mama Cash, and international women's fund, asked me to do a presentation for a group of women who had inherited a considerable sum and wanted to do something meaningful.
At the end of my speech, a woman came up to me and said: 'I think it's great what you're doing, I would really like to support you,. To my astonishment she continued: 'I'd like to donate 25.000 euros to enable you to properly establish the Donor Association.' It was the first time I was actually offered money instead of services or products, I was ecstatic with happiness, and so grateful for this generous offer, we were in desperate need of funds.

I tried to get my message across to as many people as possible. Donors, charities, policy-makers and journalists. 'Everyone needs to know that you can not just determine or communicate whether a charity is trustworthy or not. Charities will have to publish their details and finances on the internet, so donors can draw their own conclusion and make their own choices.'

I received a lot of attention from the press, almost every newspaper asked for an interview, which I was very happy to give. However, virtually every journalist was asking if I had more scandal to report about the charity sector.

## Publication of management salary makes charities nervous

### Volunteers furious about director's salaries

Two young journalists from *de Volkskrant* newspaper persisted, and I gave them a little tip: 'Ask the charities for their cost balance sheet,' I said. 'I guarantee you they'll only mention their fundraising costs.' I'd never expected Pieter Klok and Xander van Uffelen to follow up on my advice, and subsequently publish a legendary article on the salaries of the charities' managing directors. It caused such upheaval when it came out that the CEO of the Heart Foundation was receiving an annual income of 170.000 euros. The board of the foundation thought they could bury the story by simply firing him, but this only added to the controversy.

> *'Any man worth his salt will stick up for what he believes*
> *right, but it takes a slightly better man to acknowledge*
> *instantly and without reservation that he is in error.'*
> *- Andrew Jackson -*

'More transparency is needed,' I told the press. 'If the Heart Foundation had been open about why it was so important to hire an expensive cardiologist as their managing director, then the donors would have been able to decide for themselves whether they'd agreed with these arguments or not. Being transparent prevents being caught off guard by what is published in the press.'

The charity industry was at a loss and didn't know how to respond to the criticism surrounding the salaries, so they did what they always did, they closed ranks and bought themselves some leeway by establishing a committee.

© www.jessecartoons.com

To my surprise I received a call by Herman Wijffels, the chairman of the Social and Economic Council of the Netherlands. He asked me if I wanted to be the representative of the donors in this committee.

It was refreshing to work with Herman, an open-minded realist, and focussed on problem solving; an attitude which contrasted sharply with the dirty politics I had encountered so far in the charity sector. With his enthusiastic team we developed a Code for Good Chairmanship, including a salary guideline.

As a result of the committee's recommendations and increased public pressure, most annual reports now detail the salary of the manager director. This still doesn't give much insight into a charities actual overhead costs, but it shows that change is possible, even if it's achieved in tiny steps...

## Chari-Guru

As it became apparent that the 'annoying Esther Jacobs from Coins for Care' was back, I was repeatedly invited to talk about my plans for the Donor Association. At these meetings, CBF, VFI and other organizations did their utmost best to put themselves and their policies in a positive light. 'You know, ours is not an easy job,' was their reaction when confronted with my criticism.

For a while I became kind of (in)famous. In 2004, *de Volkskrant* newspaper nominated me for the election of 'Dutch citizen of the year.' I ended in 14th place, just after the prime minister. In the same year the magazine Communication put me on their cover under the header 'Chari-Guru'. The leading charity magazine proclaimed me the third most powerful person in the Dutch charity industry. In 2005 I appeared on another cover, *P+* magazine photographed me like Robin Hood, on a horse, and captioned it: '*Esther Jacobs, the charities' worst nightmare.*'

© *de Volkskrant, December 23, 2004.*

| | | | |
|---|---|---|---|
| 1 Ayaan Hirsi Ali | 10071 | 26 Arjen Robben | 1869 |
| 2 Ahmed Aboutaleb | 9749 | 27 Anky van Grunsven | 1836 |
| 3 Prins Bernhard | 9595 | 28 Ruud van Nistelrooij | 1816 |
| 4 Theo van Gogh | 8994 | 29 Tonke Dragt | 1788 |
| 5 Job Cohen | 6709 | 30 Rob Oudkerk | 1646 |
| 6 Geert Mak | 6063 | 31 André van Duin | 1584 |
| 7 Leontien van Moorsel | 5666 | 32 Arnon Grunberg | 1504 |
| 8 A.B. | 5154 | 33 Neelie Kroes | 1235 |
| 9 Wouter Bos | 504? | 34 Martin-Jan van Mourik | 1201 |
| 10 ...n de Waal | 4982 | 35 Dick Advocaat | 1154 |
| ...Verdonk | 4641 | 36 Maria Goos | 1058 |
| 12 Geert Wilders | 4275 | 37 Paul Verhoeven | 1005 |
| 13 Jan Peter Balkenende | 3829 | 38 Aart Jan de Geus | 946 |
| 14 Esther Jacobs | 3388 | 39 John de Mol | 906 |
| 15 Peter R. de Vries | 3358 | 40 Marja & Bert | 834 |
| 16 Arjan Erkel | 32.. | 41 Herre Kingma | 822 |
| 17 | | 42 Jeroen van der Veer | 711 |
| 18 Pieter v.d. Hoogenband | 2929 | 43 Heleen van Rooijen | 653 |
| 19 Remco Campert | 2897 | 44 Van Houts en De Ket | 608 |
| 20 Inge de Bruijn | 2775 | 45 Leo van Wijk | 490 |
| 21 Esther Vergeer | 2484 | 46 Monic Hendrickx | 446 |
| 22 Karel Appel | 2296 | 47 Cees Geel | 355 |
| 23 Morris Tabaksblat | 2217 | 48 Joep v.d. Nieuwenhuyzen | 295 |
| 24 Jan-Hendrik Blemond | 2022 | 49 Tjibbe Joustra | 280 |
| 25 Marco van Basten | 1920 | 50 Fons van Westerloo | 212 |

'I can just imagine Jaap, Raymond, Klaas and these charity 'hotshots', sitting at their breakfast table, opening their newspapers and choking on their toast... *There she is again*, they'll think. Another day ruined,' laughed Karel, who'd also got involved in the Donor Association.

While writing this book I uploaded one of my first television interviews about the Donor Association onto YouTube and found that, although spontaneous and enthusiastic, full of good intentions and energy, my message was some-what erratic. Over time I would become more professional and develop a polished and convincing pitch.

I must have been the terror of the establishment: they were aware that I knew about all their wheelings and dealings, and that I could generate a lot of publicity. 'You appear so trustworthy, since you do not have any personal interest or investment in the industry,' was Lucas Stassen's analysis, who was now communication advisor to the Donor Association. Lucas was right, I didn't receive any compensation for my work, I was not particularly interested in setting up a career in the charity world, and I didn't need to chum up with anybody; I was completely independent.

'They do not have any influence over you, and they are uncomfortable with that, so they want to keep a close eye on you. *Keep your friends close and your enemies closer...* That's why they invite you to take part in all these discussion groups,' explained Lucas.

At least they were taking me seriously now. That much had changed... I set out to prove the charity industry that they need not be scared of me, that I just wanted to make a constructive contribution. After various explorative meetings it became clear that the charities were not necessarily against change, but only if this could be achieved in their own space and time.

I was contacted by a student, asking if she could do her practical placement at the Donor Association. I couldn't believe my luck, I had never had a personal assistant! Noor took a seat next to me in my office at home, asked me where she should start and took care of the phone calls, arranged meetings, the e-mail and clearing up the office. Noor was a gift from heaven! Her help enabled me to focus on the most important issues and be a hundred times more produc-

Transparency; more understanding, more money

tive. I decided to place a few more ads, inviting students to do their internship at the Donor Association. It resulted in six interns working for me. My house slowly transformed into an open plan office with desks and chairs everywhere,

She won this Flair bouquet

Ellen Hensbergen (26):

My internship with Esther Jacobs was an incredibly valuable experience. Esther is a true source of inspiration, not just for me, but for a lot of others, too. We worked from her home, which was very special. It's amazing how she devotes her time and energy to her charity work: more than 13 hours a day and she doesn't even get paid for it! What she achieves is even more incredible, she is someone...

*One of my interns nominated me for this gargantuan bouquet of flowers. The womens magazine Flair chose me out of hundreds of other women dedicating themselves to worthy causes.*

242

© De Volkskrant

## Chased by begging letters

Achtergrond | Banken mogen adreswijzigingen niet doorgeven aan goed doel

and a mix and match of second hand computers, either borrowed or given. Just like with Coins for Care, we'd managed to get sponsorship for most office supplies.

### The Ombudsman

We received many reports of suspicious or unpleasant situations:

- 'I work for an exclusive design furniture supplier. Last week we had a special delivery to an expensive canal house. It appeared to be the office of a local charity, and the furniture was destined for the director's room. Surely that isn't right!'
- 'One sister Michaela keeps sending me letters with coins included, asking me to return them, including a donation. How do I stop this?'
- 'Click4Care announces on their website that with every click of the mouse a certain amount is being donated to charity. Our organization is being mentioned on their site as one of the benefactors, but we've never received any money.'
- 'When my grandfather died, I asked all charities to remove his details from their databases, however, they keep sending him letters and brochures.'
- 'I stepped down from the board of a charity, because of some malpractices going on; could you look into that?'

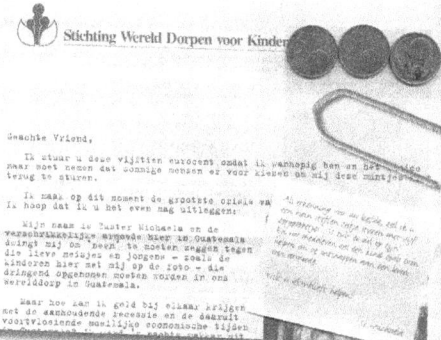

All these cases were dealt with during our board meetings. Some reports were quite serious and it would have been possible to investigate them one by one, but it would have taken all out time and resources. If we really wanted to make a difference we should aim for a higher, more structural level. We needed to use our time and resources efficiently, and decided to focus on issues which were relevant to many donors, instead of individual cases.

## Amount of charity-spam annoys donors

A small charity foundation approached us and complimented us on our initiative: 'We are a small asset fund, which means we have our own money and we don't have to raise any funds. We're currently supporting a number of projects and where possible we blow the whistle on issues within the charity world. We know, for instance, about some serious child abuse cases in Brazilian orphanages, it's very upsetting, but so far we haven't found a solution yet, do you think you can do something for us?' she asked.

'It sounds heartbreaking, these are such terrible offenses, and it sounds as if you've already tried everything possible to do something about it. Unfortunately we are not in a position to act upon these kinds of reports yet, I am so sorry,' I replied.

I made some inquiries to see if any other party could pick up these individual cases: 'Only if they would have our quality label,' the CBF answered. The VFI also said they'd only deal with complaints about their own member organizations. The government couldn't do anything unless there were indications of terrorism or tax evasion, and the press were only chasing scandals, ...nobody seemed to be willing to take responsibility for the functioning of a charity, and to make sure they do as they promise. It proved that there was an urgent need for an objective organization or independent body, where donors could turn to if they had complaints or suspicions. 'The only thing I can commit to at this stage, is that we will promote the importance of a kind of ombudsman for charities, who can investigate these kind of reports,' I promised the lady.

When I started the Donor Association, I thought I would be able to provide donors with a list of 'good' or 'bad' charities, but now my message had become a lot more complex. Transparency is harder to sell than top ten-lists or scandals.

My dilemma was how to proceed: climb the barricades and mobilize the masses (donors) to force charities to change, or stay close to the charities and

www.jessecartoons.com

guide them step by step on the long and difficult journey towards transparancy? The first scenario would raise a lot of support amongst the donors and the media, and we'd gain a lot more power, but we would distance ourselves from the charities, and our message would fall on deaf ears.

Our main objective was to unite donors and start a dialogue with charities, so we settled for the second option: close negotiations with the charity industry. By constantly aiming to be one step ahead, we were right on top of any new development, and we kept pushing the charities to review their processes. The Donor Association was on their case!

Continually navigating between giving information, raising public awareness, pushing the charities, and at the same time not burning our bridges behind us, meant we were less outspoken, and therefore less interesting for donors. Our counter stalled at three thousand members.Not many donors felt the need to take a more rational approach; their donations were simply emotionally motivated. Or they donated out of habit, tradition, or religion; or just randomly. Only a small group of critical donors demanded transparency, but they did not necessarily want to be part of a 'movement' or organization. The established charity organizations were all too eager to jump on the bandwagon: 'Who exactly is the Donor Organization representing?' they kept voicing. This strategy had the desired effect: after a while the attention shifted from the message to the messenger.

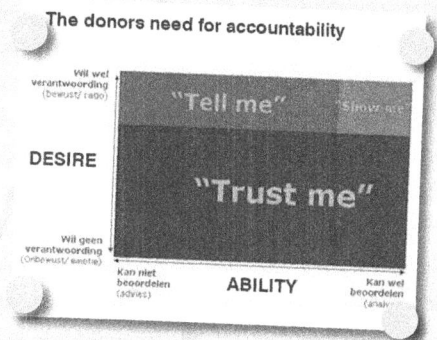

The donors need for accountability

Wil wel
verantwoording
(bewust/ ratio)

"Tell me"    Show me

DESIRE

"Trust me"

Wil geen
verantwoording
(Onbewust/ emotie)

Kan niet
beoordelen        ABILITY        Kan wel
(advies)                            beoordelen
                                   (analy

## Comfort level

Over the last few decades, the relationship between the charity sector and the donors had changed from 'Give us your money and trust us', to 'Tell me how our money is spent' This is when Oxfam Novib had introduced their do-it-yourself

*Trust me, Tell me, Show me. The model the donor organization used to explain the various types of donors.*

philosophy, steering away from 'just' giving money, and instead providing people with the means to take charge of their own situation. With the Donor Association we had arrived in the 'Show me' era: 'Show us what you do, so we can decide whether we should donate.'

It's definitely a sign of the times. A century ago you'd start organizing your funeral if a doctor would tell you you'd only had three months to live, whereas now you'd ask for a second opinion, or search for information on the internet, trying to form your own opinion. In our present western society there seems to be a lack of trust for authority.

Everybody reacts differently to change, some people build windshields, others build windmills; I could empathize with both reactions. Despite being close to stepping down, following the resistance I'd met during the Coins for Care campaign, I realized I was at last in a position to make a difference.
I noticed a deep reluctance to change amongst the established charities and other official parties: 'It's going well as it is, donors give their money and do not have complaints, so for what reason should we change the way we operate?' they would argue. These organizations derived the right to exist from their members and would not want to upset any of their followers. The government, however, was scared of having to take responsibility for the registration and controlling measures, and played the ball back to the different ministries and trade organizations. The donor's attitude towards the charities ranged from highly critical to complete indifference.

It's always nerve wracking when you enter unknown territory, to leave the security of what you know, for the uncertainty of not knowing. Some see this as a threat, others see opportunities. I would like to get the message across that you should never let these kind of insecurities hold you back.

*'If you do what you've always done, you'll get what you always got.'*
*- Mark Twain -*

## A black hole?

'How do the charities spend our donations?' concerned donors would ask me frequently. I decided to use Coins for Care as an example and together with my team of six students, I started to investigate how the money donated by Coins for Care had been spent. We approached all participating charities for a statement (to put on our website, as initiatlly agreed) and compared these with their annual reports.

Some organizations, like Liliane Fund, were able to justify to the very last cent what the donation had been used for. However, we found that there were also some charities who had not stuck to the agreement: 'We've spent the money on our objectives,' was their vague answer.
There were organizations who claimed to have spend the money on something completely different from what was stated in their annual report. Others blatantly refused to report any details of what they had done with the Coins

for Care funds: 'That is none of your business, it's got nothing to do with you,' was the reply from one of the charities. A small number of charities had even closed down. That nice lady from 'Help Ukraine,' never answered her phone, and there's been no trace from her, nor our money ever since!

Even after the Coins for Care campaign had officially ended, people were still sending in foreign coins. I had already divided this money twice over the participating charities. But with some of the charities refusing to explain how they spend our money or even closing down, I asked my board if it was still a good idea to donate the extra money to the charities. 'Considering the situation and since the campaign has finished long ago, would it not make more sense to invest this money into the Donor Association and use it for the promotion of transparency?'
'That might seem logical, but you'll have to be very careful,' was the advice of both the Coins for Care board as well as the Donor Association board. 'You're being closely watched by people from the entire industry.'

*We read our way through piles of annual reports.*

It took a few months to look into all legal possibilities and consequences. 'The campaign stopped officially three years ago, all money was paid out, including two extra payments. You've since set up the Donor Association,

*In the Coins for Care project report we accounted for each penny, including the gift to the Donor Association's transparency project. The report was send to all charities and could be found on our website.*

you're campaigning for more transparency, and still people are voluntarily sending you money. Legally, it shouldn't be a problem,' reasoned my lawyer and an attorney.

In the end Coins for Care donated 40.000 euros to the Donor Association. This gift was included in Coins for Care's project report and communicated on both websites, to all participating charities and the press. For months nothing happened and I almost forgot the donation ever took place.

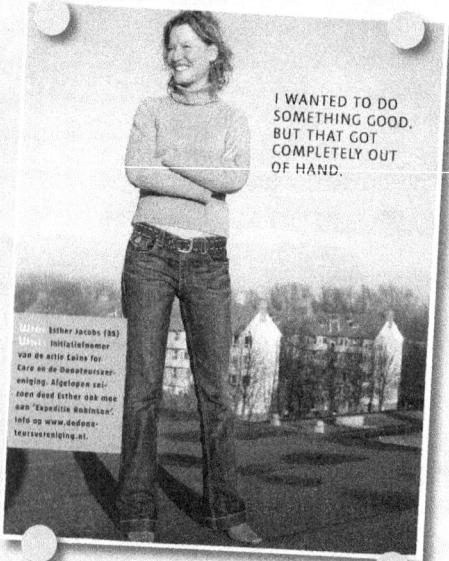

I WANTED TO DO SOMETHING GOOD, BUT THAT GOT COMPLETELY OUT OF HAND.

Esther Jacobs (35) initiatiefnemer van de actie Coins for Care en de Donateursvereniging. Afgelopen seizoen deed Esther ook mee aan 'Expeditie Robinson'. Info op www.donateursvereniging.nl.

'Seems like we made so much fuss over nothing,' I remarked to my Board. 'You better watch out,' warned a few board members of the Donor Association, and I wish I had listened to them; in hindsight it would have prevented a lot of misery.

## I want out!

After their dismissal from EuroCollecte, Jaap and Raymond had remained active in the charity industry and I bumped into them again at a conference, which was chaired by Klaas van de Poll. To my surprise Raymond was giving a workshop on ... ethics, and Jaap was present as reporter for his own fundraising magazine. It really got to me, this was completely inappropriate. I looked around. Didn't anybody understand how outrageous it was that these three men were here at all? Let alone in these prominent functions?

Confused, I tried to discuss it with a few other attendees at the conference. They all reacted indifferently: 'Esther, just cut it out, your personalities just clashed, that's all, you really need to stop making a deal out of it.'
I sensed that nobody fully understood what had happened, or worse still, didn't want to know. I couldn't stay there any longer, and with tears in my eyes I made a quick exit.
Dizzy and sick with emotion I got into the car, desperate to get away, it was the only thing I had on my mind.
Then I heard an advert on the radio which would change everything:
'This is your last opportunity to sign up for the Survivor TV show, and spend two months in the wilderness!' I quickly thought of the possibilities, two

months on an uninhabited island, without email and telephone, far away from the charity world...it was like a dream to me! On the spur of the moment I signed on, and three weeks later I found myself on a deserted island in Malaysia.

> I felt literally sick, and drove straight home.

The first two weeks were spent hidden in a cave with Marnix, a Belgian police officer, later Douwe joined us, we built a raft and rowed to another island where we joined other contestants who, until then, had been unaware of our existence. I had never thought that the welcome I received on that island would be so similar to what I was trying to walk away from.

*'You don't have to be sick to get better...'*
*- Coachingscalendar*

# Excuse 15:

# "What will people say?'

> 'Sing like no one's listening,
> love like you've never been hurt,
> dance like nobody's watching,
> and live like its heaven on earth.'
> - Mark Twain -

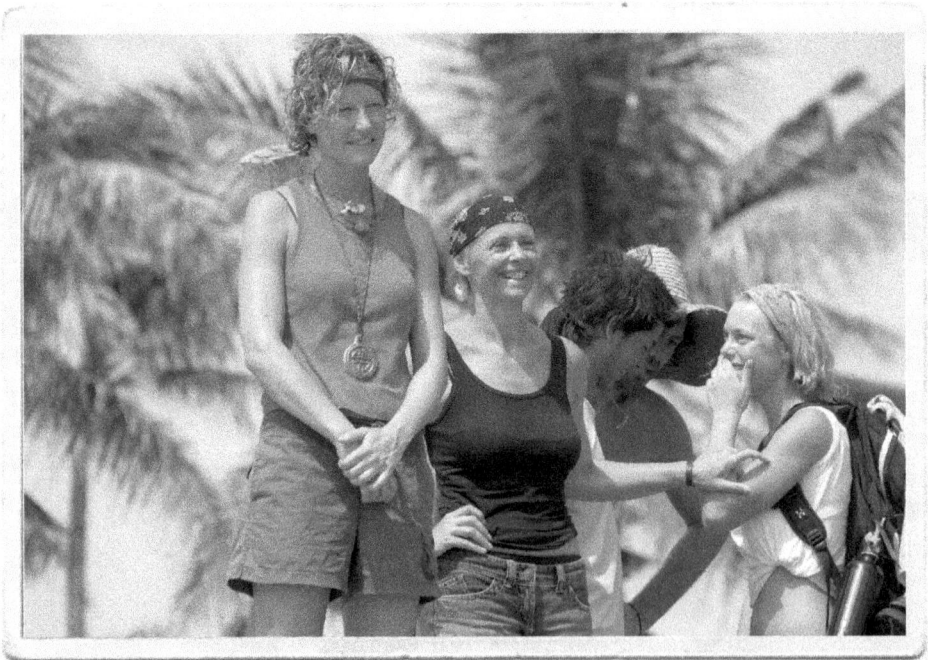

© Photo: Jeroen van Amelsvoort

## Survivor – part two

Marnix, Douwe and I had been swimming for hours, pushing the raft over open sea. The cave, which had been our home for so many weeks disappeared slowly out of sight, and the island where the other candidates were waiting for us was now getting closer and closer.

© Photo: Jeroen van Amelsvoort

The doctor, traveling on the boat next to us, kept a close eye, checking every so often for hyperthermia or sunstroke.

Halfway we were told to have a break, and were given a few pieces of fruit to eat, but Douwe was so scared of sharks that he refused to stop: 'Keep swimming, keep swimming!' he said, trying to push the raft ahead, despite the production team's boat obstructing the way.

The last length of the journey was tough, we had to swim against the current, my foot hurt with cramp, but we were nearly there, and finally landed on Mensirip Island.

Once we walked onto the beautiful white sandy beach the feeling of triumph was indescribable. 'We made it!' we yelled and I enjoyed the soft warm sand under my feet, which were sore from the rough surface of the cave and the water. 'It's seems like paradise!' I sang, doing a little dance and taking in the breathtaking views.

'Look coconuts, as many as you can eat!' I yelled, and started to collect them; this was exactly how I had imagined a deserted island to be like.

Marnix was overcome by emotions. 'This is a personal victory for me,' he said with a lump in his throat. 'This hellish journey is symbolic of the defeating of my disease,' he explained. 'Can you imagine, only eight months ago I was receiving chemotherapy.' It was a very emotional moment. As for Douwe, he was just happy to be out of the water.

We found a trunk containing a watermelon and three beers as a reward for our successful crossing, the alcohol, combined with the euphoria worked like a charm, and a few minutes later Marnix and I sat giggling on the beach.

'I think there might be a letter in the trunk,' slurred Marnix. 'Better leave it where it is...' I giggled.

© Photo: Jeroen van Amelsvoort

'Silly people,' Douwe said in disapproval. For some reason the alcohol hadn't affected him as much.

'Congratulations and welcome to Mensirip,' the letter read. 'In three days time you will be expected on the top of the hill,' were the instructions. 'Oh no,' I sighed, 'yet another three days before we meet the others.'
We thought we should make the best of it and made a huge fire on the beach, Douwe and Marnix hacked the coconuts and roasted the flesh until caramelized while I cooked some rice in the fresh milk. 'What a lovely party meal,' we sighed afterwards, relaxing in the shade.

© Photo: Jeroen van Amelsvoort

That night we slept on the beach. The sand was lovely and soft, so comfortable after the hard rocky floor of our cave.

## The others

'Fellow Survivors, here we come!' shouted Marnix and I, while walking up the hill. Douwe was very quiet. 'I was voted off last week and I don't think my coming back will be much appreciated,' he explained. 'Come on, when they hear about our challenging raft voyage, they will probably change their minds,' we reassured him. Marnix and I couldn't wait; we were full of silly jokes, trying to figure out what was going to happen next.
'The boats are here,' we heard the production team say over their radio's, while they were walking up and down nervously. Ernst Paul, the presenter of the show, was waiting on top of the hill. Marnix and I hadn't seen him since the auditions. Those two weeks that we had spent in the cave he'd only been visiting the other candidates.

© Photo: Jeroen van Amelsvoort

'Esther and Marnix,' Ernst Paul said in a ceremonious voice, 'we ask you to choose your team-members from the pictures you found in the cave.' We looked at each other, this was so exciting. 'Douwe, you'll have to decide for yourself which team you want to join,' said Ernst Paul. 'Marnix,' said Douwe quickly. 'I like him.'
While choosing our team members, we tried to take into account each others preference. Marnix let me have the 'wise Indian' whose picture had

so appealed to me, and I made sure Marnix could have the 'cool dude', who he had found interesting. Slowly it dawned on us that we would be each other's opponent from now on. 'I'd never thought I would have to compete with you,' I whispered. 'Neither did I,' Marnix answered, 'but remember, it is just a game.'

One by one the contestants were called to an open space on top of the hill. I saw their shock when they were told to join their new team. 'We had our suspicions that something was about to change,' they said later, 'because we'd been asked to take all our belongings with us.'

There was another surprise: Nicole, the girl whose picture we had used for the game of draughts, returned to the group after she's been voted off

© Photo:
Jeroen van Amelsvoort

earlier. The other contestants looked on, disapproving. They had been surviving the competitions and elimination challenges for two weeks already, and had not expected Douwe and Nicole to return, nor to be introduced to some new candidates.

'Marnix and Esther, you are now the new leaders,' Ernst Paul announced. We were both given a necklace with an 'immunity amulet', and were told to stand on a special platform next to our teams. 'As a leader, you're granted immunity, which means you cannot be voted off,' Ernst Paul said. Marnix and I looked at each other, that did sound good. Not aware of our strange position, we thought the immunity would allow us the time to get to know every one, without being voted off prematurely. But when we took a closer look at the faces of the other contestants we understood it might well work against us.

'The leaders will now receive a flag belonging to the new camp,' Ernst Paul explained. The 'wise Indian', a skinny old man with long grey hair tied into ponytail, refused to acknowledge me, pressing his lips into a thin, angry line. It was horrible, standing there on a raised platform, with this amulet around my neck and holding a flag. I couldn't wait to speak to my new teammates and tell them where we had come from. I was also dying to know what they had been doing over the past few weeks, but the opportunity to talk was being postponed for as long as possible, probably for a maximum effect.

'Shortly we'll start the challenge. Marnix and Esther, you two will be asked to compete against each other,' continued Ernst Paul. The test was a memory game, and during the game Marnix and I each had to stand on a wobbly plank held up in the air with ropes, supported by our team members.

'Esther and Marnix, please place the strongest people of your team at the ropes,' was the instruction from Ernst Paul. Carl, a sympathetic looking man with curly brown hair, who was in my team, stealthily indicated which people I should put where, by nodding his head. The wise Indian was placed right at the back. 'John is physically gone,' Carl explained later. 'He wants to go home; he's even asked us to vote him off at the next council.'

A fragile looking blond girl took up the very last position. 'Meredith,' asked Ernst Paul, 'your new leader seems to believe you are the weakest in the group. What do you think of that?' I wished Ernst Paul would stop referring to me as leader, and putting all kind of words in my mouth! To my relief Meredith said: 'I think this is correct at the moment, I do feel I'm the weakest right now.' Phew, I was saved for now, but this incident illustrated how the situation could be manipulated by the production team, and that every single word or action would be put under a magnifying glass.

Marnix and I were given a fifteen minute long detailed description of our individual team members, after which we had to answer twenty questions. I failed the first two questions; it was incredibly frustrating. I was so keen to get on with my team members and contribute to a common success. For every wrong answer, a team member would have to let go of the rope, and my little plank was now slanting dangerously. Marnix answered only one question incorrectly. ...so my team eventually lost. To be fair, we'd never stood a chance in the first place, because Elbert, the bodybuilder in Marnix' team was probably as strong as all my team members put together.

*The scene of our first test.*

The winning team was rewarded with a Spa treatment, which included a massage, and a glass of champagne in a Jacuzzi on the beach...

Within my team, the mood was sombre. 'The boats will take you now to your island,' we were told. During the trip to our new camp, I tried to lighten the mood, and bombarded my fellow contestants with questions: 'What's been happening so far? What have you been eating on the island? What kind of tests have you done? What's your daily routine like?' I hardly got any reaction, only the two youngest contestants, Meredith and Wim, every so often produced a brief answer, mainly out of politeness. John 'the Indian' kept himself to himself, as well as Carl; there was nothing left of our initial 'click'.

## Tainted leadership

Once we got to our new island, Meredith and Wim, who had spent the previous week on this island, called out: 'Hey, that's weird, that hut wasn't there when we left this morning' On the beach we saw a tiny wooden shed on poles, and when we explored it we found a mattress with sheets, a pillow and a mosquito net. A true piece of paradise on a deserted island. 'This is the leaders' hut,' said reporter Rudi the Rat.

© *hraudiovisuals.com*

The camera crew was filming everything. I looked at the wooden construction. It had space for just one person, but it might fit two, maybe even three.

I remembered the advice from the survival expert: 'If you're ever offered a bed, no matter what the circumstances, just refuse it.' I longingly looked at the hut. My back had still not recovered from sleeping on those rocks, and I tried not to think of how nice it would feel to lie down on that soft mattress, with its cool sheets. 'Can we take turns sleeping in the hut?' I asked Rudi hopeful. 'This is the leader's hut, it's meant for the leader,' was Rudi's cryptical answer. 'Is the leader allowed to share the hut with someone?' I asked, still exploring all possibilities. 'I'll have to check with the production crew,' answered Rudi.

A bit further down the beach was another hut, which was a lot bigger, but not very sturdy. 'We built that hut last week,' stated Meredith and Wim proudly. 'We all slept there. It leaks a bit when it's raining, but other than that it's fine.'

As if on cue it started raining, and we quickly took shelter in the hut. 'So, since when did you know you're the leader?' Marleen broke the silence. She was a Belgian woman in het fourties, who had remained quiet so far.

'Literally, only just now, at the same time as you were told,' I was eager to explain my situation. 'I don't really want to be a leader, it's something the production team has decided, so let's talk about what we should do,' I suggested. But nobody reacted.

'I'm sure you've also read the SAS survival book?' was John's snide remark. 'Of course, I wanted to be well prepared for this expedition,' I replied, but John looked away disapprovingly.

This is heading in the wrong direction, I thought. I have to find a way of showing I have something to contribute to the group... My mind was frantically searching for something to say. Not really thinking it through, just wanting to please, I told the others about my knowledge of medicinal plants. 'In the cave

## The contestants
### The sensible 40+

Carl (43), huisvader. Lijkt sympathiek, maar ontpopt zich meer en meer tot huichelachtig en rancuneus persoon.

Douwe (49), schipper met het uiterlijk van Robinson Crusoe. Werd er voor het spel begon al uitgeste md, maar kreeg een herkansing in het geheime kamp van de dertigers. Is geen groepsmens en kan behoorlijk zeuren.

Marleen (44), sportspecialiste. Valt nauwelijks op en houdt zich, mals bijna alle Belgen in de expeditie, angstvallig op de vlakte.

Margriet (50), zangmanager. Zij werd al direct in de eerste aflevering weggestemd.

Elsje (47), eigenaar eetcafé. Een vrouw die wil laten zien dat ze geen poppemieke is. Ze moest de expeditie vroegtijdig verlaten, omdat ze haar enkel brak.

Elbert (49), eigenaar van een sportschool. Sterk, met een klein hartje. In het eerste team ligt hij niet lekker, maar het gaat beter in het tweede team. Wordt in aflevering 5 geveld door heimwee.

John (52), rentenier. Heeft een probleem met autoriteit. Kan het niet verkroppen dat Esther de leider wordt en begint met Carl een agressieve, onmenselijke hetze tegen haar. Is trots op zijn directheid, maar verdraagt geen kritiek.

Annita (45), administratief medewerker. Moeder van twee dochters, geschieden en wil nu later ... ze sterk ge...

### The 'lost' thirties...

Esther (35), marketingconsultant. Begon gezellig met Marnix op een rots eiland, maar de expeditie werd voor haar een nachtmerrie toen ze als leider werd aangesteld en twee onsympathieke, inflexibele oude mannen tegenover zich trof. Had het onder andere omstandigheden vast beter gedaan, want is zéker sympathiek.

Marnix (37), rechercheur. Doorzetter, sympathiek persoon, zijn leiderschap in de nieuwe groep levert geen enkel probleem op.

there weren't any plants,' I joked, 'but now I'm hoping to find something edible in the jungle.' My remark was badly timed. Everybody was now staring at me, not saying a word. They probably had no idea what to think of me.

By now it was getting dark. 'Let's go to sleep,' someone said. The hut was leaking and crowded with all seven of us, there was not enough space to sit, let alone stretch out. 'Why don't we use the other hut as well, and have a few people sleep in there,' I suggested. But there was no reaction. While we got ready for the night, I persuaded Meredith and Wim, the youngest participants, to join me and sleep in the leader's hut. It seemed logical: three of us would be out of the rain and the others would have more space in the big hut. The next day three others could sleep in the leaders hut.

Even though they had agreed, Meredith and Wim did not come back after they went into the big hut to get their stuff. I walked to the doorway, feeling lonely and not sure what to do. Everything I said seemed to be misunderstood or interpreted wrongly. 'Are you coming?' I asked Meredith and Wim. 'No,' answered John in their place. 'They stay here, with us, you go and sleep in your fancy hut,' he snarled.

I quickly explained the idea of rotating a couple of people in the leaders hut each night, but there was no response. 'Well, if everybody is going to sleep here, then I'll join you,' I decided.

'No, you can't stay here, it's already too crowded here!' John said before anybody could react. Silence and tension hung heavy in the air.

I hesitated. I felt tired, cold and wet, and just wanted to lie down. Staying on my own in the comfortable, dry leader's hut was so tempting, but I knew that would be the most stupid thing I could do. So I stayed there, in the doorstep, feeling horrible.

At some point Nicole broke the silence and said: 'There's still some space next to me, Esther,' and she moved up a little. Silent disapproval for the both of us filled the hut. I wormed myself into the corner. Everything was clammy and wet. But I was so exhausted. Without saying anything I lay down, and fell into a deep sleep.

The next day the nasty comments and discussions continued, there were constant remarks about my leadership and the acquired immunity. 'Please, let's just talk about it' I offered. 'I did not ask for this position and hate it just as much as you do. Let's explore our options and see what we can do to improve the situation,' I suggested. I really did not want to be the leader.
But John and Carl, clearly the informal leaders, simply refused to be near me or acknowledge me. Only the youngsters were willing to talk, but were quickly overruled by John and Carl.
In a quiet moment Nicole came to me. 'Esther, I am so sorry about what is happening, it is not fair how they are treating you,' she said. Her sympathy made me feel a little better. 'However, you need to understand that I'm in difficult position,' she continued. 'They voted me off and now, all of a sudden, I'm back again. I just have to think about myself and I can no longer support you, I'm sorry,' she said softly. I completely understood her situation and thanked her for being so honest with me.

Maybe I could change the situation by making myself useful? I noticed John and Carl making a fishing net out of an old piece of mosquito netting. I walked over and offered to help. 'I don't believe you've spent the last two weeks in a cave,' John blurted out. 'I know it sounds far fetched, but it's the truth,' I said in defense. 'You're lying,' John said imperturbable. 'Look,' he said, turning to Carl, 'she hasn't even got hairy legs, which proves her story isn't true.' I was taken aback for a moment, but then I burst out laughing: 'Well, you can wait for hairy legs all you want, but I'am blessed with nearly invisible blond hairs.'
'Nonsense,' said John to Carl, ignoring my explanation. 'She and that Marnix were both wearing one of those red bandana's. The crew must have given those to them, to make them more credible. But it's clear they are both models, straight from a casting agency,' John raged on, while Carl nodded in agreement. I was baffled, where did he get these ridiculous ideas?
The two men, who continued to bully me, reminded me of Statler and Waldorf, those two disagreeable old men on the Muppet Show, who are always trashing the rest of the cast. 'How do I look?' John asked Carl. 'Well, uhm, I suppose like me?' answered Carl, pointing at his wild hair, beard and bruised body. 'Exactly, but both Esther and Marnix look as if they've just walked out of a fashion magazine!' John hurled like a madman. I couldn't help laughing uncomfortably, this was more stubbornness than I could handle.

© Economics/ Lex Dirkse

These kind of ridiculous 'theatrical' discussions occurred repeatedly over the next few days. John and Carl always had a different argument for why I should leave: the cave was a lie, I wasn't a real candidate, I shouldn't have accepted the leadership, I had been the last to arrive, they didn't know me so well, they didn't like me, and so on. 'Esther, if I were you I would just save my face and leave quietly,' was Carl's advice.

## Group dynamics

I tried to ignore the nasty comments, and kept looking for ways to improve the situation. At some point Wim and Meredith sought me out in secret and admitted they thought it extremely unfair how I was being treated. 'Being the youngest in the group, however, we can't just bypass John and Carl,' they explained their difficult position. 'I appreciate you coming to see me,' was the only thing I could say.

**It went wrong from the very first moment**

Esther Jacobs (35) deed mee aan het televisieprogramma Expeditie Robinson 2005. Ze werd aangewezen als een van de leiders van de twee groepen die op verschillende eilanden leefden.

Esther: "Het eerste jaar dat Expeditie Robinson op televisie kwam vond ik het geweldig. Toch gaf ik me het jaar daarna niet op om mee te doen. Het groepsgebeuren is niets voor mij. Ik ben een einzelgänger. Daar komt bij: ik kan nog geen twee uur zonder krant! Maar vorig jaar had ik het helemaal gehad met mijn drukke leven. Ik zat in de auto toen ik de radiocommercial hoorde: 'Vandaag is de laatste kans om je op te geven voor Expeditie Robinson'. Dat deed ik. Drie weken later vertrok ik naar Maleisië. Het spel begon anders dan verwacht. Op Schiphol zou ik de andere deelnemers ontmoeten. Maar alleen Marnix was er, en met z'n tweeën vlogen we naar de andere kant van de wereld waar we gedropt werden op een eiland, om in een groot te overleven. Waar de achttien andere deelnemers waren, was onduidelijk. Pas twee weken later vertelden we bij de rest gevoegd. Marnix als leider van de ene groep, ik als leider van de andere. Vanaf de eerste minuut ging het mis. Twee mannen in mijn groep accepteerden mij niet. Of eigenlijk, ze accepteerden de spelregels niet: ik werd aangewezen als leider zonder dat ik daarom gevraagd had. Maar omdat ze zich niet tegen het spel konden afzetten, projecteerden ze hun onvrede op mij. Voordat ik kwam hadden zich allang vrienden en gewoontes gevormd. Niemand wist van het bestaan van Marnix en mij. En toen werd plotseling hun vertrouwde wereld omgegooid. Door andere omstandighe-

den gaan mensen zich anders gedragen. Je zag dat heel duidelijk gebeuren. Stap voor stap werd mij het leven in de groep onmogelijk gemaakt, continu door dezelfde twee mannen. En ze trokken de andere vier deelnemers van mijn groep met zich mee. Die voelden zich allemaal ongelukkig met de situatie en hadden me best een kans willen geven. Maar niemand durfde daar openlijk voor uit te komen. Ergens snap ik best waarom: je wilt te allen tijde voorkomen dat je zelf de pispaal wordt, dus ga je meedoen. Je steekt in ieder geval je nek niet voor een ander uit. Daar komt nog bij, een ouder iemand - zoals de twee mannen in mijn team - wordt in een groep niet snel gecorrigeerd. Daardoor lukte het ze de sfeer op het eiland in een paar dagen absoluut grimmig te maken. Ik ben op sommige momenten absoluut gekwetst door de groep. We vingen bijvoorbeeld altijd krabbetjes omdat je op die pootjes uren kunt kauwen. Dan had je in ieder geval het gevoel dat je aan het eten was. Op een ochtend hadden we er ontzettend veel gevangen. Ik liep in mijn eentje nog even langs het strand om kokosnoten te zoeken. Toen ik terugkwam waren alle krabbetjes op. Niet één was er voor me bewaard! Op die momenten voelde ik me eenzaam. Na tien dagen in de groep werd ik weggestemd. Weg gepest, heb ik ook veel gehoord. Toch voel ik uiteindelijk dat negatieve van weggepesten niet zo. Ik weet dat het niet persoonlijk was, maar dat het allemaal een gevolg is van hen groepsproces. Dit is wat je in een groep mensen kunt verwachten: iemand is altijd het mikpunt. Gelukkig sta ik stevig in mijn schoenen. Ik weet wat ik waard ben en daarom heb ik aan mijn expeditie-ervaring geen complex overgehouden."

© Top Sante.

Even Marleen, the sensible older woman, came and sat with me to share her thoughts. 'Esther, I really am at a loss,' she said. 'When I was with John and Carl last week, we had a real good time. But somehow they've changed, I don't recognize them anymore,' she continued. 'Did you know that John had even asked us to vote him off as soon as the opportunity would arise?' she asked. 'Yes, Carl told me something like that during our first test; John was physically at the end, wasn't he?' I replied. 'Well, ever since John saw you standing there holding that flag, his fighting spirit has completely returned', Marleen continued. "I'm staying,' he told me through clenched teeth on top of that hill,' Marleen explained. 'I'm sorry I did not realize the impact of their behavior any sooner. Now it's too late. In the end you were the last to join, so if we would vote, we would probably vote you off. However, you have immunity...I think that's the true reason for their behavior,' Marleen concluded somberly.

How is it possible that four out of six people show their support, and still you're being bullied?' the interviewer asked me. 'I don't know either,' I said, 'I guess it's a new group and everyone fears for their own position. Carl and John clearly have the upper hand in all this.'

'And how do you feel about that?' the interviewer continued. I took a moment to think about that, glad that somebody actually cared enough to ask me how I felt. 'I feel lonely,...and powerless,' I sighed, 'I am trying so hard, but I keep walking into a wall of resistance,' I felt my throat choke up.

'Will you be okay? Do you think you can hang in there a little bit longer?' was the interviewers next question. I pulled myself together, 'Well, I start every day afresh. All I can do is just be myself; hopefully things will change for the better. So, yes, ...let's see what tomorrow brings,' I answered. Immediately the reporters attention shifted. Before I knew what was happening, she walked off and spoke in her walkie talkie to the production team. 'She's staying; the circus can start!' Then she returned to me and continued the interview.

So her questions weren't at all about my personal well being; the only thing they cared about was the show. I realized I was completely on my own.

During another interview she enquired into what kept me going. 'I try not to let it get to me personally,' I explained. 'Not personally?' she raised her eyebrows, 'but they are being personal all the time!' 'Yes, but that's been happening right from the very moment I was introduced, on top of that hill. Even though they didn't know me, they immediately opposed my position as a leader, and accordingly vented that out on me as a person,' I continued. 'The fact that they seem to have a different argument every day means they're looking to justify their feelings. I would have taken it personally if they'd said after a couple of days or even after an hour: 'Esther, we just don't like you.' In that case I would have probably left. But they haven't even bothered to find out who I am, so rationally I know that it cannot be personal. But still the way the're treating me is not fair. It makes me feel upset and lonely.

## A fair chance?

'I would like to give up the 'privilege' of leadership and immunity,' I requested Ernst Paul, the presenter and producer of the show. I was at the end of my tether, and completely fed up with the situation. 'I just want to be like the others,' I explained.

'That's not possible. These are the rules, and they simply cannot be changed,' Ernst Paul countered, without any room for discussion. 'But I don't think I'll be able to take it much longer,' I protested. 'The others clearly don't want me here,' I muttered, defeated.

My team, all extremely demotivated and weakened by the constant discussions, lost the elimination test. We had to vote someone off that same afternoon. I decided to use the Tribal Council to officially ask my team to give me a fair chance. If their answer was no, I would give up and leave the island.

I hadn't realized what consequences this would have until I told Ernst Paul about my decision. Immediately the production team called the contestants one by one for an individual chat. Apparently the producers were concerned for the reactions of the other participants during the Tribal Council and were desperately trying to control the outcome.

'Well, Esther, it's very clear that they don't want to let you go yet,' Meredith confided in me when she came back from her session, which had lasted over an hour. 'They spoke to me for ages, but I'm not allowed to talk about it,' she added. One by one the others returned, and quietly we waited for the Tribal Council to start.

I was convinced this would be my last afternoon on the island, and decided to prepare a festive meal. 'Look what I brought, I think this would be a perfect occasion for this,' I smiled while I took an unlabeled can out of my rucksack. John jumped up: 'Where did you get that?' he asked suspiciously. I explained that Marnix and I had each been given a can, during our time in the cave. 'We could have eaten them before we came to meet our new teams,' I explained, 'but I preferred to share this surprise can of food with you.' At that very moment I was called away for my interview.

When I returned a bit later, I discovered that the others had already cooked and eaten. 'There's a little bit left in the pan for you,' they indicated from a distance, as they all huddled together. Not exactly my idea of a celebration meal, or a team builder at all...

© Photo: Jeroen van Amelsvoort

It got later and later. I suspected there was a lot going on behind the scenes. By the time the Tribal Council began, it had already gotten dark. Ernst Paul confirmed in front of the entire group that Marnix and I had indeed spent the first two weeks in a cave. He even described our challenging voyage with the raft, which he called 'unique in the history of Survivor.' Then he emphasized again the rules of the show: The leaders have complete immunity. 'That's how we play this game,' he said, looking us in the eye, one by one, and we all had to confirm we understood.

'Esther asks you to give her a fair chance,' Ernst Paul continued. My heart was in my throat; my fate would be decided right then and there.

'Marleen, what's your answer?' the presenter asked. 'I'll give her another chance,' Marleen said, barely audible. John and Carls cast her nasty glances, but Marleen looked straight ahead. Then Meredith and Wim were asked the same question and they also answered positively. I couldn't believe it, what had the production team done to make them change their minds?

'Like I said before, she won't get another chance from me! said Carl. 'No,!' grumbled John, as expected, when his turn came. Nicole was on my side.

'So, the majority of you is happy to give Esther another chance,' summarized Ernst Paul. 'Does that mean you'll stay with us, Esther, and accept the rules of the game?' he asked me. 'If the group is giving me another chance, then I'll accept,' I replied. 'Okay, then we'll continue with the voting,' Ernst Paul concluded.

As was to be expected Nicole was voted off. She had to leave the island immediately. I was the only one to say goodbye to her, even though I didn't know her very well, and I gave her a big hug. 'Good luck Esther,' she said, 'you're going to need it.'

In complete darkness we were guided back to our camp. 'What did you do that for?' I heard Carl whisper through clenched teeth to the others. 'I thought we'd agreed not to give her another chance? Now we're stuck with her.'

'But the crew told us...' someone protested. 'I don't care about the production team!' Carl thundered. 'We make our own agreements and stick to them, alright? Next time everybody votes for Esther! Understood?' I felt disheartened, I had been given a new chance alright, but it had not even lasted five minutes.

The next morning the mood was hostile. 'What are you still doing here?' someone shouted at me. I decided not to get caught up in any of it, and started looking for edible shells in the surf, keeping a safe distance from the group. 'Why are they asking why you're still here?' my interviewer sounded confused. 'I

© Economics/ Lex Dirkse

thought they had given you another chance?' I told her about what I had heard just after the council, and the crew were shocked. 'I never stood a chance,' I said in desperation.

## Tipping point

When I returned from that interview, I felt the mood had somehow changed, I couldn't put my finger on it, and it wasn't until after a few minutes that I realized everyone was acting normally!

Marleen explained how she'd stood up and told the group that the situation couldn't go on like this. The mean remarks would have to stop, for everybody's sake. 'It's horrible when the mood is so bad, we all suffer from it,' she said in a motherly way.' I realized how I had, indeed, suffered under the constant bullying and was very relieved to hear it would be a thing of the past.

It was as if a little magic wand had been waved. I wasn't being ignored any longer, instead the others now involved me in the daily routine and even their conversations. The sudden change felt weird in the beginning and not only for me; I saw Wim and Meredith constantly looking at the older contestants, checking if it was really okay to talk to me.

Someone had caught a huge fish and I offered to clean it, having practiced this skill daily in the cave. 'If you skin it and cut the meat into thin slices I will cook you a delicious dinner,' suggested John. He turned out to be an excellent cook. He covered the fish slivers in flour and fried them in oil, while cooking some rice in fresh coconut milk.

During this wonderful meal we all sat together, the mood was relaxed and open, and for the first time we had a proper conversation that gave me some insights into what had happened.

'I can see you're not really a group person,' Carl said in a friendly way. The others nodded in agreement, looking at me expectantly. 'That may be right,' I said, 'but how can you tell? Is it not just the situation I have found myself in?' I asked curious. 'Oh no, it's your attitude, your reactions, it's obvious that you feel more at ease on your own than amongst other people,' they explained.

'I'm at my happiest when I'm with other people, so I'll always look for company,' Meredith said, casting a sweet glance at Marleen, who was hovering over her like a mother.

'You were also reacting a little weird on the boat,' Wim added. I looked at him puzzled. 'When we were on our way to the island, you started questioning us about who did what, and what we'd eat, and so on...' 'I guess you, sort of, overwhelmed us,' said Meredith. 'It was just too much.'

I was perplexed, they had interpreted my enthusiasm as an interrogation by a new leader... Didn't they realize that after two weeks in a cave in isolation you just can't wait to meet your fellow contestants?

'It might also have to do with you being Dutch,' was John's analysis. 'Belgians are a bit more reserved and less direct and outspoken. You're already a very outspoken person, let alone after two weeks in isolation, I think it was just too much for us,' said John.

'I'm so relieved we can talk about that openly now,' I smiled, 'I honestly didn't have a clue,' I admitted, and added diplomatically: 'The events of the past few days pushed me into a defensive mode which might have confirmed all those prejudices you had about me.' We kept talking well into the night, enjoying the discussions and the relaxed mood.

Despite all that had happened, I had intensely enjoyed the island and its nature. Even during the days with discussions I had meditated every morning, trying to release the negativity. Now, in this new situation, I could truly relax. The island looked even more beautiful than before, and felt incredibly happy to be in such a magical place.

DEAR ESTHER,
CHOOSE THE TEAM MEMBER YOU TRUST MOST FOR A CONFRONTATION WITH THE OTHER TEAM AT HARIMAU

Dearest Esther,

Shocked after watching yesterdays show, I send you a DVD with the first episodes. Cherish them, they're full of beautiful memories!

One last word on John and Carl: you reap what you sow.

Hang in there, a strong woman like you can withstand a knock or too, I'm sure.

Lots of Love
Marnix

© Photo: Jeroen van Amelsvoort

## Sleep with the fishes

The following day another elimination challenge would take place. 'Your leader needs to choose the person she trusts the most, for a fierce battle with the other team,' the instruction letter read. I could feel the mood change again, after all, I was still the leader and had immunity. If we lost, one of the others would be voted off. 'The challenge will be held in the cave at Harimau,' Carl read. 'So it will probably be a test in the water,' he analysed. Who is a good swimmer?' Wim asked. All eyes shifted towards Marleen, who was a fitness instructor and in great shape. Marleen might have been the only team member I could trust. After all she was the only one who had been consistent and rational in her behavior towards me. 'Alright then, Marleen will join Esther for this challenge,' it was decided.

It felt strange to be going back to Harimau, back to the cave where I had spent two happy weeks with Marnix. It seemed a lifetime ago...

It was great to see Marnix again, finally a friendly face, someone who knew me and understood me. I briefly explained my difficult situation, and felt a lot better when Marnix and his teammate, 'cool dude' Maxime, told me never to give up.

It was an incredibly scary challenge, I was thrown into the water with a concrete block of a hundred kilo attached to my feet. Fear was overwhelming me when the weight pulled under water, deeper and deeper. 'Don't give up,' I tried to calm myself, 'this is your chance to win something for the team. If you give up, they'll have another reason to be nasty!' After ten seconds Marleen was allowed to dive in the water and cut me loose. It may have been the scariest experience in my entire life. The time spent under water, waiting for my release, felt like an eternity. In reality, we surfaced within forty-five seconds.

However, Marnix and Maxime had been a little bit quicker, they won the price we could only dream of: an elaborate dinner on the beach.

Back in the camp Marleen and I felt bad when we saw the hopeful faces awaiting us. 'Sorry guys, we've lost. Esther tried her best, she hung in there, but it was really scary and, unfortunately, the others were faster,' Marleen said.

## Conspiracy Theory

'We stand no chance at the next voting round,' Wim and Meredith confided in me. 'You can't be voted off, so we're up against the other three,' they complained. I tried to put myself in their position. 'Why don't you try to win someone over, so you can count on at least another vote?' I said. 'No, it wouldn't make any difference, we'll just have to accept our fate,' they ignored the suggestion.

The candlelight battle: You have chosen to challenge your leader. Put the shell and the candle on top of the trunk. The leader and his challenger take a seat on either side of the trunk, while facing each other. Light the candle and put both hands on the trunk. When the flame is blown out by the wind you put your hand on the shell emblem in the middle of the trunk. The person who is the first to do so, is the winner.

Suddenly we heard a shout from Carl, who was waving a piece of paper; it was a letter from the production team. The production team regularly adjusted the rules, to make the game more 'exiting' for the viewers. 'You're offered the opportunity to challenge your leader,' it said in the letter. 'The winner will get the immunity amulet, which means they cannot be voted off. The loser will have the votes against them count double.' It took a minute before this news had sunk in, and then a big smile appeared on John and Carl's faces. 'You see, Esther,' said Carl, 'When someone wins the amulet in a challenge, it is easier to accept their immunity then when it is given to them.'

Following the instructions in the letter, we made our way to the trunk where we found a detailed description of what was expected of us: 'Two people place their hands on the trunk. A candle is being lit. As long as the flame is alight you don't move your hands, but as soon as the flame is blown out by the wind, put your hand on the shell emblem in the middle of the trunk. The person who is the first to do so, is the winner.' It seemed a simple but fair game, it wasn't about strength or knowledge. However, losing the game would have far reaching implications, as the unlucky contestant would be most likely voted off.

I waited for the others to make up their minds, but nothing happened, nobody seemed to be willing to take the risk. 'If you're not going to challenge me, can we please let the subject rest and get on with things? I'm getting hungry,' I said, hoping it would put an end to the challenge, but instead it fired up the discussion: 'It's not fair that we have to compete for it, while you were just given immunity!'

'If you just set out to be liked, you will be prepared to compromise on anything at anytime, and would achieve nothing.'
- Margareth Thatcher -

Then Meredith, simplifying to our chat earlier, said: 'Esther suggested that Wim and I could vote someone off if we had her vote.' Now the bomb exploded: 'Esther, have you sunk so low that you're now trying to plot against us?' snorted John, and he jumped up furiously: 'Either she goes, or I go,' he shouted as he ran towards the gong and gave it an almighty bang, which was the sign to challenge the leader. 'Come on, young lady,' John said authoritatively, 'let's play this candlelight game; I'll show you who's boss!' Shocked by his sudden furious outburst, the others got up and followed him meekly towards the trunk. Relieved that a decision had been made, and someone else was willing to take up the challenge, they sat down behind him. I felt completely on my own again, and took a seat at the other side of the trunk.

'How am I going to win this game?' I thought. 'You don't need to do anything,' a voice in my head said. Not do anything? I wondered. But I have to do something, I figured. 'Just sing a song,' the calming voice said again. Not knowing what else to do I sat down, placed my hands on the trunk and started softly humming a tune. John was trembling with nerves and adrenaline. I felt very calm. The candle was lit, and the challenge started...

'If the flame goes out, put your hands on the shell emblem as quickly as you can. If you take your hands off the trunk before the flame has gone out, you're out,' the camera crew instructed. A few times the flame flickered, but I didn't move a muscle. Then the flame flickered again, and John quickly slammed his hand on top of the emblem. However, the flame was still burning, which meant John had lost the challenge; he would have to go at the next Tribal Council. The voice had been right: I did not have to do anything. John had brought this upon himself.

But still, the others were angry at me and complaining it hadn't been fair. I protested: 'First you tell me that won immunity is easier to accept than given immunity. And now that I have won it fairly, you're still mad at me?' I challenged them. A sudden strength came over me, and I decided I was going to stay, on the island no matter what; I'd fight till the bitter end. 'No more discussions, I'm sick of it!' I said angrily, realizing this kind of behavior would increase the risk of being voted off. So be it, I had to stand up for myself.

'Today is International Women's Day,' announced Ernst Paul, 'and that's why only the women will participate in this elimination round.' It was a tough contest, in which we had to spin a very heavy wooden wheel, which was being pushed into the opposite direction by the other team.

Only winning the this challenge would save John from elimination, as the losing team would have to vote someone off. Marleen, Meredith and I tried our best, but we were exhausted. Unfortunately we lost. John, Carl and Wim came up to us and put their arms supportively around Meredith and Marleen.

'Doesn't matter, it was hard work, you did well,' they said, completely ignoring me. I was overwhelmed by sadness, I had worked myself into a sweat, for the team, for John; I had burnt my last bit of energy, and they did not even thank me for it. Qui-

reality show

Bye bye, John

etly I sat down under a tree and let my tears run freely. I let it all out and nobody even came to see if I was alright, except the camera crew, dutifully recording everything.

When we walked back to the boat, I was still tearful, and Marleen put her arm around me. 'It's so unfai-hair,' I cried. 'I know,' she said softly, 'just leave them be, they don't know any better,' she advised. 'Who do they think they are?' I was absolutely furious. 'This is beyond any decency.'

Further down the beach I saw Marnix looking at me worriedly, was I alright? I gave him the thumbs up sign, composing myself, trying not to let my emotions get the better of me.

That night, John was voted off, unanimously. 'John is my friend,' I heard Carl say to Ernst Paul, 'and it hurts being forced to vote him out!' What do you mean 'forced'?' Ernst Paul asked him, 'you could have voted for someone else?' Carl mumbled something about John's fate being decided anyway. 'Well, it is, and always will be, your own choice who you vote for,' Ernst Paul concluded.

After John's leaving, (he did not take my hand when I offered him a farewell handshake, by the way) the mood reached an absolute low. Everybody was reconsidering the new situation and their own position. While we were waiting for the boat, Carl suddenly walked up to me, all aggressive: 'It's all your fault!' he shouted at me, his face an inch from mine. The production team had to hold him back, and after that he didn't want anything to do with me anymore.

## Revenge

Two days later, after the mood had improved just slightly, I was challenged to a duel by Carl: 'I owe John as much as that,' he said. But we all knew that his actual motive was to win the immunity amulet.

We walked towards the trunk and sat down. I started humming my little song again, but when the flame died out, Carl was the first to slam his hand on the shell. He jumped up in excitement and let out a huge cheer, all the others came up to congratulate him. Carl finally had what he wanted, and I knew I would be voted off at the next Tribal Council. I wasn't even upset, I just felt completely exhausted by the battles of the past week.

After the challenge the atmosphere was very relaxed. Carl was euphoric, proudly parading around the camp, showing off his amulet. The others wisely kept any comments to themselves.

Now that I did not pose much of a threat anymore, Carl became his old sympathetic self again. That night we had a good chat about traveling: 'I have traveled around the world myself for the past thirteen years,' he said, 'and when I hear you talk about your charity work, I think you would be much happier if you'd follow your heart,' he advised.

For the first time in three weeks I thought about home. Carl was right: I would gradually cut down my work for the Donor Association and start traveling again, something I had always been passionate about. 'Without noticing I've got stuck in the ratrace, working in an office, for more than five days a week.' I laughed: 'it used to be my biggest nightmare! And I'm not even earning any money doing it!'

We were all feeling the effects of not having enough to eat. I had slowed down considerably, not finding much energy. Wim was suffering from stomach pains, and had not been able to eat anything at all.

Deze twee 'Expeditie Robinson'-kandidaten mochten de samensmelting net niet meemaken

DARMONTSTEKING DWONG WIM TOT VERTREK

# I WAS A HANGER-ON,
### and I feel ashamed about that now

We only had a small amount of rice left, se we added some seaweed and... snails to create a decent meal. Not having much choice, I did eat some snails. I tried to focus on the little bit of protein they provided, but I still felt horrible. After this exotic meal, I tried to rest as much as I could to preserve my energy for the next day.

Another elimination challenge would be held, it was to be all or nothing: if we would lose, I would be voted off. In some ways I did not want to go yet, having just started to feel at home on our island!

The next morning, just before the challenge, Carl came to me while I was fishing, and started up this weird conversation: 'Esther, if we lose this challenge, then maybe I can persuade the others to vote for Wim; he doesn't feel well at all, you see.' It didn't feel right, and I waited to see if Carl had anything else to say. He continued: 'in return, I'd like to ask you not ever to vote for me.' Carl looked at me expectantly.

'Well, we know Wim feels pretty bad,' I said. 'I prefer to just ask him what his plan is. If he wants to go home, then indeed we can suggest we would vote him off at the next council,' I suggested diplomatically. 'No, no, that's not a good idea, let me talk to him,' Carl said, jumping up nervously. 'Maybe it's best you don't talk to anyone about what I've just said,' and he quickly walked back to the camp, leaving me startled. Had Carl just tried to make me part of a conspiracy? He had certainly tried to turn me into one of his allies, in case I would survive the challenge. I was very surprised to find he thought of me as a realistic threat, I had so far thought Carl was very confident.

I decided not to mention our little chat; Carl would deny everything, it would be his word against mine, and I was sure the others would be on his side. If Wim decided to leave because of his ill health, I might stand a chance. Never in a million years would I ever, join an alliance with someone like Carl. No way!

For the next challenge we were told to play tag with the other team in knee-deep water. This may sound fairly simple were it not for the fact that we were tied together and also had to carry a heavy backpack. I felt determined and physically strong and was really enjoying the game but, unfortunately, Meredith struggled. We had to drag her along and at some point even carry her. I flet like Carls wasn't giving his all, but that was kind of expected. My team lost. It was game over. I knew I would be the one who was going to be voted off.

Saying goodbye to Marnix was tough. We had imagined this so differently during our weeks in the cave. His team members expressed their support: 'It's a shame you won't be joining our team, Esther!' someone shouted. 'We'd sort of counted

As guest in a TV show
about bullying.

© Photo: Jeroen van Amelsvoort

on it already,' said another. I felt a lump in my throat, hearing such kind words from these complete strangers.

My team stood back, sheepishly watching what was going on. I overheard their hushed conversation: 'Did you hear that?' whispered Carl, 'They're all on her side,' said Wim. 'How can that be? They don't even know her...,' Carl said bewildered.

I turned around: 'You didn't know me either, but had already made up your minds about me,' I snapped. I understood my team was alarmed at the positive reactions from the other team: they would have to justify themselves at some point, when all contestants would be put together into one team. So far, there hadn't been anybody condemning their unacceptable behavior, but that might not be the same in a new group of people. I guess they suddenly realized what the possible consequences were of their actions.

During the Tribal Council I was indeed voted off. 'This is probably the least unexpected result ever,' Ernst Paul said lightly. I had voted for Wim, he was very ill, and an hour after I had left, he was rushed to hospital suffering with appendicitis...

Back in the hotel I looked at myself in the mirror, and was shocked to see how much weight I had lost, fortunately there was an enormous buffet waiting for me, and it felt good to eat some proper food again. After dinner, I brushed my teeth and washed my hair, and lay down on the soft bed. I felt completely refreshed and released all the negativity of the past days. It had been nearly four weeks since I had left home, having told everyone I would be away for at least seven weeks. That meant I had another three weeks left before I needed to go back! 'Where shall I go next?' I thought, while stretching out on the soft mattress.

## Ten minutes of fame

Despite my regular appearances in the media, I had never been recognized by people in the street, although everyone seemed to have heard of Coins for Care. 'Oh, is that you?' people would ask surprised. 'I think I may have seen you on television a while ago.'

After only three Survivor episodes, however, complete strangers would stop their cars in the middle of the street to salute me. When I walked through town, students would call my name through their open windows. Other people would come out of their houses, take my hand, and say: 'We just want to let you know we support you!'
After Survivor, for at least two years I was being recognized in every train, plane, or in any other public place. Especially in a sauna; with my hair wet and not wearing any make-up, people would recognize me immediately, which could be very uncomfortable, as we don't wear any bathing suits in the sauna in Holland...
Women would tell me they had been crying in front of the television, while the men clenched their fists and said: 'If I ever get my hands on those two guys...'
My treatment on the Survivor show released a flood of emotions from the viewers, and I received thousands of supportive e-mails.

John or Esther?

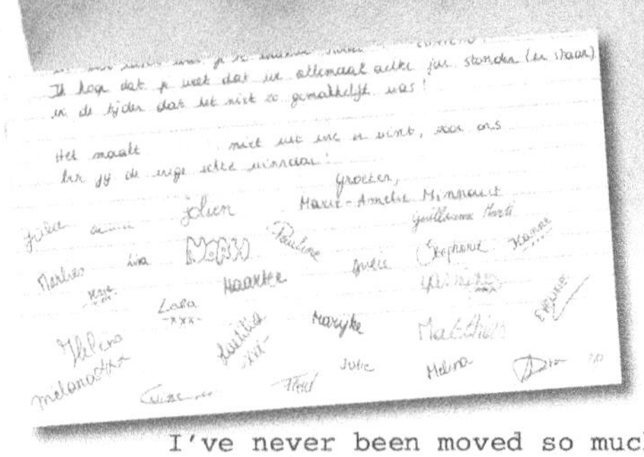

[handwritten notes, partially legible]

I've never been moved so much by a television show as this one, and my husband thinks it's hilarious...

You're achievement during this show was just amazing. I felt for you on this difficult trip in the far east, amongst a group of people of which a few were plain nasty. I admire your attitude, you stood your ground and it was obvious not everybody was ready for that.

For years I have been carrying these notes in my wallet. The dollar is a leftover from a trip to the US, the German Marks I found when we moved into our new home. I have been planning going to an exchange office, but when I heard about your Coins for Care campaign through the Survivor show, and saw that the campaign is still going, it seemed a perfect reason to contact you personally.

So I can also show you my support for everything that has been happening to you on the island. Esther, you are a top girl, with a big heart, and don't be put off by some narrow-minded, ignorant fools.

*I am not involved at all with your situation, but, as a Belgian, I am ashamed to see how they've turned against you, I am Bart, 50 years old (Belgian, but not proud of it) and I've cried at you exiting the show.*

Normally I would not bother writing a reaction, but this time I felt this overwhelming sense of shame while watching Talpa; I have to let you know I'm on your side!

This was a lot more than a psychological game, it was a psychopathic game being played, Those grown-up men should be ashamed of themselves, as well as the other contestants.

PS. I forgot to tell you how I admire your attitude during that last Island council! You knew what was coming and just stood there, shoulders straight, in fact, I have never seen you sit so upright. You made such a strong impression, showing that they were not going to get you down. Absolute class!

Every week we're on the edge of our seats and this must have been the most exciting Survivor ever. We are deeply impressed by your 'battle' with the rest of the group. I, not my husband, have been in tears a few times, but despite having to leave early, to me you are the winner, and I am sure you continue to be a winner once you come off the island. You are top class!

Here a brief note from Martin and Debby + kids
We would like to let you know that we are disgusted by these two nasty characters and those Flemish hanger-on people!!!!!
Absolutely terrible!!!!!
Really Esther, you were excellent!!!!
That's what we wanted to tell you, I'm sure you'll get hundreds of emails, but had to let you know.
Greetings from Landsmeer.

I (27 years old) and my girlfriend (Mariel, 24 years) have never felt so much sympathy for any contestant ever!

I'm impressed with how you keep standing, your head up right, and for me you're the absolute winner, regardless of the outcome!

It is incredibly courageous to have been put out there for as long as you have, in such difficult circumstances. Not many people will be able to do that.

I wish you all the best for the future. You are a true leader.
I would like to close of with a one-liner about leadership by Mel Gibson from the film Braveheart: 'Men don't follow titles, men follow courage'.

Dear Esther,
I am not someone who normally contacts a contestant of a television show, but I was so impressed with your behavior on the Survivor show that I have to send you a mail. I admire you for standing strong in such irrational circumstances. I myself have a strong personality and one way or another I was able to identify fully with you. Congratulations! I am sure you have gained some people knowledge during this TV Show!

Hi Esther,
Even though you don't know me I just want to tell you I think you are incredibly strong, gosh, when I watch those confrontations with John and Carl on TV, I get so cross, I just can't understand why they are so nasty to you!

It's also funny to read (or hear) that I am not the only soloist in this world, but that you're a star at that as well!

I have never seen a television show causing such upheaval, and when you read all the reactions on the different internet forums it is almost scary to see what your role, and those of those other, how do I put it, 'psychopaths' have brought about in normal people. How is this possible?

Compliments Esther, you have done so well in the Survivor show!
You've won the biggest price available, much more valuable than any money price ever!

I can't tell you how I admire you! I've never seen anything like it, I could have pulled John through the screen by his dirty blonde hair, what a pathetic idiot!!! I had never, ever could have stayed there. I'd rather crawl home on my bare knees. And you, you kept going, despite everything, well, well done!

*This is the first time I'm sending a mail to someone I don't know, and who takes part in a television show!*

I was invited to appear on Linda & Beau, a prime time television show. 'Our theme this week is bullying, and we'd like to hear your experiences on Survivor,' the host explained. 'It's unbelievable, but bullying does still happen, even amongst adults,' she introduced the show, and a compilation film was played containing a few of my worst moments on the island. 'Here she is, our number one Survivor!' I was announced. I got a standing ovation from the studio audience.

'The two weeks in the cave were so special,' I said, over-whelmed by the warm welcome, 'but I would rather forget the ten days after that, although I do in the end feel it has been a valuable experience,' I added. 'Judging by the many positive reactions I received since the show was aired, many people identified with what happened to me.' Linda asked me if I had been frightened during my time on the island. 'Oh yes,' I replied. 'I've seen what can happen when people's behavior is not being corrected. We were interviewed every day by the camera crew, whose questions were targeted at getting most controversy out of the contestants; they would never counter anything we said or did, let alone condemn anything, so it seemed as if they were agreeing with everything you said. I interpreted it as support, which I needed badly at certain moments, and

© Dag Allemaal (Belgium)

I'm sure, the others took it as an encouragement for their attitudes, until however they saw how the other team reacted to me. My team members had not realized they would have to justify their behavior at a later stage in the show, and now it is aired on television it must be hard for them,' I smiled.

'Everybody probably knows a Carl or John,' - or a Jaap and Raymond, or an Amal and his boss, I thought to myself - 'and I think that's what makes my story so identifiable,' I said to Linda and Beau. 'I receive a lot of e-mail from people who are being bullied at their work, sometimes so badly that they eventually have to call in sick,' I continued. 'These stories really get to me, we're talking about people's lives being ruined, I was in a show and I could have stepped out, but in real life you don't have that choice, you've got to deal with it, day in day out.' I concluded.
Apparently it helped many people to share their story with a fellow victim of bullying: the e-mail kept coming in.

I sometimes read the messages on the Internet Survivor forums, where thousands of people commented on the show. Their criticism of Carl and John was often offensive. I wondered what had brought on this aggression from the viewers. One night, after a show in which Carl and John had been extremely nasty towards me, one of the viewers asked if anyone knew where Carl and John lived, and proposed to go beat them up. Someone else answered: 'I looked up the address,...' Another one enquired 'are there still trains going at this hour?' To my amazement, I was witnessing a gang being formed. Fortunately they never executed their threat.

People must have thought I was still on the island: 'Esther, hang in there!' they wrote, or: 'I wish I could come over and help you out!' They should have known the recording was over and I was safely back home, besides, even if they were not aware of that, how was I supposed to read their e-mails on a deserted island? I understood they just wanted to share their experiences: injustice is an incredibly strong feeling which many us can identify with. And when emotions take over, all rationality disappears.

After the last episode, there was a huge finale show, live in front of a studio audience, in which the winner of Survivor 2005 would be announced. 'It will be the first time I'll see John and Carl again,' I told Marnix. 'Did I tell you that Carl has sent me an e-mail in which he offers his apology?' I asked my friend. 'Better late than never,' was his reaction.
During the live show Wim, Meredith and Marleen apologized in front of the camera's for their behavior towards me. 'I cannot believe I behaved like that, that's not me at all,' Meredith confessed, blushing with shame.

'Carl, I hear you've also apologized to Esther?' Ernst Paul asked. 'Well, yes, in hindsight I realized I might have been a little harsh in my judgement,' my tormentor, who had eventually been voted off unanimously, admitted. 'It prematurely ended Esther's Survivor experience, and eventually mine as well,' he added. The camera turned to me for a reaction. Even after three months it still made me furious: 'During those ten days on the island you didn't show any remorse; In the three weeks after I was gone, you were asked twice on camera if you had any regrets, and you replied that you still thought your behavior had been acceptable. Even when you came home you did not change your mind. It was only after the show was broadcast on television, that you became aware of the reaction of the public, and decided to contact me,' I summed up fiercely.

'And John, what about you?' asked Ernst Paul. 'Oh well, I thought it would make some good television, stir things up a little, it's only a game you know, it's just the way I am,' John said casually.

Ernst Paul now turned to me: 'Esther, what's your response to this?' 'John, you say this was just a game, but I have seen the real emotion in you,' I said. 'You told the others you were willing to go because you were physically at the end of your reserves, but once you saw me, you changed you mind and seemed to have renewed strength to continue the competition. What's happened in your life, how can you treat someone like that, someone you don't even know?' I had not intended to say that, it just came out, but the audience got up from their seats and gave me a huge applause. John mumbled something like: 'Hooray, we've got a new Mother Theresa,' at which the crowd started jeering at him.

'How weird,' I thought, during the expedition we didn't have any feedback at all, and now it was crystal clear, who the audience had supported. Carl and John didn't say another word, they were infuriated and stared at their feet. After the show, John had to be escorted out of the building by security, as he had received threats from the audience. Carl later emigrated with his family to Spain.

The finale show was, of course, all about the winner. I had a lump in my throat when it was announced that Marnix had became the 'Survivor'! Everybody thought it was a well deserved win, and Marnix himself was overcome by emotion and could not utter a single word. Winning the show meant so much to him; he had, after all, completely overcome and defeated his disease. Tears ran down my cheeks when I saw my Harimau-buddy struggling to keep it together, while his wife and children ran up to him flung their arms around him.

At the after party I was approached by so many kind people, showing their support, and complimenting me on my performance during the show, and also that night in the studio.

One of the highlights of the evening was Marnix and I presenting a huge gingerbread man to the camera crew. Rudi the Rat was the honorable receiver, and a smile appeared on his face when he read the decoration: '361'. It was the magical code with which we had managed to unlock the trunk. 'How is this possible?' Rudi said, struggling to understand. 'I knew you'd taken something out of our box, but not that you'd cracked the code!' he shook his head and burst into laughter.

Three years later I was driving through the Namibian desert, when a Dutch family came up to me and said: 'You must be Esther! We recognized you straight away. Good to see you are doing so well!' I had joined Survivor to get away from the spotlight, however, the show had the complete opposite effect, and given me more fame than I had ever wished for.

## Tiny Spark

'It's as if I am on the psychiatrist's couch,' I said to the two journalists who were interviewing me for Carp magazine. I'd just returned from Antwerp, where I'd joined Marleen for an interview with a women's magazine, and on the way back I'd stopped at the border station of Roosendaal where I had arranged to meet the two Carp reporters. Our meeting was supposed to take an hour, but we'd already been talking for four hours! Stephanie and Marieke came up with such sharp questions and clever evaluations that I seriously felt as if I was in psychoanalysis instead of taking part in an interview!'

'I've followed the Survivor show closely and there's one thing I just have to ask you: please tell me, how did you manage to retain such a friendly outlook towards everybody?' asked Stephanie, 'I was, honestly, so impressed by this,' she added. 'I don't know, I haven't really thought about it. I guess it was just the best way to react,' I explained. 'If six people are nasty towards you, twenty-four hours a day, there's not much you can do. I was just hoping that someone would see the light eventually, and start behaving normally again. If I'd lost it, and got really mad at them, I'd have wasted any chance I had,' I explained.

'Are there any similarities between Coins for Care, the Donor Association and the Survivor show?' asked Marieke. 'Uhm,...that's a tough one, I think they are all completely different projects except, of course, that the launch of the Donor Association was a direct result of the Coins for Care campaign, I can't see a direct link with the Survivor show,' I said, my brain working hard.

'I do see a resemblance between the three,' Stephanie said. 'Just think about how people have reacted to you?' She was right, for every supporter there had always been an opposer, someone who hadn't liked me. 'Is that always the case?' asked Marieke. 'how were you when you were growing up, did you easily interact with other people?' 'I've always been an outsider,' I admitted. 'On my first day at Nyenrode I wore yellow fluorescent cycling trousers, plastic cherry earrings and had a fresh perm in my bleached hair. I came straight from the fitness club. The outfit was entirely inappropriate for such a traditional and conservative environment, you should've seen the looks I got....' I blushed with embarrassment. 'One of the older girls took me aside and gave me a bus ticket, and said: 'Esther, do me a favor and please go back to wherever you have come from, you don't belong here.' I thought it was part of the initiation ceremony, but she actually meant it, she really wanted me out of there!'

'I'm not sharp with things like that, I am more of a loner,' I added, 'and I'm sure people sense that, because I always seem to produce very intense reactions from others, both negative as well as positive.'

'So, actually you can't go through life as inconspicuously as you'd like,' Stephanie concluded. I thought about this new insight for a moment, these two girls had really looked at everything I had done and they had chosen an interesting angle for their interview. I complimented them both: 'You're so right, where ever I go, there are always people who really like me, as well as a few who turn against me, without any apparent reason.' 'People feel threatened by you,' said Marieke. 'You have a strong personality, confident in your views and actions and that can be intimidating,' Stephanie continued. 'That's why someone like John was against me even though we had just met,' I thought aloud. 'Maybe that is why Nitza and Louise, the two marketing girls at Interglobe, didn't like

Fitness girl.

278

me either,' I added. 'And, of course, certain people in the charity industry feel threatened when a young girl turns up and changes their little world beyond recognition,' giggled Stephanie. The two reporters came to a beautiful conclusion: I am a small spark, the spark has the potential to light a fire, some will be grateful, they love the fire as it brings light and warmth, but there are also people who are frightened by the roaring flames. The spark, however, won't go unnoticed, and doesn't leave anyone in the dark.

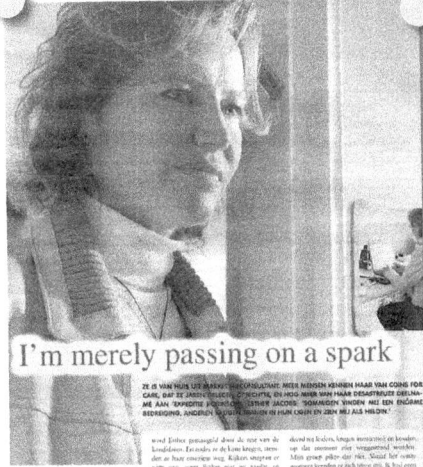

I'm merely passing on a spark

'Be who you are and say what you mean. Because those who mind don't matter and those who matter don't mind..'
– Dr. Seuss –

# Excuse 16:
## 'This is not the right moment.'

*'If you wait for the perfect moment when all is safe and assured,*
*it may never arrive.*
*Mountains will not be climbed, races won, or*
*lasting happiness achieved.'*
*- Maurice Chevalier -*

## Tons of money

The Survivor show had brought me a lot. It had been a magnificent experience, a serendipitous adventure in which I had a taste of true freedom. I had become one with nature, and for the first time in many years my life was not ruled by my agenda. The second half had been difficult, but the problems with Carl and John had made me stronger; I felt a lot more confident.

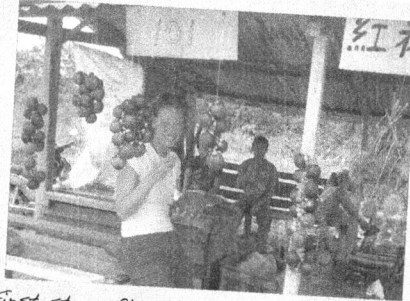

*First stop after the Survivor show: a fruit stall en route to the airport*

After being voted off I traveled to the US, to pay my brother an unexpected visit, feeling completely recharged, ready to get back into the real world.

'I'm not so sure I want to go back into charity,' I said to Marnix, my Survivor buddy. 'So why don't you just quit your work with the Donor Association?' he asked. 'You've been a philanthropist for long enough, haven't you?' 'I can't simply drop everything, that would mean it's all been for nothing,' I replied. 'I do want to quit, but not without handing over properly, so others can continue on with what we have achieved so far,' I decided.

My house was now being used as the Donor Association's head office. Every morning five interns and volunteers arrived at my doorstep. It took a heavy toll on my work-life balance, and I realized we needed to move, especially if I was going to withdraw from the organization. So I started to look for a new office space, hoping I could find sponsorship for this as well.

My second mission would be to find a successor, which was challenging because we didn't have any money to offer. 'Nobody will be prepared to take over all that work without being paid for it,' one of my student workers warned me when I told them of my plan.

A friend advised me to contact Ton aan de Stegge, a Dutch telecom-investor-turned-rich. 'He has had a lifelong interest in the charity sector,' she said. 'Is he aware that we are in need of funds?' I asked wearily. 'I've spoken to so many people already and I don't really have time for another chit chat,' I said. 'Yes, he does, and he's just sold all of his Telfort stocks, so money shouldn't be a issue. Just give the guy a call,' my friend proposed.

The evening before meeting Ton, we had our regular board meeting. 'If we don't get sponsorship for at least two projects, we will have to pull the plug,' we calculated. 'We simply need funds, otherwise it's game over.'

This clearly wasn't the right moment to announce I was thinking of stepping down. 'First I need to make sure the Donor Association is out of danger, before thinking of myself,' I decided.

The burden of our tenuous financial position weighed heavily on my shoulders and the meeting with Ton was an important one. I was hoping he would want to consider sponsoring our DonorInformer. If I could at least get his commitment to sponsoring this project, I would be content.

Ton was waiting for me in his large spacious office in the modern Telfort building. He was tall, slimly build, and energetic with bright, intelligent blue eyes. We made small talk for a few minutes, and then Ton got to the point: 'So, Esther, tell me something about yourself.' I'd done this so many times, and knew my pitch inside out. I briefly summarized my personal background and skillfully switched the conversation to the Donor Association. '...and, right now I am looking for sponsorship for an amazing project...' I concluded, ready to provide more details on the project.

Ton put his hand up: 'Hang on, not so fast, did you just say you looked after your brother for a while? Please, tell me more about that.' Surprised at Ton's interest in that particular fact, I briefly told him that after my parents got divorced, my brother Michael lived with our mum until he was twelve years old. 'Then Michael decided he wanted to live with our dad, but my dad was just moving to Curacao. My dad's girlfriend suggested that Michael should live with her in Amstelveen, so her house became the center of our 'long-distance' family life. Michael lived there for a happy three years, but when my dad and his girlfriend broke up, he had to move out. By that time I had nearly finished my Anthropology course at Florida University - I only had to write my final thesis - and decided to move back to the Netherlands to take care of my brother. I looked after him until he was seventeen, when he moved out to live on his own.

I thought this was enough detail about my personal life, but Ton said: 'So may I ask you how old you were when this happened?' 'I was twenty-six when he moved in, and twenty-nine when he left,' I answered, not fully understanding where this was leading to. 'That's quite something,' Ton said in admiration. I still thought it was odd that he'd be interested in this particular detail, while the purpose of our meeting was the Donor Association.

When I got to know him better, I discovered that Ton has the tendency to steer a conversation into unexpected directions, just to see how people react. I must have done alright, because when I brought up the Donor Association for the third time, he let me speak. 'Our DonorInformer project is very important,' I explained. 'There is currently no database available which includes details of all registered charities, We're looking for a sponsor for part of the *DonorInformer* project, which will create this online tool.

'How much do you need?' Ton asked, not beating around the bush. 'Uhm, about 10.000 euro per year,' I said, slightly taken aback. 'We can do a lot with such amount' I added quickly when I saw Ton was contemplating. 'And how much will it cost to run the Donor Association for a whole year?' Ton asked. I hadn't thought about that, and made a quick calculation of all the projects. 'We probably need about 100.000 euro per year,' I replied.

'100.000 per year,' Ton thought for a moment. 'Alright, then I'd like to support the Association for three years, I want my sponsorship to have a lasting effect. Just one year won't do anybody any good...' he continued as if it were an every-day occurrence to donate 300.000 euro. 'What do you think?' he asked, his eyes twinkling.

Do you still have any of these old addresses in your address book?

Bosch en Duin:
Hesdaglaan 12d

Nieuweglin:
Kameraarswede:
Landouwerdriff 74
Hertewede 7
Hindeweide 6

Breukelen:
Straatweg 25
Nw Nijarcode

Londen:
68 Hurstwood Road
6 Petherton Road

Curaçao:
P.O. Box 6202
Royal Palm Resort

Gainesville:
999 SW 16th Avenue
3515 SW 39" Blvd

Amsterdam:
Apollolaan
Rijnstraat 197

Amstelveen:
Keizer Karelweg 363
Gooreegspad 109

Utrecht:
Oudegracht 91

Parijs:
Quartier latin

You can cross them out!!!
Because...

After nearly 10 years of roaming about, we have finally found a home for ourselves...

een eigen huis

you can write this one down in pen please feel free to pop by.
1181 XG Amstelveen
Tel./Fax 020-4451518
lot eind feb
020-647798:
Kom je snel een keertje kijken ???

# Business is good for Ton

Als je wat centen hebt, valt het nog niet mee om die op een goede manier kwijt te raken", verzucht Ton aan de Stegge. De voormalig Telfort-topman stuitert, door de verkoop van zijn bedrijf aan KPN, met een geschat vermogen van 58 miljoen euro op nummer 401 de rijkenlijst Quote 500 binnen en zoekt goede doelen waar zijn miljoenen effectief aan de slag kunnen. Hij was het spoor al zo'n beetje bijster toen een kennis hem aan Donateursvereniging Nederland koppelde. Het is een club die gevers inzicht biedt in wat er te koop is in de goededoelenbranche. "Niet sexy", zegt Aan de Stegge, "maar het pakt wel een kwestie aan die sterk speelt: je wilt weten wat er met je geld gebeurt." Hij stopt de Donateursvereniging drie jaar lang een ton toe en denkt mee. Initiatiefneemster Esther Jacobs zette eerder de euro-actie Coins for Care op en leerde daar hoeveel geld er bij andere fondsen opging aan onkosten. Nu ijvert ze voor meer transparantie. "Het CBF-keurmerk biedt schijnzekerheid. Het controleert de besteding van de inleg niet volledig. Een kwart daarvan mag opgaan aan wervingskosten, op overige kosten is geen zicht." Het is opmerkelijk dat Aan de Stegges bijdrage aan de grote klok hangt. "Ik had het liever anoniem gedaan, maar Esther heeft me overtuigd dat het gebruik van mijn naam dingen losmaakt", zegt Aan de Stegge. "Ik doe al wat voor weeshuizen in Kenia, voor Indiase tsunamislachtoffers, en ik kijk naar investeringsfondsen." De goede werken worden geen hoofdjob. "Investeringsmaatschappijen, die komen af op de tovenaar die van 25 miljoen een miljard maakt. Maar zo simpel lag het niet" ■ PB

De Donateursvereniging is 'niet sexy', vindt Ton aan de Stegge.

'Sorry?' I was stunned. 'What if I commit to three years, 100.000 euro each year, that will enable you to continue the good work for a while,' he said. 'Well, that..., that would be fantastic!' I replied. I couldn't believe what was happening. 'Don't you need some more time to think about it?' I asked. 'Oh no, I'm absolutely sure. Just put your proposal into 1 A4, and mail it to me. I would also like to meet the rest of the board to discuss my role in this project. Then I'll forward the money into your accounts so you guys can get going!' said Ton. 'I think you're doing a very important job, and you've got much better things to do than looking for sponsorship,' he concluded. I was baffled: 'Okay,...uhm.. yes, I'll send you a mail,' I stumbled.

Just before I walked out of the door Ton said: 'I do have one condition, if I support the Donor Association I want you to be involved in it. I think you play a pivotal role and that is why I want you to continue.' I was so overwhelmed by what he was saying, and I just nodded, realizing this was again not the right moment to tell him I actually wanted to stop.

Walking to my car I had to pinch my arm, was it really true? I called Diane and told her everything. 'Tons of money from Ton,' she laughed. 'Who would have thought?' We were ecstatic, the Donor Association was saved.

But what about me...?

# Bad news

I had a heavy workload, and having the office at home wasn't making it any easier, I also had to fit in a paid job every so often to stay afloat. My body had withstood a lot during the Survivor show, but now I really started to feel the strain, I caught one cold after another. The other contestants were also having health problems; loss of hair, irritable bowels and tooth decay wasn't uncommon, and most of them were put on a course of antibiotics. In hindsight we realized we were paying quite a high price for a reality TV-show.
During a general check up, my doctor discovered I had an increased risk of cervical cancer. 'It isn't something we should worry about yet,' he said, 'but the abnormal cells will increase while your resistance is low, so you need to make sure you live healthily,' was his advice. It was quite a scare, and I was aware I would have to change my lifestyle drastically.

'I have found us an office space!' one of the Donor Association shouted when she came in one day. 'Someone at the tennis club has a friend who runs his own tax collection agency, and he's quite happy to put us up!

'It's only a small gesture, I'm glad to be of help!' said Anton Groot when he showed us around. 'We don't mind having a few ladies around,' he added with a wink. The office had everything we could wish for, it was bright and spacious, and conveniently located close to public transport, and the best thing about it was that the volunteers had organized it themselves, without my assistance. We moved in a few weeks later, and it was great to be returning to a normal house at the end of the day; no more desks in my living room, no printers in the kitchen, finally I had a place to relax!

Once the news of Ton's contribution got out, a few suppliers withdrew their sponsorship and asked to be paid for their services. We also became a target for companies who called us with all kinds of commercial offers.
'Welcome to the world of commerce,' Ton smiled when I complained about this. 'I often see dollar signs appear in people's eyes once they know who I am,' he confessed, 'you'll just have to accept it,' he added, but I found it hard to deal with.

When my loyal assistant graduated, faced with the choice to either stay with the Donor Association, or find a properly paid job, she decided to ask me for a moderate compensation. She was important to me, without her I would be in trouble, and I didn't want to lose her, so we came to an agreement. I was in a similar position, and discussed the possibility of receiving a monthly compensation with Ton and the board. I would at least be able to cover my fixed costs without the stress of having to find a paid job every now and then.

When we drew up a balance after a few months, however, it became clear that we hadn't progressed much. Ton's donation had resulted in some of us getting a small salary each month, but we still didn't have a sufficient budget for a suitable successor. 'For that money you might find a recent graduate, although they would probably be too inexperienced to do the work,' our accountant summarized.

My doctor was still seeing me regularly for check ups. 'The number of abnormal cells is increasing,' he told me. 'You really need to start taking it easy, and allow your body to recover. Stress causes these cells to grow, and if they're not receding on their own, we'll have to operate,' he said. The news wasn't good, and left me very distressed.

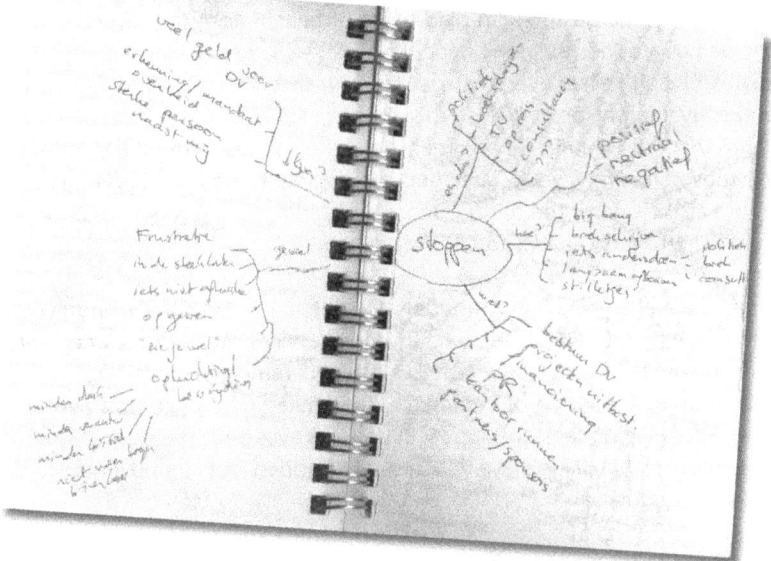

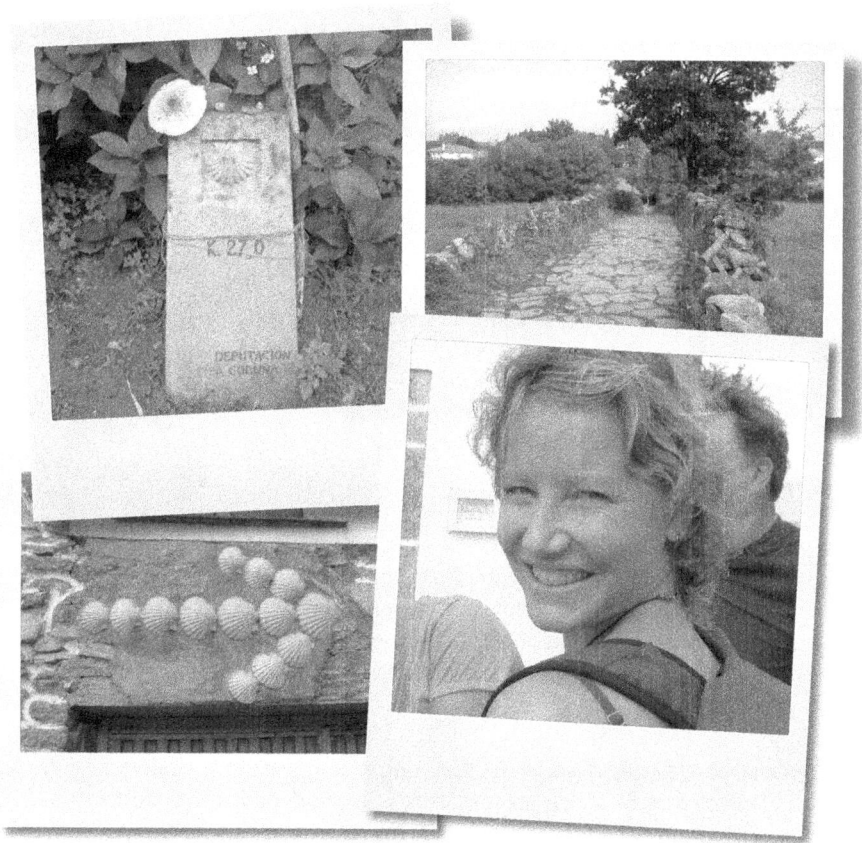

## The battle

I thought about Judith, wife of Kluun, the Dutch writer. A few years ago I had done a project for her, during which she was diagnosed with terminal cancer. I remembered her incredible strength, and her ability to deal with the disease and eventually bravely accepting her fate. 'You know,' she said one day, while catching her breath halfway up the stairs, 'I am thirty-six, and I've come to terms with not making thirty-seven, but I just think it's so awful for my daughter and Raymond.'

*Don't wait.*
*The time will never be just right'*
*- Napoleon Hill -*

When I asked Marnix how he had felt when he was diagnosed with cancer, he recommended reading Lance Armstrong's book. I found it so inspiring, and although my situation was completely different, and far less serious, I did gain a lot of strength from it. 'Anything is possible, you need to fight,' Armstrong says about his battle with the disease, and I ate as healthily as possible, took vitamin pills, tried to get plenty of exercise, and slept a lot; unfortunately, the stress was out of my control.

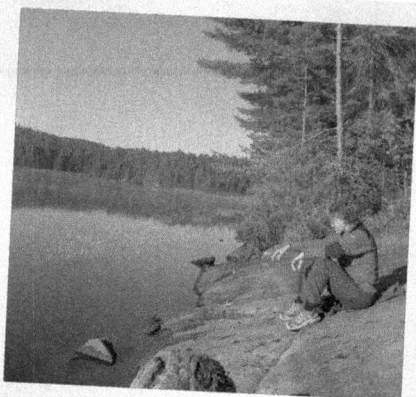

'I'm not sure I know what to do,' I said to Marnix during one of our long telephone conversations. 'Esther, your health is the most important thing you possess,' he said. 'You did want to quit the charity world anyway, so let this scare be the incentive to really cut down and not be drawn into driving things forward constantly,' he said wisely.

I decided to clear my head in Spain, during a long walk to the famous Santiago the Compostella. It was an amazingly relaxing experience. Unfortunately, I picked up an injury after only four days. My foot was so swollen that it didn't fit into my shoe anymore. I flew back to the Netherlands and had it checked, but the doctors couldn't find anything wrong. 'You might have a small hairline fracture in the bone,' they said. 'We can't do anything about that, only rest will help, so take it easy,' they said.

I had heard that advice before, and it drove me insane; my body told me to take it easy, and stop running around like a headless chicken, but the truth was that I didn't know how to, I had never done it.

'Should I just let go of everything, drop it, just like that? What about the students I've helped into their first job? What about Ton who's just committed to a three year sponsorship, and what about all these charities and donors?' I asked my friends, but of course, nobody had the magical answer, although they were all concerned for my health. 'Can't you just say you're forced to quit because of ill health?' they said.

The power to get things done

I didn't want to worry my family so I did not tell them about my health issues. As for the Donor Association, I didn't want to stop out of weakness, I couldn't let everybody down, but I had already decided to cut down gradually. I now had enough arguments for doing so, without having to mention my health which, according to me, was more of a personal issue. 'Just keep going, a few more weeks aren't going to make that much difference,' I told myself.

## Not now!

In the summer of 2006, my boyfriend and I went hiking for a month through West Canada, we camped out in the wilderness, enjoying the beautiful sur-roundings and friendly people. It was an amazing adventure, we even kayaked with killer whales! I was very aware of the need to relax, and had forbidden myself to check any e-mails, I just had to switch off completely, so I could recharge my batteries for my last few months at the Donors Association.

One morning I received a strange message from a friend back in the Nether-lands, who texted: 'Esther, I'm on your side, you can count on me!' I wondered what it was about, I then received another text from someone I hadn't spoken to in a long time: 'I am so sorry, let me know if I can do anything for you!'
'It sounds serious, I need to get online and find out what's going on,' I said to my boyfriend.
I located a tiny internet cafe, and through an incredibly slow connection I discov-ered what was going on. Jaap had pub-lished a critical article in his *Fundraising* magazine, about the donation of Coins for Care to the Donor Association. 'That can't be too bad, that's more than six months ago,' my friend said.
Unfortunately, the *Volkskrant* newspaper had picked up on Jaap's criticism, and run the story on their front-page: 'Money for charity diverted to fund own association' it said in big letters. They had made it look as if I had used the money for my own benefit! It spelled the end of our peaceful

### Charity money used for private funding

| datum ontvangen | 18-08-2006 22:30 | | leuke reacties | |
| forward/reply met | <info@estherjacobs.info> standaard e-mailadres ▼ | publiek: | deze e-mail is publiek toegankeli |
| acties | ← ⏎ ⏎ ⏎ 🗑 ✂ ✎ | | | |
| | - meer acties - ▼ | | | |

During the organization of my administration (I am a professional organizer), I bumped into the Volkskrant from August 9, in which you appear on the front page cover. I meant to keep the paper for a completely different reason, but because I find you such an inspiring personality I immediately read the article. I understand you are being chased up again, curious, that the Volkskrant is only too eager to put this on their front page. That Mr. Krol needs to take a good look at himself.

I googled your website (excellent site!!) and I -a complete stranger- would like to show you my support with the following words: Where there's light, there will be darkness.

I wish you a lot of light and love and keep going with your inspiring activities,

Best greetings,

Diana

---

*and the internal troubles with the management team. People are desperate for trying to save their own reputation. Am disappointed. Trying hard not to take it personally, or go for the defense (sometimes hard). There must be a way to come out of it stronger. I should not be lead by the negative (fear) but by my own strength, the light. That must be possible, I just know. Just give me the power to search for it, find it, and use it!*

*A bit earlier I already had the feeling that I should not stretch the elastic any further, but need to veer it back. No forced attempts, but go with the flow.*

*12 Aug*
*Upset, because of bad publicity*

---

*Coins-for-Care*

*Projectverslag 2000-2004*

---

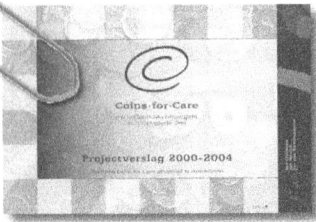

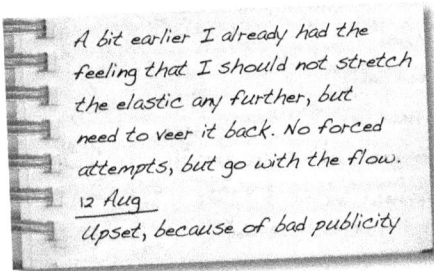

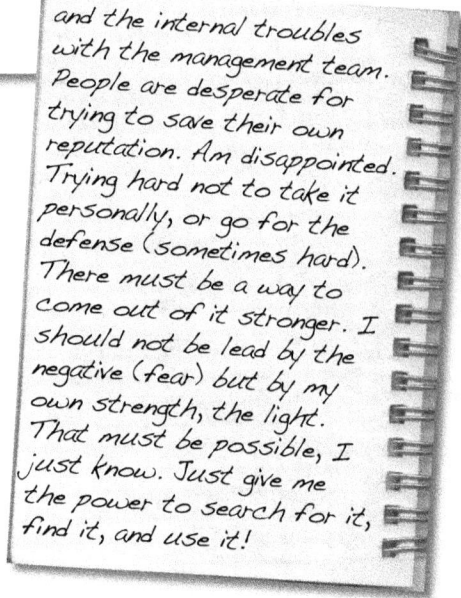

*Waiting is a trap. There will always be reasons to wait.*
*The truth is, there are only two things in life,*
*reasons and results, and*
*reasons simply don't count-*
*- Robert Anthony -*

holiday, from that moment onwards I was glued to the computer and phone, trying to find out what was going on and whether I could rectify the situation.

I spoke to the board, who were equally as shocked. 'You need to admit that you were wrong paying that money into our account,' someone suggested. 'Hang on, it was a justified decision, completely transparent and openly communicated!' protested someone else. 'Well, I am still behind our decision to pay the leftover money to the Donor Association,' I replied, 'remember that a number of Coins for Care charities don't even exist anymore? And that some others simply refused to tell us what they had done with the money? Our decision to spend the forty-thousand euros on the promotion of transparency was a legitimate one,' I insisted.
A few board members, obviously worried about their own position, kept pressuring me to admit that I had been wrong, but I simply refused; I was not allowing myself to be drawn into any political games, it went against everything I believed in.

The doctor's results were getting increasingly worse and he strongly advised me to take it easy. 'If your situation doesn't improve over the next three months, I will not have any other option but to operate,' he said. Three months...it was a tight deadline...

At the next board meeting I finally announced that I wanted to stop my work with the Donor Association. 'I feel my work is done. The charities who are searching for transparency and involvement of their donors have been given the tools to work with. Unfortunately, there are still quite a few organizations who are not interested, but I don't think they will ever change, not even if I spend another seven years promoting transparency.' I explained. 'Furthermore, attention is shifting from our objectives to me personally, and I think it's time for someone else to take the baton.' It was a tough call, we still hadn't found a successor, and me stepping down could mean the end for the Donor Association.
My decision was not accepted, everybody tried to change my mind, encouraging me to stay on, saying it could not be that bad, that there was still a lot of work to be done, and I was eventually persuaded. A few of the other board members,

*'Make a difference or get out!'*

however, were dropping out. 'At least they aren't afraid of making their own decisions,' I thought enviously, and I realized that even more work was likely going to end up on my plate.

> **INTERVIEW** She didn't manage to enforce financial control on the charity world, but **Esther Jacobs** is tired of the battle. After seven years she is ending her work for the Donor Association. '27.000 charities are still a mystery; no details available.'

# Esther is tired of fighting

A donor needs to know where he stands.

ORKUN AKINCI
EEMNES

Esther Jacobs: 'Niemand gaat met hetzelfde fanatisme goede doelen tot transparantie bewegen, ook niet tegen een kleine vergoeding.' FOTO PIM RAS

Ik kan vanmiddag een goed doel oprichten, een leuk bedrag ophalen en ermee naar de Bahama's vertrekken. Ongestraft. Er zijn geen regels, ieder toezicht ontbreekt en geen organisatie hoeft jaarcijfers te overleggen. De overheid hamert op zelfregulering, maar dat is lastig in een branche waarin de mensen achter veel organisaties onbekend zijn. Mondjesmaat worden sommige goede doelen transparanter, maar ik heb geen zin om hier nog jaren mee door te gaan. Een vervanger is niet te vinden. Ik ben mezelf zeven jaar lang dagelijks voorbijgelopen. Niemand gaat met hetzelfde fanatisme goede doelen tot transparantie bewegen, ook niet tegen een kleine vergoeding. Dan houdt de Donateursvereniging dus op te bestaan. Partners uit het bedrijfsleven nemen onze projecten over."

"De vereniging is ooit opgericht uit Coins for Care. Ik had een actie opgezet om oude munten uit het guldentijdperk in te zamelen voor goede doelen. Omdat de stichting Eurocollecte hetzelfde deed, ontstond een samenwerking. Maar bij die club gebeurden zulke rare dingen dat ik me in de gang van zaken bij goede doelen ben gaan verdiepen. De directeuren van Eurocollecte declareerden miljoenen aan onkosten en werden ontslagen. Ze lopen nu trouwens nog steeds rond in de branche.

"Bij Coins for Care gingen sommige dingen ook niet goed. Er waren 118 doelen bij ons aangesloten met het CBF-keur (Centraal Bureau Fondsenwerving). Maar ik wist toen nog niet dat zo'n keurmerk geen garantie vormt dat het geld goed terecht komt. Een aantal goede doelen weigerde gewoon verantwoording af te leggen over de miljoenen die wij voor ze binnenhaalden. Andere hielden al snel op te bestaan, bijvoorbeeld Help Oekraïne en Health Care Albania. Anderhalf jaar lang heb ik gebeld en gemaild om erachter te komen wat er met het geld gebeurde. Dat heeft me als persoon wel geraakt, hoor. En sommige van de organisaties die geen inzage wilden geven, sommeerden me ondertussen wel zo snel mogelijk het beloofde geld over te maken.

"De Donateursvereniging heeft bereikt dat er voorzichtig een cultuurverandering gaande is. Donateurs zijn er altijd vanuit gegaan dat goede doelen worden gecontroleerd, wij hebben duidelijk gemaakt dat het niet zo is. Onze boodschap aan organisaties is: communiceer eerlijk. In 2004 is de Hartstichting in opspraak geraakt, toen het salaris van de directeur (172.000 euro) bekend werd. Misschien was er wel een heel goede reden om juist die dure directeur te hebben. Maar communiceer dat. Na de tsunami hadden de samenwerkende hulporganisaties duidelijk moeten maken dat het geld over een groot aantal jaren wordt besteed en dat het in de getroffen landen heel moeilijk werken is. Dan waren de berichten in de pers ook beter te verklaren geweest. Een donateur moet weten waar hij aan toe is, dan accepteert hij het ook sneller. Die realistische communicatie is zich nu voorzichtig aan het ontwikkelen.

"98 procent van de mensen die ik ben tegengekomen, is heel bevlogen. Er zijn echt heel veel mensen die goede dingen doen. War Child heeft onlangs de Transparant Prijs gekregen, die organisatie is echt aan de slag gegaan met de criteria die de Donateursvereniging heeft opgesteld. Maar ook heel veel kleine organisaties doen dat. De Egelopvang Zoetermeer heeft een jaaromzet van 7800 euro, maar heeft een fantastisch jaarverslag op internet gezet. Er staat zelfs op hoe het met alle dieren gaat, dat is toch prachtig?

"De Donateursvereniging, waarvan ik de kar heb getrokken, heeft mensen en organisaties aan het denken gezet. Het is nu aan de branche om te laten zien dat ze echt met onze ideeën aan de slag wil. Voor mij is het tijd me terug te trekken, ik heb er veel meer energie in gestoken dan ooit de bedoeling was. Ik had gehoopt de politiek zo ver te krijgen dat het overleggen van jaarverslagen verplicht werd gemaakt. Dat is niet gelukt. Van de 30.000 goede doelen in Nederland weet het publiek in 27.000 gevallen niet wie erachter zitten. Het zij zo. Deze drammer heeft haar best gedaan."

| **Paspoort** |
| --- |
| **Esther Jacobs** |
| **Geboren:** 28 juni 1970 te Utrecht. |
| **Burgerlijke staat:** Alleenstaand. |
| **Studie:** Bedrijfskunde op Nijenrode, studies over Latijns-Amerika in Florida. |
| **Hobby's:** Reizen, heeft al meer dan 100 landen aangedaan. |

---

© *de Volkskrant, Oct 10, 2006.*

If it hadn't been for the increasingly serious health warnings, I think I would have gone on indefinitely with my work for the Donor Association, there had never been a right moment to stop, but now my health was at stake it just did not seem worth it anymore.

## 'You can't stop now!'

Terminating the Donor Association wasn't going to be easy. My lawyer advised me to call a general assembly of all our members, whose approval was needed. I organized a meeting and was immediately confronted with a fierce protest from some of the members, who were already in the process of putting up a court case, to have the decision to terminate declared void. 'The invitation was not sent before the obligatory eight days, but only seven days and twenty-three hours,' was their counterargument.

In the meantime, a workgroup had been created by another group of members, to research a possible restart of the Donor Association. This workgroup, however, fell apart after only a few days, and the next work group could not come with a proposal either. In the meantime I had to look for a party who could take over our projects, luckily PricewaterhouseCoopers showed and interest, and soon I found myself discussing a possible takeover of the *Transparency Award* and *DonorInformer*.
While all this was going on, the Donor Association could not be disbanded, I had a three month deadline, I could feel the stress mounting, and I was desperate to bring this to a conclusion.

In my haste to abolish the Donor Association I had done something stupid, I had completely forgotten to inform the generous lady who had granted us 25.000 euro. She felt, quite rightly, let down by us, and found a sympathetic reception in the group who were putting together a court case against us.
I discovered that there were other people who had joined this group out of purely personal motives. The lady who had asked us for help regarding the child abuse cases in Brazil, was one of them. She was after our database with addresses, and her request was added to the vast list of demands. Another member who had not been voted into the board, after putting himself forward, had also joined the group.

The preparations for the court hearing took a lot of money, time and energy. I was at the end of my tether and I was tired of this group of stubborn people, who caused me quite a few sleepless nights. My stress levels went sky high and I could almost feel my 'abnormal cells' grow, so to speak.

In hindsight I think it might have been a huge mistake not to show my weaknesses, the stronger I appeared, the more resistance I met, and by now, some wanted to bring me to my knees, but I was adamant not to use my health as an excuse. I had to do this on merit, without pity and without help.
I guess most people sensed something was not right, but they were misreading the signs, I wonder if it would have made a difference had I been honest about my motivation for wanting to quit.

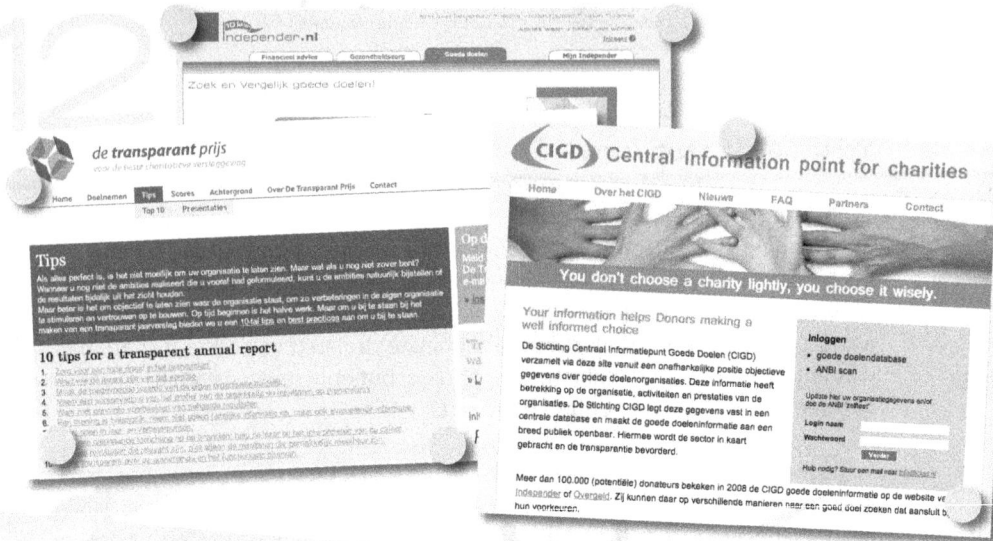

To cut a long (and emotional) story short: we won the court case. The judge found in our favor on every single issue. All we had to do now was to organize a final meeting to officially close down the Donor Association. Six of the 'rebels', however, used this occasion for a weak repeat of the court case, but eventually a majority agreed with the termination of the Donor Association. I was exhausted, but hugely relieved that this ultimately sad chapter had come to a close.

I 'retired' from the charity industry and immediately turned my back on it. 'I'm only going to invest my time on things I really enjoy,' I promised myself. I tried to ignore what was written about me in the press, and avoided articles like 'Slink Away' and 'Scandals force Esther to leave' which were appearing in the newspapers.

Over the following months, I focussed on getting my life back on track. 'I feel as if I have ruthlessly exploited my poor body over the last seven years,' I said to my doctor. 'You definitely need to allow yourself some time to get completely fit again,' he agreed.

After two years I was given a clean bill of health. 'There is no trace of abnormal cells, but you will still have to be careful in future and continue with a healthy lifestyle, avoiding stress,' he emphasized.

*'It's never too late to become what you might have been.'*

# Looking back

It took me a full year before I was able to look back with pride on my achievements with the Donor Association. I managed to establish the *DonorInformer* and the *Transparency Award*, both projects are still going strong today. I had also raised awareness around the need of critically engaged supporters, which is now recognized by the donors and the press, as well as by the industry itself. Still much remains to be done however, there still isn't a controlling body in place, we do not have an obligatory registration system, and the charity sector doesn't have an ombudsman yet. Also, lobbying for political reasons rather than charitable purposes still thrives in the industry, and there remains a critical role for the government in the realization of more transparency.

'It's never too late to become what you might have been.' I have learnt some important lessons: I no longer wait as long for others to act as I have done; I will not accept a postponement so easily anymore; I've also learnt to recognize when to stop, to listen to my body and to be aware of any subtle signs of emotional or physical distress. If you keep ignoring these signals, eventually you're body will start rebelling, forcing you to slow down.

*'Some people change their ways when they see the light,*
*others when they feel the heat.'*
*- Coaching Calendar -*

Many people who have faced a health challenge make a dramatic life change afterwards: Marnix started traveling the world and is enjoying life intensely; and Lance Armstrong and Kylie Minogue made their come backs, stronger than ever. Also Steve Jobs, the well known driving force behind Apple, came close to death when he was diagnosed with a rare type of cancer and, when asked about this, he said: 'Death is very likely the single best invention of life. It is life's change agent...' Although Steve admits nobody wants to die, he says that the knowledge we are all going to die one day, should be a motivation for living our lives as best as we can. 'Your time is limited, so don't waste it living someone else's life, have the courage to follow your own heart and intuition, as they somehow already know what you truly want to become.'

# Excuse 17:
## 'I have responsibilities towards others.'

*'Responsibility is the price of freedom.'*
*- Elbert Hubbart -*

My cats as kittens on
the tropical island of
Curaçao

## How to become a motivational speaker

'Our managers used to complain about not having enough budget or people in order to meet their annual targets, but since your Coins for Care presentation everybody has been full of enthusiasm, and by being creative they have been able to achieve much more!' the director of a big sales company confided in me. I was taken aback; it had only been my first paid speaking engagement.

During my time working for the Donor Organization I was frequently invited to speak on the topic of philanthropy and, of course, my involvement with Coins for Care. I did not charge for these seminars but by means of speaking publicly I hoped to achieve engagement in, awareness of, and ultimately sponsorship for my organization.

Surprisingly, my speeches became very popular. I was booked nearly every night and this simply took too much of my valuable time. Not charging for any of my work, I was coming to the end of my resources. When I reluctantly started asking for a compensation I got mixed reactions. 'We're doing this for charity!' would be the usual reply. 'And I have been working as a volunteer, mor ethan fulltime, for nearly seven years now,' I reacted sometimes irritably, forgetting these private banks and others organizing their philanthropy evening did mean well. 'If you want to use my knowledge for your customers, surely it's more than logical it is being paid for.'

I could not help feeling awkward having to decline an invitation or charge for my speeches. 'Of course it isn't about the money,' a friend of mine tried to help me, 'But by asking for a remuneration you can manage the number of requests your getting,' she analyzed. 'Why don't you register with a professional speakers agency, and forward them all your invitations so as to manage your diary?'

I followed up on her advice. And thanks to 'Sprekersplatform' (a Dutch speaker agency), I now got paid for all my speaking engagements. At first I would mainly talk about Coins for Care, which was a great example of achieving big results with limited resources, but soon I expanded my material using my Survivor experience as well.

> *'If you don't have the strength to impose your own terms upon life,*
> *you must accept the terms it offers you.'*
> *- T.S. Elliot -*

After one of the sessions a woman came up to me and took my hand. She had tears in her eyes when she confided: 'I am so moved by what you said. It's all clear to me now. I so needed that!' When I asked her what part of my speech had affected her so much, she mentioned something that I had not intended in the way she had interpreted it. Just as I was about to explain she had been mistaken, I realized it would probably be better to leave it as it was, and I gratefully accepted her compliment.

People continued coming up to me after my presentations, telling me what had struck them most about my experiences. And sometimes it became obviously clear they had completely misunderstood or misinterpreted what I had said. I learned to accept this as, according to the speaker agency, my story seemed to release a type of energy which stirred all kinds of emotions in people.

From that moment onwards I took a more relaxed approach. I decided to simply share my anecdotes, and not worry about a strict storyline or theme. 'My Coins for Care and Survivor adventures have so many aspects, I don't think I need to rationalize or direct these too much,' I told my confused clients at the intake. 'It's evident my listeners pick up on what's relevant to them personally, And that will differ from person to person,' I tried to assure them.

'Esther, would you be willing to share your personal journey with us?' I was asked to speak at an event organized by the 'Women in the Financial Industry' group from Lehman Brothers. They were the first to specifically ask for a personal take on my experiences. 'Of course we would like to hear about your Coins for Care success, but more so about your personal life and the choices you have made,' they summarized during our preliminary meeting. I felt very vulnerable adding my emotions to the facts, but by doing so my story became a lot more passionate and intense. The audience of women remained captivated throughout, and the reactions afterwards were exuberant. These high flying career women told me they would not have been able to do what I had done. It was clear my tale had moved my listeners deeply.

The next day I received an e-mail from one of the women who had been in the audience. 'Thank you so much for your inspiring talk,' she wrote. 'I just wanted to let you know that I have resigned from my job to finally go on that trip around the world. I have been dreaming about this for such a long time!' 'Oops,' I thought, 'do I need insurance for this?' As if she had been reading my mind, she continued: 'Don't worry, I have been thinking about this for a very long time, and your story yesterday was the last push I needed to make it happen.'

*Barely a year later, Lehman Brothers filed for bankruptcy and the global financial crisis started to spread, but I have been assured this incidence was unrelated!*

## Practice what you preach

I take my audiences onto a virtual journey nowadays. 'Close your eyes and travel five years into the future,' I will instruct them. 'Imagine all your dreams have come true. How does this feel? Look around at what you have achieved, and then take a step back to see *how* you got here. You're already there, so you don't have to wonder *if* you're going to make it."

*Follow your intuition, follow your dreams.*

Next, I let people discuss amongst each other their own excuses for **not** pursuing their ambitions. My listeners will then discover everyone has their personal aspirations, but also reasons for not committing to them. 'It's an enormous relief to find that we all seem to share the same dilemmas,' I often hear, as well as: 'Your story and questions have inspired me unbelievably.' 'I get it now, and this encourages me to chase my own dreams.'

'I am concerned people see me as some kind of Guru,' I recently confessed to a good friend. 'It seems they think I can do anything, know everything, but they forget I'm only human too...' I carefully tried to put my doubts into words. 'What if they take to heart what I'm saying, and then make a decision which is totally unrealistic,' I said despondently.
'But you just said yourself things seem to happen spontaneously during those evenings, regardless of what you say or do,' my friend reassured me. 'It's as if you're lifting a curtain which allows people to have a glimpse of what else is on offer out there. Once you've broadened your horizons, you can't go back to your former, limited perspectives,' was her analysis.

Most of the reactions I receive confirm my friend's thoughts. Even people who I have never met, but who have visited my website seem to experience something to this effect.

'The knowledge that I actually do have a choice, and not always have to do as is expected of me, makes me a stronger person,' an anonymous e-mailer explained to me. 'Sometimes, when I'm faced with a difficult situation at work, I'll think *what would Esther do?*' my landlord on Curacao told me. My outlook on life seems to be a source of strength for many. I will simply accept that, and I'm not even going to attempt explaining why.

After my seminars, people like to stay on for a bit and have a chat, and I'm always asked if I have any dreams left myself. 'Of course I still have my dreams!' is my answer. 'I would like to go traveling indefinitely, without planning anything beforehand. I know I travel a lot already,' I say quickly when seeing the surprised look on their faces, 'but that is usually for a few weeks or months at the most, after that I really need to get back home.'
Most people leave it at that, but about a year ago someone asked me: 'So, why don't you realize your own dream? Traveling for an unlimited period of time?' It put me on the spot. 'Well, hum, that's because of my...ehhh....my cats...' I did not sound very convincing. 'When I travel, I need to find someone who can look after them, which needs planning and prevents me from staying away for very long.' It sounded very weak after my powerful 'no excuses!'-speech. 'I just feel guilty towards my pets!'
Suddenly the coin dropped: my personal excuse was not fear for the unknown, or a steady job, or even a relationship, but my two lovely cats, who had been

**Close your travel guide, turn your intuition on**

Esther Jacobs:
"Je kunt mij overal neerzetten, zonder geld, ik bouw zo weer een leven op"

Esther Jacobs (34) is marketingconsultant. Dat wil zeggen: af en toe. Goede doelen is haar passie. Ze stond aan de wieg van drie benefietorganisaties, met Coins for Care als bekendste.

**Grootste droom:** Dat iedereen eerlijk en open is. Geen verborgen agenda's meer
**Sterkste punt:** Doorzettingsvermogen
**Zwakste punt:** Dingen kunnen me enorm raken. Als het goed gaat, krijg ik ontzettend veel energie. Maar ben ik teleurgesteld, dan raakt me dat tot in het diepste van mijn ziel
**Trots op:** Coins for Care. En dat ik er een lintje voor kreeg
**Bewondering voor:** Nelson Mandela. Als iemand verbitterd zou mogen zijn, is hij het. Het tegendeel is waar: hij blijft positief, blijft openstaan
**Levensmotto:** Je gevoel volgen
**Dol op:** reizen

**Esther:** "Ik ben Coins for Care begonnen zonder te weten waaraan ik begon. Op een dag had ik het gevoel: ik heb het zelf zo goed voor elkaar, ik wil iets goeds voor anderen doen. Eigenlijk heb ik zowel in mijn werk als privé-leven altijd iets gehad van: het komt zoals het komt. Als marketingconsultant werk ik maar af en toe. Ik weet nooit wanneer ik iets verdien en hoeveel. Dus soms verdien ik bijna niets. Net genoeg om van te leven. Ik ben een vrijbuitster. Onafhankelijk. Dat heeft soms nadelen, soms voordelen. Als ik aan een nieuw project begin, zoals Coins for Care (inzamelingsactie van munten bij de komst van de euro - red.) verdiep ik me vaak objectief kijken. Zonder grenzen. Daarna kwamen de Donateursstichting, waarin het aantal goede doelen in Nederland in kaart zijn gebracht. En Weetikprestatie, een organisatie die adviseert aan mensen die een avontuurlijke reis willen maken voor een goed doel en daarvoor zelf voor sponsoring zorgen door familie, vrienden en andere bekenden te benaderen. Een ontzettend leuk idee dat me direct aansprak, omdat het een combinatie is van reizen, goede doelen én avontuur..."

**"I have always wanted to contribute something"**

Esther Jacobs (31) is oprichter van Coins for Care. Deze organisatie houdt zich bezig met het inzamelen van het buitenlands geld dat...

**Esther Jacobs**, freelance marketing consultant en oprichter van Coins for Care en De donateursvereniging

**Focus on what you can influence**

'Ik heb een sterk rechtvaardigheidsgevoel en de neiging overal in te duiken. Dat kost veel energie. Soms blijken dingen ook niet zo belangrijk als ik in eerste instantie dacht en dan kun je ze beter laten liggen. Soms kun je beter je mond houden. Dan sta je veel sterker en je verspilt je energie niet aan dingen waar je op een bepaald moment toch niks aan kunt veranderen. Concentreer je op de dingen waar je wel wat mee kunt.'

**Doing is the best way of dreaming**

IN MIJN 'SNELLE' PERIODE WAS IK NOOIT IN HET PRIVÉ-VLIEGTUIG VAN DE RIJKSTE MAN VAN GUATEMALA BELAND

PLAATSELIJKE SJAMAAN UIT. DAT HADDEN ZE NOG NOOIT GEDAAN!

301

with me for over twelve years. I could not get rid of them just like that, could I? At the same time I realized they were the one and only reason for me compromising my dream.

*'If you don't run your own life,*
*somebody else will.'*
*- John Atkinson -*

I became increasingly self-conscious having to answer questions on why I was not following my own ideals. Other people had excuses far more serious, like having a family, a job, or health issues. I always encouraged them to look beyond that and chase their dreams, but personally I was not pursuing mine... because of my *cats*?

Deep down I knew it was not really about my cats at all. I used them as an excuse for not breaking all ties with my native country, something that does stop a lot of people in their tracks. I suppose I was scared of completely surrendering to my dreams.

'It's up to me,' I said to myself. 'I will surpass my last excuse and will feel how wonderful it is to be truly free or I continue like this and not live life to the full.'

*'Practice what you preach,'* I thought, and I came to a decision.

We all have a natural tendency towards postponing new and exciting things. Dieting will always start tomorrow; new hobbies and beautiful journeys are planned for after a career switch or retirement. There will always be an important deadline waiting to be met before we allow ourselves to have some fun. I believe looking for excuses is integral to being human, and it will never completely stop, but I do think it is possible to become more aware of this process and break the pattern.

> *'Take your life in your own hands and what happens?*
> *A terrible thing: no one is to blame.'*
> *- Erica Jong -*

Even after deciding to let go of my cats, I was still looking for reasons to postpone my trip. 'How much money would I need for a year of 'doing nothing'?' I asked myself. I made a careful calculation, and then counted my savings. I appeared to have enough savings, but before I knew it, I was backtracking again. 'Actually, that would never be sufficient, I need to save a lot more, so I have some reserves,' I reckoned. I recalculated, expecting to call off my plans.

But then I discovered I had made an error in my original calculation. When I corrected my mistake I found the amount in my bank-account was enough to even meet my new 'requirements'! 'No more excuses!' I smiled.

photo: Marco Okhuizen

After having found a new home for my beloved cats, I made the impulsive decision to move to Curacao. That is where I would plan my next move. I had not been to my favorite island for seven years, and immediately felt at home again. My dad had moved to Miami, but I still had many of friends over there. Some of them had returned to the island after spending some years in the Netherlands. 'It's just a much better quality of life over here,' one of them said with a blissful smile, and I agreed.

'Look, it's the *fruit girl*!' someone cheered at me at a party; they still recognized me, even after fifteen years.

On Curacao I found the peace I needed to quietly contemplate everything that had happened in the past few years.

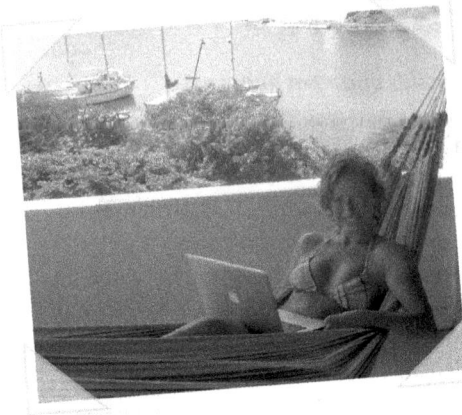

At the end of 2008, I found the first draft of a book on my laptop. I had started writing it a long time ago, and I was surprised to find my story was actually very interesting, exciting and inspiring. It was mainly about my experiences setting up the Coins for Care project and, contrary to what I remembered, the part about my troublesome relationship with the charity industry made up only a fraction of it. It contained a lot more storylines and details than I had been able to remember during my speeches, after which people had often said I should write a book. I was pleasantly surprised to find I had already started that!

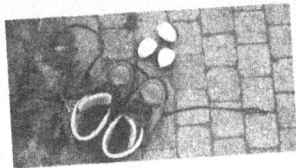

NRC, June 17, 2007

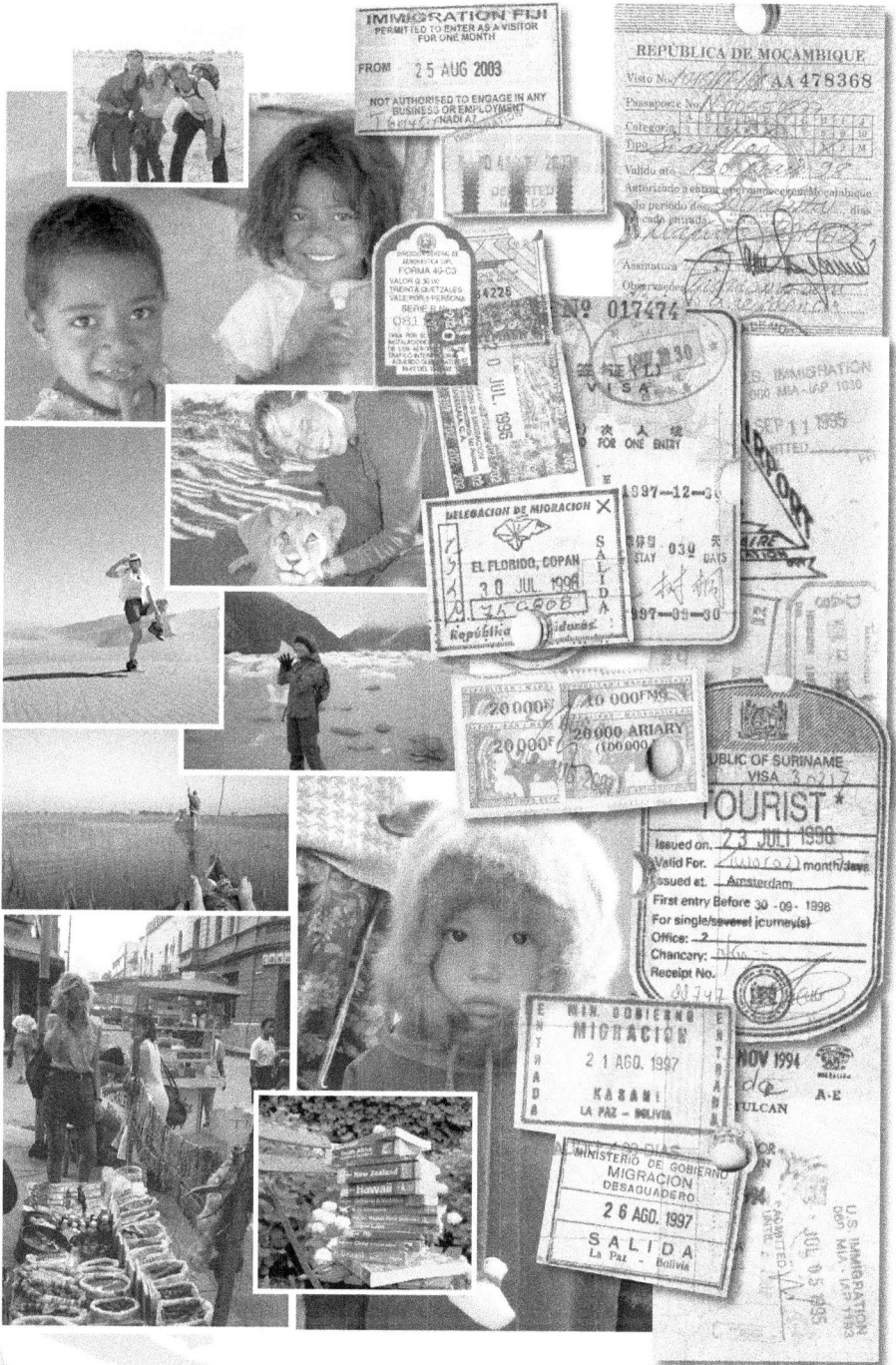

I decided to rewrite the book, and to include my Survivor experiences as well. Many people think that everything comes to me easily and my main goal for the book was to show that everybody, including myself, has to go through deep 'downs' to get to the 'ups'. When chasing your dreams, you will find many obstacles and dead ends on your way, you might even encounter opposition and feel completely dejected. However, my message remains the same: you can make anything happen, as long as you know what it is you want, and as long as you have the confidence, willpower and patience to persist. And, ok, let's be honest, a bit of good luck might come in useful.

Writing my book was a truly therapeutic experience. I had to rise above the insignificant details, emotions and frustrations in order to get my story across. I do hope I have succeeded in that and that my experiences will be inspiring for many of you out there.

Now I have finished writing I will travel through the Caribbean for a while. I can not wait to find out what else I will find on my path. I am living my dream at last!

What's yours? Start realizing your dream today. What's your excuse for not doing so?

*'Don't make excuses.*
*Make something incredible happen in your life right now!'*
*- Greg Hickman -*

# Excuse 18:

# 'I don't know what I want.'

'You have to set out in good faith for elsewhere
and lose your bearings serendipitously.'
- John Barth. -

Serendipity
noun ser·en·dip·i·ty \,ser-ən-ˈdi-pə-tē\
'Luck that takes the form of finding valuable
or pleasant things that are not looked for.'

'Serendipity is looking in a haystack for a
needle and discovering a farmer's daughter.'
- Julius Conroe Jr. -

'Serendipity is when you look for something, find something else,
and realize that what you've found is more suited to your needs
than what you thought you were looking for.'
- Lawrence Block -

# What makes you happy?

'Congratulations! You've won the jackpot!' What would you do if you win millions in the lottery? Quit your job, make that long longed for trip around the world, or finally start your own company?

If you were told you had only one year to live, what would you do? What if it was a month, or only one more day...?

If you could live your whole life again, without having to worry about money, or other people's expectations, is there anything you would do differently?

What made you happy when you were a child? What did you love doing most and when were you at your happiest?

What do you want from life? What are your dreams? Many people seem to struggle with these issues. If you want to know where your heart lies, spend some time with the questions above; your answers will provide the key to your dream.

Take your time, write anything down that comes to you, no matter how irrelevant it might seem, be completely honest with yourself, and it will become clear what appeals to you most.

Your answers might not be clear cut, but it will point you into a certain direction, and if you start exploring this area further you will notice there will be more signs and even opportunities along the way.

So take that first step! Sign up for a course, create a mood board, meditate, talk about it with those closest to you, or do something else that makes you feel good. You don't have anything to lose while chasing your passion.

Making a mood board

'Don't make excuses.
Make something incredible happen in your life,
right now!'
— Greg Hickman —

This is what I am going to do.
Right now!:

# Acknowledgements

There are more people I would like to thank than fit on this page; especially the sponsors, volunteers and other supporters of Coins for Care and the Donor Organization. Some have been mentioned in this book, but unfortunately it was impossible to mention everybody and all contributions. To me it felt like the entire country of The Netherlands was participating! So I'd like to say 'Thank You, Holland!', with a special wink in the direction of Abcoude.

Despite our age difference of almost 35 years, Karel and I have worked together very intensely for many, many months. I am eternally thankful to have met such a beautiful human being. I have learned so much from Karel. The most important eye-opener for me were his wise words: "There's a differente between being right and being acknowledged."
Our work together evolved into so much more than his original idea of 'helping some charities in my spare time when I retire'... Karel's sense of humor and his faith in the inherent good in people kept us both going through the most diffi-cult times. And of course his wife' Trudi's lovely spagetti!

I'd like to thank Erik van de Merwe, Eurocollect's treasurer, for his honesty and sense of righteousness. He was the only one who did not give in to the pressure exterted by the established charities, and he wasn't afraid to put his own rep-utation on the line. Even under the most difficult circumstances he remained honest and fair. Chapeau!

Capgemini has financed my charity work for many years. By hiring me as a free-lance facilitator for their Design Center-workshops, they provided the oppor-tunity for me to a lot of time on unpaid activities, and to travel, of course.

I could not have imagined a better companion to spend two weeks in a deserted cave than my Survivor-friend Marnix. 'We would gladly do it again, but this time we'll bring plenty of food and a bunch of friends', we joke nowa-days. I love Marnix vitality and admire the way the strives to balance his new-found sense of adventure, his family and other responsibilities. To me, Marnix is the Belgian Lance Armstrong...

A special mention to my old neighbor Berna Ooms, who gave me an important message, which became the basis for my lifestyle of trying to live life to the fullest and be in the moment. Even though I bow to her wisdom and know that she is usually right, I sincerely hope that her prediction for the end of the world will not come true (yet).

Curaçao, the island and my friends there gave me the peace and inspiration to write: thank you for that. Whenever I got stuck, I went swimming in the warm, clear sea. The rhythm brought me into a kind of trance. The fish I saw along the way helped me put things back into perspective. After my daily swim I would always know how to solve a difficult dilemma.

One day this habit made me stumble upon the most brilliant of excuses: I asked a friend if she wanted to join me for a swim. She answered: 'I'd like to, but I won't. Swimming usually results in one getting wet and I don't want to get wet.''

Thanks to Joost, the original publisher of this book, you don't have to read yet another hundred pages. My first draft of the document was much, much longer.... :)

My friend and designer Marieke, another Capgemini freelancer, took care of the beautiful design of this book.

My parents, the rest of my family, my friends and even my 'enemies' (of whom I know some will also read this book, be it with different motives) deserve a special mention. Thanks to all of you I became who I am today.

Finally a special word of thanks to my cats. 'Sorry that I had to let you go after 12 years. Please forgive me. Try to imagine how many people we might inspire to realize their dreams by sharing our story...

PS you are getting more attention now than I could have ever given you, so it did not turn out too bad, did it?

Esther ☺

# About the author
# + other books

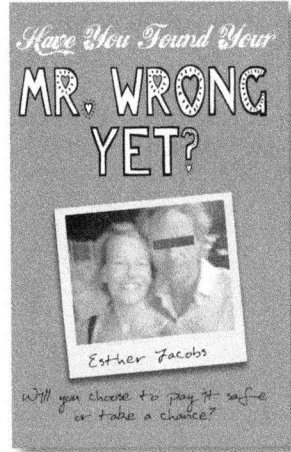

www.estherjacobs.info

# Who's That Girl?

Photo by www.eefphotography.com

Esther Jacobs (The Netherlands, 1970) is an international (TEDx) speaker and (co) author of 21 books. Without a budget, this 'No Excuses Lady' managed to raise €16 million for charity; an accomplishment for which she was knighted by the Dutch queen.

Esther gave more than 1000 keynotes, inspiring entrepreneurs and decision makers worldwide to take control and transform their challenges into opportunities. As a 'digital nomad' she has lived, worked and played in over a 100 countries and continues to travel.

Esther has been on the European 'Survivor' TV show, is an important influencer on social media and was featured in the international media over 500 times.

Check her website to attend her next presentation or workshop, to hire her as a speaker or to book a one-to-one RESULTant session.

**Turn it around.**
**Get it done.**
**Feel alive!**

www.estherjacobs.info

estherjacobs

noexcuseslady

**Linked** in estherjacobs

You Tube noexcuseslady

estherjacobsnl

# What Is Your Dream?

*Make your dream come true. Start today.*

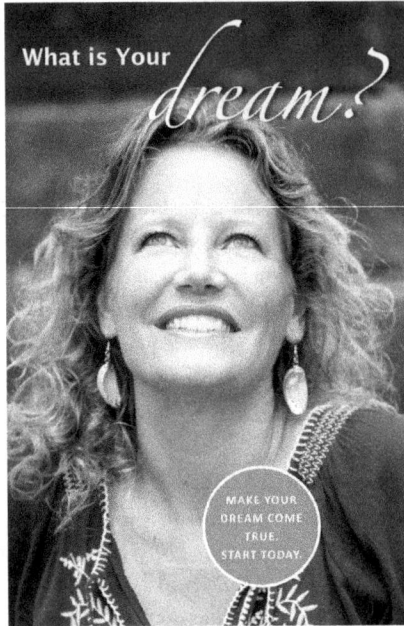

**Reader reviews**

♡ "I've got the uncontrollable urge to go out and make my dreams come true, right now!" **Isa**

♡ "This book has taught me to ask for what I want" **Sabrina**

♡ "Of course, your book is inspiring, but what it brought me is renewed courage to continue pursuing my dreams." **Kirsten**

♡ "I read the book straight through. I admire you and the other dream seekers for the way you have lived up to your dreams. Now it's my turn..." **Cateleine**

♡ "This book makes you start to dream about what you really would like to experience." **Ineke**

♡ "I have started my own business! This book helped me take this beautiful step." **Marco**

*Congratulations!*
*By picking up this book, you have just taken the first step toward realizing your dream! Don't let go of this momentum. Keep focusing on your dream, make conscious choices. That's the only way to avoid that moment, looking back, when you think' If only I had"*

What would you do if you weren't limited by time, money, responsibilities or other restrictions?

- Travel the world
- Start your own business
- Find your dream job
- Make more time for fun stuff
- Live abroad

Whatever your dream is, start today, is Esther's advice. As an expert in enjoying life, she inspires, offers practical tips and food for thought.

The other part of the book is filled with the personal stories of ordinary people who, just like you and Esther, are trying to pursue their dreams through life's ups and downs. The combination of tips and colorful interviews gives hope and confidence that ANYTHING is possible. Moreover, it makes you want to try it for yourself.

**www.whatisyourdream.us**

# Digital Nomads

*How to Live, Work & Play around the world*

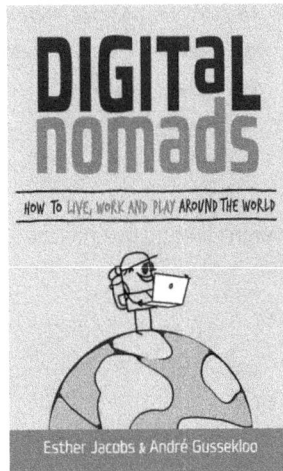

**Praise and reader reviews**

♡ *"The most complete guide to quitting your job, going on the road, traveling the world and having the most amazing time."* **Natalie Sisson – author of The Suitcase Entrepreneur**

♡ *"This book is accessible and practical. Your first task is to turn the page, your second task to begin packing your bags."* **Chris Guillebeau – author of The $100 startup**

♡ *"This is a book about freedom. Even for those of us who are not so 'digital', it provides valuable insights."* **Adrian Hector Luna, from Buenos Aires, Argentina**

♡ *"I liked the tax & financial advice - a lot of other books just skip this topic."* **David Schneider on Amazon**

♡ *"Lots of practical information to help you transition into this lifestyle."* **Nolibell on Amazon**

♡ *"The best gift you can give to students, young professionals and anyone tired of the daily commute to an office every morning."* **Kim Brooks on Amazon**

♡ *"The digital nomad lifestyle is real and achievable. This guide tells you how to work from anywhere, using the Internet as a tool."* **Ingrid on Amazon**

♡ *"it is realistic, it does not just paint a glamorous picture of the DN lifestyle."* **Shivan Dana Jalal on Amazon**

♡ *"This book has so much information that I am surprised about its low price."* **Amazon Customer**

Distance is an illusion. We are lucky to live in an age where planes and communication technologies have made the world smaller than ever. New opportunities galore. We are at the brink of a revolution that changes the way we live, work and play. And the good news is – you can be part of it.

Life doesn't have to be a rat race. Why toil away in an office when you could be working from a hammock? Why postpone that round-the-world trip until your retirement? Why retire at all when work can be fun?

A growing army of digital nomads are finding their own answers to these questions. Armed with a laptop, they follow their dreams and live unforgettable adventures. Are you ready to join in their footsteps and make the world your playground? This book takes you by the hand:

- Inspiring stories from digital nomads in the trenches
- A step-by-step guide to setting up your online business
- How to design your own international masterplan
- Productivity tricks for working while on the road
- The countries your money stretches furthest
- Discover where digital nomads meet and chill

Don't waste any more time in that office prison. This book is your way out. But be warned - your life is about to change, big-time!

**www.digitalnomadbook.com**

# How to write your book in a week
*A 7 step guide to writing and self publishing for entrepreneurs and non-writers*

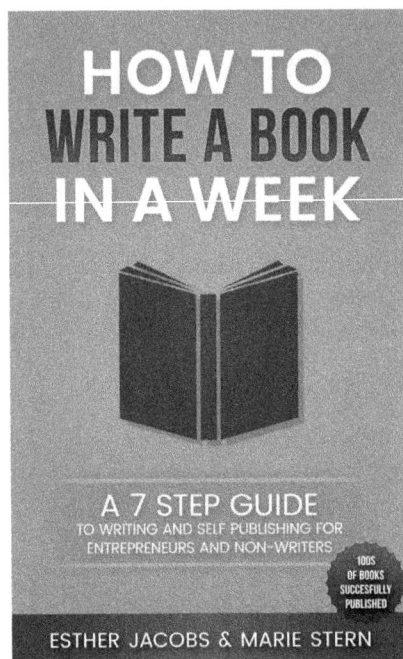

**Readers reviews**

- ♡ *"I just published my book. What I haven't been able to achieve in the past three years I did in just 7 days!"* **Chris**
- ♡ *"I am currently writing a book and it has taken me well more than a week! If I had had this detailed how-to guide available I would have cut my time way down. And avoided some mistakes along the way."* **Michael on Amazon**
- ♡ *"Writing the back cover material first seemed weird and I realized it is a stroke of genius."* **Entrepreneur M.**
- ♡ *"It is well written and edited, which is not an easy feat for a book that has been written and published in a week."* **David on Amazon**
- ♡ *"Everything you need to know in an afternoon reading session!"* **Amazon customer**
- ♡ *"Wish I'd seen the list with 10 book ideas before I wrote my book.."* **Andrew**

Is this the year you are finally going to share your message with the world?
Don't let the idea of having to write a book hold you back. It's easier than you think, and you don't even have to actually write the book yourself...

Never thought about writing a book? Maybe you should consider it! Publishing a book will give you expert status, help spread your message and increase sales of your other products and services. It may even kick-start or boost your public speaking career.

Writing, publishing and promoting a book has never been easier. You can do it in a week.

This guide will teach you:
• The best kept secrets to a quick start for writing, promotion and sales
• Smart writing process hacks
• Alternatives to writing the book yourself
• Self-publishing
• The keys to launching a successful book, superfast

The authors Esther and Marie met at a conference, where they were giving a book writing workshop. They decided to write this book in just one day, using their own tested method. And now they're inviting you to try it, too!

# Have you found your Mr. Wrong yet?

*Will you choose to play it safe, or take a chance?*

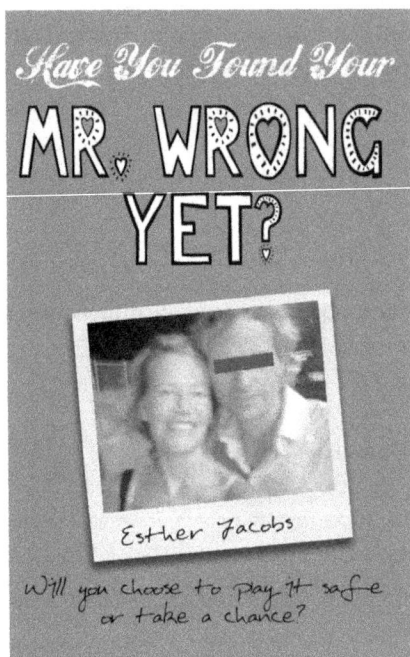

**Readers reviews**
- ♡ *"Surprising insights for anybody who has been involved with (or still is) a Mr. Wrong."* **reader Anette**
- ♡ *"Great to read about the experiences of people who dare tread outside of the beaten paths."* **Trucella, Bol.com**
- ♡ *"Planning to re-read this book several times. One thing is for sure, Esther's (love) life is definitely not boring!"* **Lanella op Bol.com**
- ♡ *"I'm impressed by the amount of work and research put into this book - all the extra factual information, surveys, research...it is definitely eye-opening and informative with a load of alternative views. Read this for something unconventional!"* **Amazon customer**
- ♡ *"Esther is not afraid to take responsibility for her own role and does so with complete honesty"* **reader AvL**

"I never imagined that a smart, independent, confident woman like me could fall for the biggest womanizer on the island. Would this former(?) playboy break my heart with his charming ways? Or was our relationship really special to him? Do I choose to play it safe or do I risk taking a chance? Can a person truly change? Is that even something to wish for? What does this inner turmoil say about me, my desires and my fears? Slowly I began to realize that this personal journey was far more important than the final destination. There was so much I did not understand yet. I needed to learn to enjoy the moment and let go – really let go."

Motivational speaker and author Esther Jacobs is determined to get to the bottom of the Mr. Wrong phenomenon. Using her own story as a springboard, she takes off on a groundbreaking odyssey through the various types of playboys and the women who fall for them, alternative relationships, Mr. Right and wise and wayward women. She challenges readers to reconsider their assumptions and choices. Do they follow their head (security) or their heart (adventure)?

Have You Found Your Mr. Wrong Yet? offers a candid look at a trailblazing woman forced to come to grips with life's deepest questions when she finds herself falling for... Mr. Wrong.

This book is not only about relationships, but contains many (management) lessons about switching perspectives, taking risks, breaking with traditions, letting go and taking control of your life under any circumstance.

www.mrwrong.us

I hope you enjoyed reading my book and wish you lots of success and fun with realizing your dreams.

Esther

Liked it? I would really appreciate if you could leave a review on Amazon.com.

Spelling errors, typo's or translation hiccups??? I'd love to hear from you! Please help to improve this book by emailing me any suggestions you have on info@estherjacobs.info

More free tips, videos and adventures? Sign up for my '5 minutes of inspiration' newsletter: bit.ly/esther-inspiration